The Mystical Mind

"[An] exhilarating study of religion and the science of mind.... D'Aquili and Newberg make difficult scientific concepts understandable and accessible as they formulate this fresh approach to religion and science."

—*Publishers Weekly*

TITLES IN THE SERIES

The Mystical Mind

*Probing the Biology
of Religious Experience*

Eugene G. d'Aquili
Andrew B. Newberg

FORTRESS PRESS   MINNEAPOLIS

THE MYSTICAL MIND
Probing the Biology of Religious Experience

Cover image: © Tony Stone Images.
Cover and book design: David Meyer
Typesetting: Ann Delgehausen

Library of Congress Cataloging-in-Publication Data
D'Aquili, Eugene G., date
    The mystical mind : probing the biology of religious experience /
    Eugene G. d'Aquili and Andrew B. Newberg.
      p.   cm.
    Includes bibliographical references and indexe.
    ISBN: 0-8006-3163-3 (alk. paper)
    1. Mysticism—Psychology. 2. Experience (Religion) I. Newberg, Andrew B.,
1966– . II. Title.
BL625.D29 1999
291.4'2—dc21   99-24089
                                                          CIP

The paper used in this publication meets the minimum requirements of American National Standard for Information Sciences—Permanence of Paper for Printed Library Materials, ANSI Z329.48-1984.

Manufactured in the U.S.A.   AF 1-3163

Mysterio tremendo et fascinanti
mentique mysticae id quaerenti
duobus ab auctoribus
conlatis delectatione veritatis
hoc opusculum dedicatur

To the tremendous and spellbinding mystery,
and to the mystical mind seeking it,
this modest work is dedicated
by two authors united by a love of truth.

Contents

Preface

The Mystical Mind is the culmination of almost twenty-five years of research on the relationship between the brain and religious experience. It strikes at the heart of questions such as: What makes something spiritual? Why are religious experiences so powerful? How can we understand religious experience from a biological perspective? and What can religious and mystical experiences tell us about the mind and reality?

Eugene d'Aquili initiated this groundbreaking research with an analysis of religious experiences in ancient cultures. As human beings and human culture developed, he found, so did religions and associated religious experiences. Today there is a tremendous amount of information about the myriad varieties of religious experience. We also have a much greater understanding about how the brain and mind work. *The Mystical Mind* uses this knowledge to forge an integrated approach toward understanding religious and mystical experiences. It explores what biology can tell us about religious experience and examines the implications that such experiences have for the study of biology as well as theology.

This book is based, in part, on brain imaging and other neuroscientific research that have investigated how the brain works under a variety of circumstances. These studies have advanced our understanding of how different parts of the brain work together. Research over the past two decades has also begun to explore the relationship between brain function and body physiology. As a result, we can describe what is happening in the brain and measure the changes in the rest of the body that accompany various brain states. With this information, we can begin to explore, in detail, how religious and mystical experiences affect our minds and bodies.

It should be mentioned with sadness that Dr. d'Aquili passed away prior to the publication of *The Mystical Mind* and so could not enjoy the completion of this book. The ideas he expressed here, however, reflect his creativity and intelligence. He was a true pioneer in the field of science and religion, particularly in the study of the biological experience of religious phenomena. Fortunately, Dr. Newberg will continue to pursue these issues and seek an even greater biological understanding of religious experience.

The implications of this research are far-reaching and profound. They allow us to consider religious experience in new ways that will present challenging issues for biology, religion, and theology in the twenty-first century.

Part One

Prelude to the Mystical Mind

Chapter One

Introduction

A HISTORICAL PERSPECTIVE ON THEOLOGY

Throughout the ages, human beings have endeavored to understand their place in the universe. They have sought many different answers to the questions: "Why are we here?"; "How does the universe work?"; "What determines good and evil?"; and a myriad of other compelling queries. Of all the answers considered, perhaps none has been so pervasive and so persistent as those that invoke some higher being (or beings) or higher state of being. The notion of a higher being or state of being has usually fallen into the realm of the religions and, more specifically, to the systematic study of the theologian. To this end, numerous complex ideologies and religious systems have developed to guide human beings toward a higher order of things.

At the outset, we must state the obvious: some higher being or higher state of being has taken on innumerable forms in various religions and cultures. In the Western religions and in Hinduism, the higher being has been called "God." In all theistic religions, God is perceived as the ultimate externality (transcendent), the ultimate internality (immanent), and sometimes both simultaneously. Often, God is not perceived simply as a higher being but in many ways has been described as the ground or substance of all being. Thus, God is not only the higher being but also a state of higher being or ultimate reality. In fact, in the mystical traditions of the Western religions, the goal of the practice of meditation is to become intensely united with God and in so doing to become, in a sense, a part of ultimate reality involving release from the cycle of birth and death.

Eastern traditions such as Hinduism and Buddhism have tended to move away from the notion of a higher being per se and simply focus their beliefs on a state of higher being or ultimate reality. This state, which can be achieved through intense lifelong meditation (and sometimes over many lifetimes), has also been given many names, depending on the specific tradition. For example, in Hinduism, the ultimate state (which can have personal characteristics) is Brahma, and in Buddhism, the ultimate state (never in any way personal) is Nirvana. The important point is that no matter how this ultimate being or state of being is described, its fundamental characteristics are remarkably similar across traditions and cultures.

The Mystical Mind is the culmination (to date) of a line of research and scholarship that began in 1975 when Eugene d'Aquili and Charles Laughlin published "The Biopsychological Determinants of Religious Ritual Behavior" in *Zygon: The Journal of Religion and Science*. Their thesis was that all religious phenomenology arose from neuropsychology, but in a way that was much more complex than simple materialistic reductionism. The first ten years of this scholarly movement were very difficult indeed. The attempt to integrate neuropsychology and theology was extremely controversial in the mid-1970s and was often dismissed as an attempt to integrate incommensurables. Among those who became involved in relating neuropsychology to religious phenomenology were, in addition to d'Aquili and Laughlin, John McManus, the Nobel laureate Roger Sperry, Colwyn Trevarthen, Solomon Katz, Victor Turner, James Ashbrook, and several others, including James Austin and Laurence McKinney. Indeed, Ashbrook first used the term *neurotheology* in an article he published in 1984, also in *Zygon,* titled "Neurotheology: The Working Brain and the Work of Theology." Ashbrook painted neurotheology with broad strokes in terms of the split-brain research being conducted at that time. His was a vision begging to be realized, not an accomplished fact. We hope that Ashbrook's vision is realized here some fifteen years later by a substantive integration of neuropsychology and what we might call theological phenomenology.

In keeping with this integration, we will explore the issue of how "ultimate being" is perceived and experienced by the human brain and mind. We will try to be specific when referring to the ultimate being within any given religious tradition. Whenever we refer, however, to God, ultimate reality, absolute unitary being, void consciousness, and so on, we are referring to essentially the same thing. The particular name that we use will be consistent with the particular cultural or religious context that we are considering. It has become fashionable in the social sciences to eschew any comparisons of meaningful similarity among the various religions. The assumption has been that religions are so culturally complex and idiosyncratic that there could be nothing but a superficial comparison between them. Indeed, the generic term *religion* has all but fallen out of use, having been replaced by *the religions*. There can be no doubt that the surface structures of *the religions* are very different and very complex. But, as we will demonstrate, the neuropsychological approach to religious phenomenology will establish that there are certain core elements that appear to be universal and that can be separated from particular cultural matrices. In view of this, we will sometimes use the unfashionable generic term *religion* even though we are perfectly aware that "the religions" manifest great diversity among themselves. The current scholarly attitude toward "the religions" is very similar to the attitude toward cultures just a few decades ago. Under the influence of Franz Boas, in the first half of the twentieth century a vast cultural relativism developed that made it impossible to develop a nomothetic anthropology. Over the past twenty to thirty years, however, sociobiologists and biogenetic structuralists have gone a long way toward establishing some universal core aspects of human cultures in spite of their diversity.[1] It is our intention to bring just such a nomothetic approach to the science of religion. This global and nomothetic approach to "the religions" we call neurotheology, and it often allows us a glimpse of the "religion" lurking beneath "the religions."

In many instances, the search for a God or an ultimate reality and the related practice of religion involves ritual. Ritual behavior has been previously defined as a subset of formalized behavior that represents the reciprocal communication between two or more individuals.[2] Ritual must be structured so that it has various components that comprise the overall behavior. Ritual is usually stereotyped or repetitive over time. Thus, ritual is something that is done more than once and involves doing the same things over and over again, usually in a rhythmic pattern. The final criterion for ritual is that it results in some greater coordination between individuals toward some common goal or purpose. Ritual behavior occurs in many animal species, including human beings, and is critical to the development of behaviors of a social or integrative nature. Thus, ritual might be performed by a group of people through song, prayer, dance, or the telling of stories. The telling of stories specific to a particular religious tradition forms its myth structure. Many scholars use the term *myth* to refer to the primary narratives of a religious tradition. Thus, myth refers to the stories (sometimes recorded in ancient texts or scriptures) that form the foundation of a given religion. The term *myth* has more recently taken on the derogatory meaning of false ways of believing about God or the universe. For our purposes, however, we will use the earlier and stricter definition and consider myth to represent the basic stories of a religion without regard to the issue of their factual or literal truth.

Ritual might also be performed by the individual through contemplation, meditation, or prayer. These private rituals bend the original criteria, since they do not involve communication with other human beings. However, communication (not necessarily verbal) in private rituals occurs between human beings and a putative higher being or state of being. Private rituals fulfill the other criteria in that they are usually structured, involve repetition, and help coordinate the individual toward the ultimate goal of the higher reality. Rituals, whether performed by a group or by an individual, are thus designed to help bring the practitioners closer to the higher being or state of being. These rituals often surround various mythopoetic themes such as good and evil, right and wrong, and justice and injustice. As time passes, human rituals become more clearly defined. Furthermore, elaborate systems tend to develop in order to explain the rationale behind rituals and myths. So was born the study of theology that helps explain the philosophical, epistemological, and ontological basis of myth and ritual specific to a given religious tradition.

We must pause here to consider the various senses by which the term *theology* can be understood. In a very strict sense, theology is the study of a *theos* or God. Both the Jewish and Greek philosophical understanding of God was in personal terms. The Jewish God was definitely personal, but the philosophical Greek *theos* was considered to be a "rational hypostasis." The Hellenistic philosophical concept of a rational hypostasis would describe *theos* as an "ultimate center of awareness" who possessed rationality in a transcendent way, that is, without the sequential states of reasoning characteristic of the human person. Since both Christianity and Islam proceeded out of a conflation of the Jewish and Greek concepts of God, they could not help but see God in personal terms (in some sense at least). Thus, theology can be seen as the intellectual quest for this ultimate transcendent person. Given this historical context, the word *theology* should be reserved for theistic religions only, and even more specifically, for those arising out of the Greco-Jewish tradition (i.e., Judaism, Christianity, and Islam). With the development of comparative theology in the early part of the twentieth century, however, it became apparent that the nonpersonal Oriental religions possessed many of the formal characteristics of the classic Western religions. It became academically fashionable to use the term *theology* for the formal study of any belief system centered on an ultimate or absolute, whether personal or nonpersonal, whether understood as God or as an ultimate state. It is now acceptable to speak of a theology of Buddhism, a theology of Hinduism, and even of a theology of shamanism.

Within each religious tradition, the word *theology* can be used in two senses: natural theology and theology proper (or dogmatic theology). Natural theology is not really theology at all but rather a branch of philosophy. It attempts to prove, or at least prove probable, the existence in reality of the hypothesis-God, or of the hypothesis-the Absolute, by reason alone, without any appeal to divine revelation (in the West) or to fairly rare esoteric experiences (in the

East). In the nineteenth and twentieth centuries, this enterprise has attempted to enlist science. With or without science, it is a thoroughly rational discipline, theoretically without any axes to grind.

Theology proper represents intellectual deductions from a foundational myth (or the primary myth on which the religion is based), as well as "reasonable" extrapolations on such a myth. The beginning point of theology proper, at least in the West and in primitive societies, is a belief in the transcendent truth of the foundational myth, either at the literal surface level or at a deeper symbolic level. It is the belief in the truth of the foundational myth that motivates the deductions and extrapolations from that myth to create a body of knowledge that is dependent on the truth of the myth. In the East, theology proper often develops from a rational attempt to derive meaning and understanding of reality from the esoteric and mystical experiences of holy men. In Hinduism, however, there is, in addition, a marked admixture of deduction from ancient foundational myths.

In the past fifty years, there have been a few attempts to develop a "metatheology" utilizing various general scientific or philosophical themes such as evolution and process theory. A metatheology should be an overarching approach that can explain the essential features of any theology arising out of any specific religious tradition. We intend to present here the most comprehensive metatheology to date. In addition to its being a metatheology, however, this book assumes some aspects of natural theology and considers a number of ancient basic truth claims of many religions in what we hope is a novel and exciting way.

It seems that much of religious and theological study today focuses on the basis of religion, the nature of God, and the relationship between human beings and God. These studies are based primarily on philosophy, epistemology, and ontology, and they therefore take place in a more theoretical realm. Furthermore, these studies often use ancient religious texts to help validate their conclusions.

Theology in its more rigorous form has been dominated by Christian thinkers; thus, Christian theology has developed into an extensive study of the relationship of human beings to God and God incarnate. Much of the focus of Christian theology has been on the Bible, including both the Old and New Testaments. As the study of theology evolved, various other texts were included as well as the dicta of the church's magisterium. Christian theological thinking slowly evolved from the writings of the church fathers into medieval concepts of religion and God, through the Renaissance, the Reformation, and eventually to the postmodernism of the present. Today, theological studies have become a formal academic pursuit as well as a religious one. First-rate modern systematic Christian theologians seem to be producing systems that lie somewhere between deduction from the foundational myth of Christianity at a deep symbolic level and a true metatheology. Much of the work in present-day theology consists of analysis and understanding of existing texts in a consistently hermeneutical context.

In comparing philosophy to modern theology, Paul Tillich suggests that philosophy is a "cognitive approach to reality in which reality as such is the object."[3] Philosophy, then, is directed toward the external reality of the universe. Theology, on the other hand, is directed toward the "ultimate concern" of human beings. This "ultimate concern is that which determines our being or not-being." In some sense, theology is directed inward toward an individual's ultimate concerns. While this duality should not be regarded as rigid, it does demonstrate what the fundamental issues of theology are and how they differ from philosophy. This distinction is similar to the one between theology and science, since science is an empirical philosophy that is directed toward our objective cognitions of the external world. The theologian, however, also must start from the state of being in external reality, since theology must begin with human experiences if they are to be interpreted.

The duality between science and theology has received much attention in recent years, but there appears to be a historic struggle between scientists and theologians. Ian Barbour outlines the ways of relating science to theology as consisting of four possible relationships.[4] The first is that science and theology are considered to be essentially opposite and antagonistic to each other. Examples of this conflict include scientists who support scientific materialism, such as sociobiologist Edward O. Wilson and biologist Jacques Monod.[5] In their view, religion is perceived to have an adaptive advantage from an evolutionary perspective, but it does not represent objective reality as does science. The religious counterpart in this conflict involves those who believe in biblical literalism. Here the Bible is considered to be literally true, and thus it supersedes any scientific data that conflict with the statements of the Bible. This has led to great debate in many scientific and religious areas, the most notable of which has been the argument between supporters of the theory of evolution and the adherents of creationism. Either science and scientific theory are absolutely accurate or the Bible is absolutely accurate. Because of the vast differences between their descriptions of the origins of life and of the universe, both systems seem to be mutually exclusive.

A second interaction between science and theology is a mutual independence from each other. In this way, religion and science function in totally distinct domains. They do not conflict because science interprets human understanding of the world while religion interprets God's activity in the world. A story of a Kalahari bushman who was bitten by a mosquito illustrates this point. After the mosquito bite, the bushman promptly went to the medical doctor to get the medications to prevent malaria. The bushman told the doctor that after his appointment, he had to go see the tribe's medicine man. The doctor could not understand why the patient was going to go to a spiritual adviser if he had so much faith in modern Western medicine. The bushman replied, "I go the medical doctor because I got bitten by the mosquito, I go to the medicine man to find out why." This short tale indicates that science and religion (or spirituality) need not conflict, since they cover different parts of reality. The only problem with this interpretation is that it also forces science and religion into exclusivity, and the domain of each becomes essentially off-limits to the other.

The final two relationships between science and religion are dialogue and integration. The dialogue consists of boundary questions that exist in both science and religion. Examples include the big bang cosmology and quantum mechanics. Investigation in these fields eventually results in religious questions that are unanswerable by scientific analysis. Questions such as what existed before the big bang, why did the big bang occur, why is the universe here at all, and does God play dice with the universe, all appear to be out of the realm of present-day scientific inquiry. Some of these questions may never be answerable from a scientific perspective. David Tracy suggests that there are more subtle examples of boundary questions that occur in everyday human experience.[6] Examples of such experiences include anxiety, joy, basic trust, and death. Science and religion share certain methodological principles that are not identical, but similar enough to allow for meaningful dialogue. Holmes Rolston suggests that religion interprets and correlates human experience while science does the same with experimental data.[7] Science and religion also function within certain paradigms that form the basis of the accepted practice and can only be changed with great upheavals. Again, while science and religion are certainly not isomorphic, they are similar enough that a beneficial dialogue can exist between the two.

The final relationship that may exist between science and religion is integration, in which the two come together to explain each other. As noted earlier, natural theology (such as that described in some of the work of Thomas Aquinas and other scholastics) attempts to explain the existence of God and religion entirely by human reasoning. A classic approach of natural theology is the design argument, which proposes that the inherent order of the universe implies the existence of God. The anthropic principle, which has gained some support recently among noted scientists, suggests that the conditions of the universe are too perfectly attuned for the development of human life and that there must have been divine intervention, if only to get things started. Another attempt at integrating science and theology is the development of a "theology of nature." This differs from natural theology in that it begins with a firm religious basis that is then modified in order to accommodate the influx of new scientifically derived information. Finally, science and religion are integrated in "process philosophy" as developed by Alfred North Whitehead.[8] This philosophy was formulated with both scientific and religious concepts in an attempt to develop a overarching developmental metaphysics that is applicable to the universe as a whole.

Of course, each of these four relationships between science and religion—conflict, independence, dialogue, and integration—has its own shortcomings. For the purposes of this book, however, we do not feel it is necessary to critique each of the theories regarding science and religion. We simply want to establish a framework within which an analysis of theology from the perspective of the mind and brain may be considered. This framework is important because the concepts that we will put forth fall into the category of the integration of science and religion. Thus, science and religion will be explored in a complementary manner in order to develop a coherent analysis of the world. But, as we will see, our model goes one step further in that science and religion not only are brought together but also are essentially considered to be one and the same thing without either being reduced to the other. This result will be derived from our analysis of the mind and brain, and their relationship to human experience in general and religion in particular. Thus, we would suggest that one cannot understand religion without understanding the mind and brain and one cannot understand the mind and brain without understanding religion. This is part of the reason that we have referred to the mind as "mystical," because the analysis of the mind eventually leads to a holistic or unitary understanding of both science and theology. However, before beginning such a consideration, we must continue our brief introduction to theology in order to understand the relevance of the mind and brain to the theological enterprise in general and to the development of a scientific metatheology in particular.

SOURCES OF THEOLOGY

Paul Tillich indicates that there are three main sources of Christian theological education.[9] The Bible is the original text upon which the church was founded, and it is thus the primary source of systematic Christian theology. Over time, other texts have become embodied in Christian theology, particularly the corpus of patristic writing. All of these texts must be considered in the context of human culture since they must be received by human beings for any revelation to occur. Church tradition is also seen as a source of theology, since it is the church that has formulated Christian teachings and theology throughout history. It is not a particular church's teachings that should become the basis of theology, however, but the object of all churches in general, that is, God. The third source of systematic theology, according to Tillich, is historical religion and culture. These are important sources because they yield the perspective from which any given theologian develops theological concepts. This, in some ways, forms the hermeneutical basis of theology. Knowledge of the language, culture, and economic and political climate from which a theological work has been generated is necessary to adequately study that particular theology.

Of course, theology is not limited to Christianity and has been extensively studied in other Western religions as well. Judaism has a long history of theological studies. This includes ancient texts such as the Torah, the haftarah, the Mishnah, and the Talmud. In fact, much of the basis of Jewish teaching is the emphasis placed on the study of the Torah to determine specifically the relationship of God to human beings. Much of Judaism concerns itself with the notion of God and the meaning of God's covenant with the Jewish people. This transmitting of Jewish teachings is usually understood as part of the covenant itself.

Islam has also generated theological accounts based on both the Bible and the teachings of Muhammad as recorded in the Koran. Islamic theology is also derived from sources similar to those mentioned by Tillich. Thus, the culture, language, and social structure of the people who have embraced Islam allowed for the evolution of theological studies.

The Eastern traditions of Buddhism and Hinduism have a very different basis compared to the Judeo-Christian and Islamic theologies. Nonetheless, in keeping with the criteria Tillich sets forth, the Eastern traditions also have the same types of sources as those generating Western theologies. The cultural component of the Eastern traditions is clearly different from the culture within which Judaism, Christianity, and Islam arose. Both Hinduism and Buddhism have numerous texts that describe the tenets of the religion and the various ways in which it can be practiced. The distinguishing feature of the Eastern religions is that they not only have a tradition of group rituals such as those found in the West, but they also use meditation as an integral part of their teachings. Even though meditation and contemplation are part of the Western religious traditions as well, these methods are seldom practiced by the general populace. Only a few isolated Western sects practice meditation as a primary and essential component of their religion.

Traditional theologies consist of cognitive elements derived from extrapolations from foundational myths. Thus, in traditional religions a distinction is made between the purely intellectual components of the religion that are defined as theology and religious practices such as ritual and ethical behavior. The latter two, as examples of praxis, are rarely considered parts of theology, practically speaking. In developing a metatheology, however, a rational, and if possible scientific, understanding of religious practices must assume its place in the corpus of rational thought defining a theological enterprise. Traditional theologies could in no way account for religious practices such as ritual except by appeals to faith. As we shall see, modern neuropsychology can do better than that.

The word *theology* has always evoked the rational element in religion. Although any given traditional theology is based on belief in a foundational myth, the process of theology itself is based on rational inference or deduction from that myth. Faith may involve the beginning assumption, but theology itself is always a rational process. We justify the use of theology, as in *neurotheology*, because it brings all the elements of religion, even those formerly considered irrational and thus not within the purview of theology, under a single rational explanatory mechanism, namely, neuropsychology. Thus, for neurotheology, rationality resides not so much in the logical inferences and deductions from myth as in the fact that other elements of religion, formally considered irrational, can now be explained rationally in their causes and consequences. These include an understanding of the necessity for humans to structure myths, an understanding of the brain mechanisms involved in their structuring, an understanding of the need for ritual, how it is generated by the brain, how it incarnates myth, and its personal and social effects. Neurotheology also can explain the need for and effect of ascetic practices and the nature and consequences of meditation. All of these elements, formerly considered irrational aspects of religion, can be brought under the umbrella of rationality and hence constitute part of a new theology that now includes all aspects of religion. Admittedly, this metatheology vastly increases the theological enterprise, but it is a logical expansion of the concept of theology that has been defined as a rational discourse on religious concepts. Philip Hefner presents a metatheology intended to subsume all former theologies deriving from specific myths in *The Human Factor: Evolution, Culture and Religion*.[10] Hefner's overarching paradigm or scientific myth from which he develops his metatheology might be called scientific ecology, just as ours is neuropsychology. In any case, there is an increasing tendency for many theologians to think in terms of a metatheology, and the appropriation of the term *theology* is made without apology. This seems to be generally accepted except by conservative theologians within the Christian tradition who insist that the term be reserved for inferences and deductions from a specific historical myth (i.e., the story of the life and sayings of Jesus of Nazareth).

And so, the underlying principles of religious practice such as ritual and liturgy become part of the overall theological apparatus in developing a metatheology. Crucial to this approach is an understanding of ritual behavior, since we shall see that human ceremonial ritual incarnates myth, foundational or otherwise. Likewise, a neuropsychological understanding of meditation and meditative practices is equally crucial to an understanding of religious systems and their theologies.

Social historians such as A. E. Barnes and his colleagues have emphasized the supposed inverse relationship between group ritual and individual meditation.[11] They point to the popular performance of liturgical and paraliturgical religious ceremonial prior to the Reformation and Counter-Reformation with its minimal emphasis on private devotion and/or meditation. Conversely, both the Reformation and the Counter-Reformation were marked by a decreased emphasis on popular religious ritual and an increased emphasis on private religious devotion and meditative practices. These historians also note the evolution of various pietistic movements both within and without the Roman Catholic Church, the rise in popularity of private devotions related to the printing of prayer books, and the development and popularization of the Ignatian retreat and of Ignatius Loyola's *Spiritual Exercises*.

This rigidly inverse relationship between public religious ritual behavior and private devotion and/or meditation is difficult to support on the basis of religious and historical evidence in other times and places, even within the Western tradition. Furthermore, if one looks at a variety of cultures, the inverse relationship between public ritual and private meditation becomes considerably more tenuous. In the Eastern traditions, in both Hinduism and Buddhism, there is usually a complementary relationship between ceremonial ritual and meditative practices that seems to render the inverse relationship between ritual and meditation anything but a cultural universal. Indeed, it could be argued that the supposed inverse relationship between ritual and meditation is a unique condition arising from particular cultural circumstances of modern European history. Again, we can see the significance of the cultural milieu within which a given theology and set of religious practices evolve.

Whatever may be the case concerning the complementarity versus the reciprocity of these two cultural practices, part of the purpose of this book is to show that they both tap into the same or similar neurophysiological mechanisms. A phenomenological analysis reveals that group rituals and private meditation (or devotion) are similar in kind, if not in intensity, along two dimensions. Both involve intermittent emotional discharges that are related to the subjective sensations of awe, peace, tranquillity, or ecstasy; and both involve varying degrees of unitary experience that correlates with the emotional discharges just mentioned. The result is a decreased sense or awareness of the boundaries between the subject and other individuals. This breakdown of boundaries allows for a heightened sense of community among individuals. If the process arising from both types of practices becomes more intense, there is a breakdown of the distinction between the subject and external inanimate objects, between the subject and putative supernatural beings, and, at the extreme, the diminution and abolition of all boundaries of discrete being. This final state generates a state of altered consciousness that we have previously termed absolute unitary being (AUB).

All of these states or altered phases of consciousness are involved in the development of various religious beliefs. The significance of mystical experiences has been attested to by both Eastern and Western traditions. We have already mentioned the mystical aspects of Eastern traditions such as Hinduism and Buddhism. Meditation is also practiced in Christianity, Islam, and Judaism but has been defined somewhat differently based on the culture and religious structures within which mystical practices developed. Mystical experiences are generally regarded as the mechanism by which a human being can enter into the realm of God or ultimate reality, depending on the particular religion. It is logical that such experiences eventually become incorporated into the theology of any given religion. Although early theoreticians such as Friedrich Schleiermacher, Rudolph Otto, and William James would have supported mystical experiences as a primary determinant in the development of religions, there has been a tendency by many philosophers of religion within the past fifty years to move away from this position. Findings by sociologists such as Andrew Greeley have shown, however, that more than 40 percent of individuals in the United States claim to have had experiences that they define as mystical.[12] Furthermore, a Gallup poll showed that 71 percent of Americans believe in life after death and more than 90 percent believe in God. In the face of such pervasive experience it is hard to imagine how mystical experiences do not support religion. And if the prevalence of such experiences were at least that pronounced among our primitive ancestors, then it is very hard indeed to see how such experiences were not at least partial determinants in the evolution of the religions. Furthermore, if the frequency of people believing in God or an afterlife can be documented in a country of universal education with a strong scientific and technological orientation, then one must assume that the prevalence of mystical experiences was at least somewhat higher among our primitive ancestors. In fact, mystical experiences must be explained and rationally incorporated within a religious tradition so that there is a coherent explanation of precisely what is happening when one enters into mystical states. Most religions have had to find a way to deal with mystical phenomena in relation to the more general religious structure, foundational myth, or theology. Thus, most religions have been forced to address the significance of mystical phenomena in relation to their ancient texts as well as in relation to their conception of God or the Absolute.

Based on the significance of mystical experiences in religious practice, it seems that a fourth source of theology should be added to Tillich's original three, namely, the individual's personal experiences of mystical or unusual states. Perhaps this source should, more appropriately, be considered as part of an expansion of the source that is derived from the church, synagogue, or mosque. These institutions, perceived as congregations as they originally were, not buildings, represent the manner by which groups of people come to understand and partake in rituals pertaining to their religion. Meditation and its related mystical states are the means by which individuals can come to understand and partake in ultimate reality, or even, as some have suggested, the realm of God.

WHY NEUROTHEOLOGY?

One of the primary purposes of this book is to develop the concept of neurotheology that refers to the study of theology from a neuropsychological perspective. The question that must first be answered is, Why should we consider theology from a neuropsychological perspective at all? To begin with, as we have mentioned, the theologian must begin with the human experience of religion. This is based on a variety of religious experiences that have been categorized by several authors. Ian Barbour accepts six distinct types of religious experiences first suggested by Frederick Streng: the numinous experience of the holy, the transformative experience of reorientation, the courage of facing suffering and death, the moral experience of obligation, the experience of order and creativity in the world, and the mystical experience of unity.[13] These experiences are where most of theology, especially metatheology, begins. We would suggest, however, that all of these experiences are just that, experiences, and, like all experiences, they are eventually interpreted and modulated by the human brain (we will later consider the basis for the experiential functioning of the brain). Thus, before one begins utilizing religious experiences for theological purposes, it seems most important to consider the significance of the relationship of the mind and brain to those experiences. This is why we suggest that the concept of a neurotheology is particularly relevant to the analysis of religion and religious experiences.

We have already mentioned that part of our intent here is to develop the notion that the experiences of religious ritual in general and meditative practices in particular involve similar neuropsychological mechanisms. In previous works, we have begun to develop a neurophysiological model of the brain activation that occurs during intense meditation. Furthermore, we have already been gathering empirical evidence that supports this model. More important, the model suggests a similar mechanism for a wide variety of mystical and unitary states. Even experiences that anyone may have during standard church liturgies likely involve similar areas of the brain as those in meditation, only to different degrees.

The result of the development of a neuropsychological model of mystical experiences has also led to an exploration of how we as human beings experience reality. We have argued that reality is necessarily interpreted by the brain, which gives us our sense of that reality. There is no manner in which we can come to experience or know reality other than through the functioning of the brain. This fact brings us to the ancient philosophical question about what is really real. Furthermore, since the answer to this question is in large part based on the brain, we have termed the study of what is really real "neuroepistemology." The neuroepistemological approach is also crucial to the study of theology, which is based on what is of "ultimate" concern.

More important, we have mentioned that the mind and brain are what allow human beings to develop and experience religious ritual and spirituality. Since the experience of religion, spirituality, myth, and ritual has its basis in the functioning of the mind and brain, it seems appropriate to begin an analysis of theology from the perspective of neuropsychology. In fact, if the mind and brain are responsible for all of our experiences, then they are also the mediator for our experience of God. Thus, it may be absolutely necessary to employ the study of the mind and brain in order to understand fully the relationship between human beings and God. This being the case, it seems that the concept of neurotheology may be crucial to our understanding of the theologies of religions in general and essential to our understanding of any possible metatheology.

THE PRESENTATION OF THE MYSTICAL MIND

We will begin our exploration of the nature of the human mind and brain and how they relate to religion, ritual, mysticism, and traditional theologies by considering how the brain works. This will require a review of the basic structure of the brain from its most primitive to its most highly advanced parts. While the structure of the brain is quite complex, we will try to focus our analysis on the parts of the brain that are most relevant to the study of human experience, emotion, and cognition. In particular, we will begin to explain how the brain allows us to have mystical experiences. The study of mystical experiences has particular relevance because these are what ultimately lead us to an understanding of the relationship between human beings and any higher state of being.

Once we have established an understanding of the function of the brain, we can begin to explore how the mind functions in a mystical way. It is important to note that the brain and the mind may be considered together in a "mystical union." As a whole, this mind/brain functions to give us our advanced methods of experiencing and interpreting the external world. We will also examine the significance of the mind in relation to intelligence. In the end, this overview of how the mind functions will allow us to explore in greater detail the mystical mind.

Once there is an understanding of the basic function of the mind/brain, we will consider the more complex function of myth formation. Myths themselves play a significant role in our overall understanding of the universe. Therefore, myth formation is an integral part of the functioning of the mystical mind. Furthermore, myth formation is not only a crucial aspect of the development of religion and theology, but also, as we shall describe, is necessary for the development of science.

With a new insight into the workings of the mystical mind, including how the brain and mind function and how myth formation occurs, we can begin to explore specific aspects of theology and religion from this new neuropsychological perspective. This will likely have profound implications for theology in particular since the very basis of specific theologies will be rethought from this new vantage point. We will consider the basic components of liturgy and ritual to try to ascertain why these play such an important part in religious practice. We will attempt to unravel the neuropsychological mechanisms that underlie ritual behavior. We will explore why ritual has the effects that it does and why it is so important to the development of religion. We will also consider how future ritual and liturgy might be modified according to its possible effects on the human mind/brain.

While ritual and liturgy pertain to more mundane practices within religion, meditation with its associated mystical phenomena also relies on neuropsychology. In fact, it may be that profound mystical experiences deriving from meditation involve neural pathways very similar to those involved in ritual and "lesser" mystical states. To that end, we will present a neuropsychological model for meditation, focusing particularly on the attainment of the highest levels of unitary conscious awareness. This model will also refer to the experiences attained during "lesser" mystical states. All of these mystical states have significant implications for religion and theology in general. Thus, a thorough understanding of how the mind/brain functions to generate mystical states will be extremely useful in considering theology from the neuropsychological perspective.

In addition to mystical experiences attained through meditation or ritual, it is important to understand other types of mystical experiences in reference to neuropsychology. These other mystical experiences, which are often spontaneous, throw an interesting twist into the study of religion and theology. It is difficult, at times, to incorporate the mystical experiences of an individual or group of individuals into the overall framework of a given religion or theology. In order to explore these types of experiences, we will focus on the near-death experience (NDE). These NDEs have received much publicity in recent years, and there has been a growing body of literature regarding their nature and cause. We will present a review of the relevant literature of NDEs and also propose a possible neuropsychological mechanism as their cause. While it is difficult, if not impossible, to make any conclusive statements about an afterlife based on the phenomenology of the NDE, we feel that we can analyze what the human mind/brain experiences when a person is near death and perhaps make some tentative conclusions. An analysis of the NDE will also help emphasize several of the points made regarding the nature of the mystical mind and mystical experiences in general. Again, with this new neuropsychological perspective, we can rework the meaning of such experiences into an overall theological framework.

In the last section of this book, we will integrate many of the concepts that were developed regarding the mind/brain into a new approach to theology, that of neurotheology. By neurotheology, we mean that we will examine how the mind/brain functions in terms of humankind's relation to God or ultimate reality. We will consider the significance and necessity of ritual and myth in terms of the function of the mind/brain and the implications of this analysis for the study of religion and the formation of specific theologies. We will also explore how mystical states, as experienced by the mind/brain, have altered religion and theology. Given the nature of the mystical mind to have such experiences, we will see how they must be fundamentally integrated into religion. We will also explore traditional approaches to theology and put them in the perspective of neurotheology. This will show how theological and religious principles may be understood somewhat differently when considered from this new perspective.

We will demonstrate the intriguing paradox that although God or pure consciousness is generated by the machinery of the brain, nevertheless a strict phenomenological analysis can logically and coherently see absolute unitary being or pure consciousness not only as primary over external material reality but as actually generating it. We will present the paradox of two very different approaches to the nature of fundamental reality actually being complementary and not opposed. We will explore how a phemonenological approach to various levels of reality is not only compatible with neurotheology but actually demanded by it.

Based on the concept of neurotheology, we will explore theology in a greater context, incorporating some traditional theological concepts with new ones based on our neuropsychological approach. This metatheology will incorporate various aspects derived from both Eastern and Western traditions and integrate them with neuropsychology. It will be based both on the mundane aspects of everyday life, rituals, and myths developed in religion, and on more intense mystical phenomena that arise either spontaneously or through meditation.

We should mention that many of the concepts pertaining to the mind/brain are based on existing research in neurology, psychology, and psychiatry. Furthermore, experiments on animals and human subjects have also yielded information regarding how the mind/brain works. Recently, imaging technologies have been developed that are capable of observing the brain while it works. Although a tremendous number of studies have explored the inner workings of the mind/brain, there remains an even larger amount of information that is unknown. For this reason, it is difficult to describe with absolute certainty the intricate neurophysiological mechanisms underlying human ritual, myth, mysticism, and religious phenomena in general. It is therefore, important to state at the outset that the mechanisms we present are models of how the mind/brain functions in such instances. There is good empirical evidence to support these models, but they are far from proven. We suspect that some aspects of these models will be proven true while others may be shown to be incorrect. It is our purpose, however, to show that the function of the mind/brain is a significant factor in the development of religions and theologies. We strongly encourage the continued study of how the mind/brain is related to theology and religion so that the concept of neurotheology can become a rigorous study of how human beings relate to God and to the world in the context of an Absolute.

In this book, we will explore a nontraditional approach to religion and theology that is based not so much on highly abstract concepts or ancient texts as on that part of human beings that allows us to study all of these concepts and to contemplate, and perhaps experience, the higher being or state of being—the mystical mind.

Chapter Two

The Brain and Central Nervous System

Before beginning our investigation of the mystical mind, we must first develop a foundation in the neurosciences. We will review various aspects of how the brain functions and then determine how the brain's functioning leads to various aspects of the mind. We will then consider the functioning of the mind and brain in such a way that both can be considered as mystical. While this concept may be difficult to understand at first, it will become more apparent that the brain and mind have developed in such a way that we should not be surprised at the ability of human beings to generate ritual, myth, and mystical states of consciousness. Thus, we will consider how the brain and the mind have evolved to function in a mystical way. To that end, the notion of the mystical brain and the mystical mind will be elucidated. In later chapters, we will use this foundation to explain the neurophysiological basis of myth, ritual, and theology.

It is important to state here that it is difficult to define accurately what the mind is and what the brain is. For that matter, it is equally difficult to distinguish precisely how the mind and brain are related—where one ends and the other begins. Certainly, the mind/brain question has been considered by philosophers, scientists, and theologians throughout history. Here we would like to use the following definitions for the brain and the mind. The brain is the substantive underlying part of human thought, experience, and emotions. In other words, it is the bodily organ that allows us to think, feel, and receive input from the external world. The mind is generally considered to be the thoughts and feelings themselves. Thus, the mind is the product of the functioning of the brain.

We believe, however, that it is important to get beyond such a simple dualistic definition and would suggest rather that the mind and brain are simply two different ways of looking at the same thing. This is analogous to the particle-wave model of light that is described in physics. In this model, light can sometimes appear to function as a particle and sometimes can appear to act as a wave, depending on how one tries to measure and analyze the light. Thus, if one looks for a wave, one finds a wave, but if one looks for a particle, one finds a particle. Similarly, depending on what one is looking for, one might describe thoughts and feelings as originating from the structure of the brain or from the product of that structure—the mind. Regardless, the mind and brain are intimately intertwined in human behavior and thought.

In addition to the interrelationship of the mind and brain, we should mention that science can demonstrate no other mechanism by which the mind comes about other than the brain. One common aspect of human existence that has often been implicated in the generation of human behavior is the human soul. The concept of the soul has significant implications with regards to theology, myth, and ritual. We will not consider whether or not there exists a human soul that is involved in human behavior. We would argue, however, that if there is a soul that can be experienced, our only experience of it is likely by means of the human brain and therefore the human mind. After all, we have no method of experiencing the world, which includes the soul, other than through our senses, emotions, and thoughts. These are certainly functions of the mind and brain. Thus, even if there is a sensible soul, our cognitive and emotional experiences of it must be mediated ultimately by the brain. Every other aspect of human experience that can be documented in living human beings must also be generated and modulated by the human brain and mind. This includes our daily experience of baseline reality (our family, job, possessions, the "world"), any "extrasensory" abilities that might be possible, near-death experiences, emotional responses and feelings, attitudes, thoughts—in short, any and all elements of subjective awareness. That the brain underlies all experiences of living human beings is an absolute statement. It subsumes all religious phenomena and all mystical experiences, including hyperlucid visionary experiences, trance states, contemplating God, and the experience of unitary absorption into any absolute whether personal or nonpersonal.

As we have mentioned, as far as modern science can ascertain, the brain is the origin of the "mind." By this we mean that the brain is responsible for receiving input from the outside world, analyzing that input, informing us what that input is, feeling an emotional content toward that input, creating a behavioral response to that input, and acting out that behavior. For example, when we look at our mother, our brain receives the image through our eyes; analyzes the colors and shapes and interprets the image of "mother"; informs us that the image is, in fact, our mother; decides on a specified type of emotion or behavior toward this image; and initiates, generates, and determines that behavior. This general format of brain functioning holds for everything we experience. This is true of everyday experiences as well as profound religious experiences. This brain function, as well as several others that we will consider, will eventually reveal the underlying mystical nature of the brain such that it quite easily allows for the formation of mystical experiences of many different kinds. Given this basic understanding of how the brain works, we can now explore the underlying structure and mechanism of the brain.

THE AUTONOMIC NERVOUS SYSTEM

The most basic part of the nervous system is the autonomic nervous system. The autonomic nervous system is responsible, with input from the rest of the brain and central nervous system, for maintaining baseline bodily function. It also allows the body to respond to various external stimuli. Thus, the autonomic nervous system helps connect the brain to the rest of the body. The autonomic nervous system also plays a crucial role, however, in the overall activity of the brain, as well as in the generation of fundamental emotions such as fear, joy, and shame. As we will consider later, it appears that the autonomic nervous system is required for the generation of the mystical mind.

The autonomic nervous system is traditionally understood to be composed of two subsystems: the sympathetic system and the parasympathetic system.[1] The sympathetic system subserves the so-called fight-or-flight response and is the physiological base of our adaptive strategies either to noxious stimuli or to highly desirable stimuli in the environment.[2] In short, the sympathetic system causes a sense of arousal. We have sometimes referred to the sympathetic nervous system with several other associated structures as part of an overall arousal system. We will use the term *arousal* throughout this book since we are primarily concerned with the arousal activity of the sympathetic nervous system even though there are other functions. In fact, this system has also been called the ergotropic system because the term *ergotropic* refers to the activation of this system, which results in the release or expenditure of energy.[3] Anatomically, the arousal system integrates the functions of the sympathetic nervous system, the adrenal glands, and its connections to the lower parts of the brain. Finally, it has extensions into the higher cognitive parts of the brain. The principal function of the arousal system is control of short-range adaptation to events in the environment. It initiates and carries out action directed at either acquiring or avoiding stimuli of survival interest to the animal. Among the functions of the arousal system are expenditure of vital resources, stopping digestion, opening the airways in the lungs, increasing heart rate and blood pressure, increasing muscle efficiency, dilation of the pupils, erection of body hair, ejaculation, decreased salivation, and increased respiration.

The other part of the autonomic nervous system is the parasympathetic system. This system is essentially the antithesis of the sympathetic or arousal system. The parasympathetic system is responsible for maintaining homeostasis and conserving the body's resources and energy.[4] It regulates physiological maintenance activities and vegetative functions such as growth of cells, digestion, relaxation, and sleep. The parasympathetic system is part of a more global neuronal circuitry that we have often referred to as the quiescent system. We will use the term *quiescent* throughout this book since we are primarily concerned with this function, even though this system has other roles in body regulation. This system includes the functions of the parasympathetic system, various endocrine glands, and various structures of both the lower and the upper parts of the brain. Quiescent system functions include a storage of vital resources, digestion and distribution of nutrients, constriction of bronchi, decrease in heart rate and blood pressure, collection of waste products, penile erection, increased salivation, and slowing of respiration. Since the quiescent system is involved in the conservation of the body's energy, it has sometimes been referred to as the trophotropic system.[5]

The arousal system and the quiescent system are usually described as "antagonistic" or "inhibitory" to each other.[6] Normally, increased activity of one tends to produce a decreased activity in the other. Thus, each system is designed to inhibit the functioning of the other under most circumstances. This helps prevent an excess of the activity of either system. Over the years, however, it has become apparent that the interaction between these two parts of the autonomic nervous system is highly complex. There is also evidence that these two systems can sometimes function in a complementary manner.[7] Such a functioning may occur when one of these systems is driven to maximal activity despite the protective antagonistic mechanism. When this occurs, one can induce a "reversal" or "spillover" phenomenon.[8] This spillover effect occurs when continued stimulation of one system to maximal capacity begins to produce activation responses (rather than inhibitory) in the opposite system. This state is relatively rare and requires intense driving of one of the systems, beyond its normal capacity and beyond the inhibitory effects of the other system. If intense stimulation of the same system is continued, one can attain the even rarer state that involves maximal simultaneous activation of both the arousal and the quiescent systems.[9]

The specific balance between these two systems under particular environmental circumstances is amenable to conditioning, and there is evidence that the characteristic balance is established as early as pre- and perinatal life. Our baseline state represents the emotional setting we bring to the world—that is, whether we are "uptight" or "laid-back." This baseline balance can be altered, however, by conditioning with the eventual result of a new emotional balance.

It has been argued that ritual control of the arousal/quiescent balance is fundamental to virtually all primitive healing techniques because ritual can help to reset the original balance. It also has been argued that ritual or meditation may generate alternative phases of consciousness via the activation of the arousal and the quiescent system.

We have proposed in previous works four basic categories of arousal/quiescent states that may occur during extraordinary phases of consciousness.[10] We will review them here since they contribute to the generation of a wide variety of states spanning a continuum of experiences.

1. *The Hyperquiescent State.* Quiescent activity is exceptionally high, resulting in an extraordinary state of relaxation. This type of activity happens during normal sleep, but may paradoxically occur during meditative phases accompanied by heightened alertness and vigilance. It also may occur during "slow" ritualistic behavior such as chanting or prayer as opposed to "rapid" or frenzied ritual behavior such as Sufi dancing. In extreme form, the hyperquiescent state may be experienced as a sense of oceanic tranquillity and bliss in which no thoughts or feelings intrude on consciousness and no bodily sensations are felt. In Buddhist psychology, this state is called access concentration or *Upacara samadhi.*

2. *The Hyperarousal State.* Arousal activity is exceptionally high, resulting in an extraordinary state of unblocked arousal and excitation. This state may occur under various circumstances in which motor activity is continuous and rhythmic such as in "rapid" ritual behavior, dancing, long-distance running, or swimming. It may also occur during a state in which continuous processing of information becomes so voluminous that interjection of thought and ego-centered decision making would prove disadvantageous. Examples of such experiences are car racing or piloting a jet fighter. This state will also be associated with keen alertness and concentration in the absence of superfluous thoughts and feelings. The person may feel as if they were channeling vast quantities of energy effortlessly through their consciousness, resulting in what has been called the quintessential "flow" experience.

3. *The Hyperquiescent State with Eruption of the Arousal System.* Quiescent activity is so extreme that "spillover" occurs and the arousal system becomes activated. In this case, a person who is meditating, for example, enters a state of oceanic bliss, and, by intensifying concentration upon the object of meditation, experiences absorption into that object. This has been called *Appana samadhi* in Buddhist psychology. This experience is usually accompanied by the sense of a tremendous release of energy. Thus, the meditator may experience an "active" bliss or energy rush. Occasionally, this may occur in people during "slow" ritual behavior, which can result in a brief eruption of the arousal system with consequent brief states of altered consciousness.

4. *The Hyperarousal State with Eruption of the Quiescent System.* "Spillover" phenomena may be attained by the opposite route mentioned above such that arousal activity is so extreme that the quiescent system becomes activated. For example, a meditator may experience a discharge of the quiescent system in the midst of a hyperarousal state as a consequence of enhanced concentration or of arousal drivers such as rapid and intense rhythmic stimuli. The person may experience an orgasmic, rapturous, or ecstatic rush arising from a generalized sense of flow and resulting in trancelike states. This experience may occur as a result of practices such as Sufi dancing and marathon running and even occurs briefly during sexual climax.

We will add to these four arousal/quiescent complexes a fifth, which we have alluded to earlier, in which there is simultaneous maximal discharge of both the arousal and the quiescent system. There is evidence that this occurs during the state in which there is a complete breakdown of any discrete boundaries between objects, a sense of the absence of time, and the elimination of the self-other dichotomy. In other words, it may be related to the *unio mystica,* the perfect experience of the void or Nirvana, or other absolute unitary states.

The relationship of these five levels of arousal/quiescent states to an assortment of altered phases of consciousness and mystical states is one of the major themes of this book. While we believe that the interaction between the arousal and quiescent systems is important for the manifestation of spiritual experiences, however, these experiences are highly complex and involve a number of brain structures and functions, as we will describe throughout this book. In addition to relating these states to various types of meditation, we will explore related issues of whether the state of simultaneous maximal stimulation can be achieved via religious ritual, whether the rhythmicity of ritual behavior can ever extend beyond the hyperquiescent state to include a subsequent eruption of the arousal system in the case of "slow ritual" or beyond the hyperarousal state with eruption of the quiescent system in the case of "rapid ritual."[11]

It is important to note that in describing the arousal/quiescent complexes, we have made a distinction between "slow" and "rapid" ritual behavior. Careful analysis of the possible neuropsychological mechanisms underlying the effects of ritual behavior suggests that a distinction can be made between the slow rhythmic movements of a Christian or Shinto ritual and the rapid, frenzied movements of Sufi or bushman rituals. Slow rhythmicity seems to drive the quiescent system to increasing intensity while "rapid" rhythmicity seems to drive the arousal system to ever increasing intensity. Either way, when the maximum capacity of one system is reached, there occurs the "spillover" and eruption of the other system. We will consider the effects of this type of ritual behavior in a later chapter, in addition to its implications for liturgy and theology.

For all of these states to occur in conjunction with higher brain functions, there must be some way that the arousal and quiescent systems communicate with the parts of the brain responsible for higher-order cognitive functioning. While we have implied that the body and the autonomic nervous system are extensions of the brain, they are generally not thought to be part of the brain proper. Therefore, we will now consider several of the parts of the brain specifically involved in generating our higher sensory and cognitive processes.

THE STRUCTURE OF THE BRAIN

Neuroscientists have divided the brain into numerous subdivisions in order to make locating parts of the brain easier. The first subdivision is the left and right hemispheres. Anatomically, the hemispheres look almost identical. Each hemisphere contains the cerebral cortex, which is generally considered to be the seat of higher-level cognitive functions as well as sensory and motor control (see Figures 2.1 and 2.2). The vast majority of the cerebral cortex is also called the neocortex (the "new" cortex) because it is the most recently developed part of the brain from an evolutionary perspective. It is this part of the brain that is believed to separate human beings from other animals, since it is the seat of our most distinguishing characteristic, our intelligence. It is also the evolution of the neocortex that has resulted in the concomitant development of language, myth, art, culture, and society.

The hemispheres also contain subcortical (i.e., below the cortex) structures such as the thalamus, the hypothalamus, and various midbrain structures (see Figure 2.3). These subcortical structures are involved in basic life support, hormone regulation, and primal emotions; thus, these structures are critical for connecting the brain with the rest of the body. In addition to the neocortex and the subcortex, there is a group of structures that are collectively referred to as the limbic system. This system initially was derived from subcortical structures, but it has come to incorporate parts of the neocortex in human beings and in some other primates during the course of evolution. The limbic system is associated with complex aspects of emotional expression and is involved with assigning emotional valence or content to various objects and experiences and directing these emotions to the external world through our behavior. The limbic system is also intimately connected to the autonomic nervous system to aid in eliciting various emotional responses. For example, when we cognitively become aware of something to be feared, the limbic system relates the feeling of terror and causes a release of adrenaline via the arousal system. This reaction causes us to feel our heart pound, our alertness increase, and our stomach to knot. In this way, we not only become aware of our fear, we experience the whole body's reaction to it.

The interaction of the neocortical, subcortical, and limbic structures with the autonomic nervous system and with each other is crucial to our understanding of how the brain generates human experience and behavior and eventually how myth formation occurs. Thus, we will consider each of these parts of the brain individually as well as how they are interrelated to each other. Ultimately, we will consider how the parts of the brain function together as the mystical brain, and later will observe how the mystical mind arises.

We have mentioned that there is a similarity between the two cerebral hemispheres. This seems entirely appropriate because both hemispheres have similar functions. For example, the left cerebral cortex receives and analyzes sensation from the right side of the body, and the right cerebral cortex receives and analyzes sensation from the left. The left cerebral cortex generates movement in the right side of the body, and conversely, the right hemisphere generates movement in the left side of the body. Despite the similarities, there are also many differences between the two hemispheres. The classic teaching is that the left hemisphere is more involved with the analytical and mathematical processes as well as the time-sequential and rhythmical aspects of consciousness (for example, this sequential aspect allows us to perceive what we sense as the passage of time). The left hemisphere is also the usual site of the language center, which is that part of the brain that understands and produces written and oral language. It is because of its language capability that the left hemisphere has often been referred to as the "dominant hemisphere" while the right has been termed the "nondominant hemisphere." The right hemisphere is usually more involved with abstract thought distinct from language, nonverbal awareness of the environment, visual-spatial perception, and the perception, expression, and modulation of most aspects of emotionality.

It has even been shown experimentally that the differences between the two cerebral hemispheres can create what appears to be two separate consciousnesses.[12] Furthermore, these consciousnesses can function independently of each other. In order to truly understand how the brain works, however, we must consider the cerebral hemispheres as they work both separately and together. For example, even though the major language center may be in the left hemisphere, the right hemisphere also has an area that concentrates on language (which happens to be in the brain area that mirrors the major language center in the left hemisphere). The language area in the right hemisphere comprehends and generates emotional inflections in the language. Therefore, the left and right hemispheres work together so that the left hemisphere can understand what is being said, and the right hemisphere can understand how it is being said in terms of emotional nuances.[13]

In order for the left and right hemispheres to work together, there must be a connection between them. The two hemispheres are able to interact with

FIGURE 2.1
Top View of the Brain

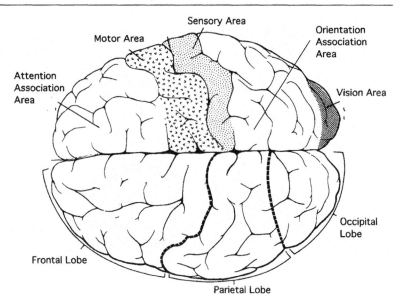

FIGURE 2.2
Side View of the Brain

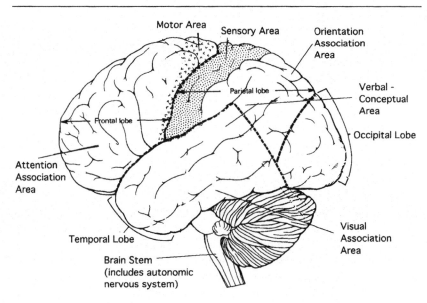

FIGURE 2.3

Side View (Cross Section) of the Central Part of the Brain

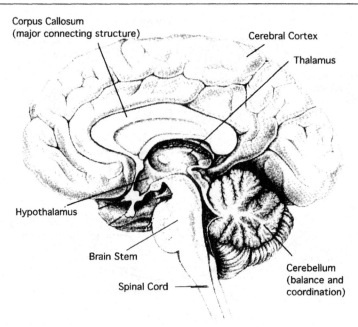

Corpus Callosum
(major connecting structure)

Cerebral Cortex

Thalamus

Hypothalamus

Brain Stem

Spinal Cord

Cerebellum
(balance and
coordination)

each other via three structures called the corpus callosum, the anterior commissure, and the posterior commissure. These connecting structures contain
nerve fibers that link the left and right hemispheres. These connecting structures do not allow all information to be transferred from one hemisphere to
the other, however. Only certain types of limited information can cross
between the hemispheres. Complex thoughts or perceptions in one hemisphere cannot be transferred to the other. Only simplistic representations or
nuances of a thought or perception—the general activity of one hemisphere—
can be transferred to the other hemisphere via these connecting structures.[14]
This will be important in the development of our neurophysiological model
of the mystical mind, since, as we shall see, both hemispheres must become activated in order to generate certain meditative or mystical states. Evidence for
the transfer of activity from one hemisphere to the other can be found in
epilepsy patients. Epilepsy, an overexcited brain state that results in seizures, can
cause seizures that originate in one hemisphere and travel via the connecting
structures to the other hemisphere. The result is a generalized seizure involving
the entire brain. It is interesting to note that some of these patients have been
cured by cutting the connecting structures in a surgical procedure called a
commissurotomy. This procedure is designed to prevent seizure activity in one

hemisphere from spreading to the other. A number of studies have been done on these "split-brain" patients to see how the two hemispheres interact when they no longer are in direct communication. But we will consider these experiments later when we discuss a model for consciousness.

In addition to the cerebral hemispheres, the cerebral cortex is divided into four major regions or lobes: the frontal lobe, located at the front of the brain; the parietal lobe, located near the top of the brain; the temporal lobe, located near the side aspect of the brain; and the occipital lobe, located at the back of the brain. Within each lobe exist smaller regions that either have names such as the hippocampus or amygdala, or are categorized according to a cerebral map that was first developed by Korbinian Brodmann (these regions have names such as Brodmann's area).[15] Over time, neuroscientists have tried to determine which brain functions are associated with what parts of the brain. This localization of function has been accomplished primarily by two methods. One method involves the study of patients who have had strokes or brain tumors with concomitant neurological problems. For example, in the past, if someone suffered a stroke and was partially blind in one eye, the determination of the location of the stroke, and therefore the part of the brain responsible for sight in that eye, could be made by autopsy findings. Researchers were then able to correlate the areas of the brain that were affected by the stroke with the neurological sequelae observed while the patient was living. Today, neuroscientists utilize various brain-imaging technologies such as magnetic resonance imaging, which locates damaged parts of the brain while the person is alive. The end result is similar, however, since a comparison is made between the neurological deficits and the findings on the brain images. The second method for determining how the brain functions will be considered in detail later, but it involves neuroimaging studies on normal subjects while they perform various tasks or receive sensory stimuli. These are called activation studies and directly show the areas of the brain involved in various activities.

Before returning to our description of specific parts of the brain and how they work, we need to consider how the brain structures are organized in terms of their overall functional characteristics. As we mentioned earlier, the brain is responsible for analyzing incoming stimuli, determining a response, and acting according to that response. To do this, the brain is made up of primary, secondary, and tertiary sensory areas.[16] The primary receptive areas are parts of the brain that receive the outside input directly. Thus, the primary visual receptive area does not receive an image so much as it receives various patterns of lines, shapes, and colors. This level of sensory reception does not allow for a conscious understanding and identification of the actual image. All of these lines, shapes, and colors are then relayed to the secondary visual association cortex, so called because it associates the various parts of the primary receptive area and generates an image—for example, the image of a small, four-legged animal. It is only through the secondary association cortex that we come to consciously "know" of the image. In fact, there is an unusual condition in which people lose their secondary visual cortex and will claim to be completely and wholly blind.[17] They will have no consciousness of sight whatsoever. These same people, however, will be able to navigate through a congested room without bumping into any objects, furniture, or walls. Thus, they will act as if their vision is intact, which it is on the primary level, but will have no awareness of that vision. The same holds true for all sensory modalities, including touch, taste, smell, and hearing.

We are still left only with the image of a four-legged animal and have not gotten any further identification of the image. This is how the tertiary association areas function. It is in the tertiary association areas that the sensory information from one sense is combined with that of the other senses. Further, there is an identification of the sensory input using information from the memory centers in the brain. This may identify the object as "your dog." But in our response to objects in the external world, there is also emotional content that can be directed toward these objects. The tertiary association areas, in conjunction with the limbic system and autonomic nervous system, help generate these emotional responses to the objects that are identified by the tertiary centers. Thus, it is the tertiary centers that allow us to understand and organize the external world and allow us to respond to whatever objects are in the external world. There are a number of tertiary areas in the brain to which we will refer in the development of our model of how the brain works. Again, we will consider them separately, but it is important to also consider how all of these areas function together in the eventual development of the mystical mind.

THE TERTIARY ASSOCIATION AREAS

We will focus on four of the tertiary association areas in structuring our model of the neurophysiological basis of human behavior and eventually the development of ritual and myth: the visual association area, the orientation association area, the attention association area, and the verbal–conceptual association area.

The Visual Association Area
The visual association area is located in the inferior temporal lobe (because it is located toward the bottom of the temporal lobe). The neurons in the visual association area receive highly processed input from the secondary visual areas (in the occipital lobes) from both hemispheres. These neurons scan the entire visual field that comes from the secondary visual association areas so as to alert the person to objects of interest or motivational importance through the inter-

connections with the limbic system and the autonomic nervous system.[18] Remember that this is the function of the tertiary center—to help identify an object and determine an emotional response. Thus, visual association area neurons are activated when an object of interest enters the visual field. This, coupled with an area of the brain that helps in visual fixation and orienting ourselves with regard to the object (the orientation association area), allows for objects of interest to be detected and fixated upon.

Overall, the visual association area appears to be involved in the highest level of visual function and analysis. It contains highly developed neurons that seem to be the end station of a hierarchical system that mediates the perception and recognition of specific and particular shapes and forms.[19] Finally, it allows for an emotional response to be directed toward the objects within the visual field.

Situated within this visual association area are two other structures called the amygdala and the hippocampus, which have functions beyond just visual processing. These two structures are part of the limbic system, which we have already considered briefly and will discuss in detail later. Suffice it to say here that the amygdala and the hippocampus maintain extensive interconnections with the rest of the visual association area. The importance of these interconnections is that the limbic system (which modulates emotional responses) is connected to the inferior temporal lobe's visual association area and, subsequently, to the rest of the cerebral cortex (or neocortex).

The Orientation Association Area
The orientation association area is located in the posterior superior parietal lobe (posterior because it is located toward the back and superior because it is located toward the top of the parietal lobe). This area receives somaesthetic (referring to touch and body position) information from the body, but it also receives input from the visual receiving areas in the occipital and middle temporal lobe, from motor and nonmotor areas, auditory areas, and the verbal-conceptual association area, which we will discuss below.[20] Thus, the orientation association area is heavily involved in the analysis and integration of higher-order visual, auditory, and somaesthetic information. In fact, a single neuron in this area can monitor activities occurring in many different parts of the body simultaneously. For example, this area is able to inform us of the position and movement of the arms, trunk, and legs at the same time.[21]

Through the reception of auditory and visual input the orientation association area is also able to create a three-dimensional image of the body in space.[22] Further, this region helps determine our position in space and can compare our internally felt location to the coordinate system of the outside world. This ability to generate a body image might allow for the generation of phenomena such as out-of-body experiences. This region of the brain is also responsible for fixating on visual objects, the determination of the three-dimensional position of various objects in our visual field, and the identification of the relationship of these objects to the body and to other objects in the external world. The rare ability to rotate objects in space to see the other side almost certainly arises from the orientation association area. Although this phenomenon can occur spontaneously, it usually occurs during intense meditation with a visual focus.

Certain neurons in the orientation association area have been described as exerting "command" functions.[23] When these nerve cells fire they can be motivationally responsive, can direct visual attention, and can become excited when certain objects are within grasping distance. Once this is done, the same neurons can motivate and guide hand movements, including the grasping and manipulation of specific objects. Further, most of these cells stop firing when the object fixated upon is actually grasped, suggesting that they may be exerting some type of "driving force" or "alerting function" so that objects of desire will be attended to.[24]

There are some differences in function between the orientation association area on the right and the orientation association area on the left. Studies have found that patients with strokes or tumors in the right orientation association area have deficiencies involving depth perception and the ability to determine location, distance, spatial orientation, and object size.[25] Further, many of these patients suffer from visual-spatial disorientation. The right parietal lobe appears to play an important role in creating a sense of spatial coordinates and body location, the left orientation association area exerts influences with regard to objects that may be directly grasped and manipulated. Further, it seems that in the left orientation association area, some neurons respond most to stimuli within grasping distance, whereas others respond most to stimuli just beyond arm's reach. It is such evidence that has caused some researchers such as Rhawn Joseph to postulate that the distinction between self and world may ultimately arise from the left orientation association area's ability to judge these two categories of distance—objects within grasp and objects beyond grasp.[26] Therefore, it seems likely that the "self-other" or the "self-world" distinction that philosophers and theologians have discussed throughout the ages may be a function of the left orientation association area that evolved from its more primitive ability to divide objects in space into the graspable and the nongraspable.

The Attention Association Area

The attention association area is situated in the most forward aspect of the brain, the prefrontal cortex. No other area of the entire cerebral cortex is as intimately and richly interconnected with the limbic system as is the attention association area.[27] Likewise, this area is profusely interconnected with all the secondary and tertiary sensory association cortices.[28] Only the attention association area receives fibers from all sensory modalities (vision, hearing, touch, taste, and smell) as well as from the tertiary association areas.[29] However, there are only a few connections with the primary sensory areas.[30] The attention association area is involved in forming conceptual thoughts by means of its rich interconnections with the verbal-conceptual association area and can also help in forming complicated visual images. Also, the attention association area of each hemisphere is connected to the attention association area of the other by fibers running across the corpus callosum.[31] Thus, it seems that part of the function of the prefrontal area is as a multimodal association area; we can assume, therefore, that the attention association area is involved in the integration of a wide variety of sensory data. Further, this area functions to help give us a sense of "egocentric spatial organization" or how things are spatially oriented to ourselves.[32] We have already considered, however, how another area, the orientation association area, is responsible for generating our sense of sensorial space itself. As one might presume, there are many interconnections between the attention association area and the orientation association area.

A complete functional picture of the attention association area in human beings is far from clear, nor has the case been clarified by experiments with animals. Animals with surgically removed frontal lobes become very hyperactive in their purposeful movements, increase their spontaneous movement, and have difficulty orienting themselves in space. Such animals have erratic behavior that seems to be stimulus bound, meaning that they respond primarily to outside events without any internal integration and coordination.[33] It should also be noted that the attention association area is situated in the larger structure of the frontal lobe, which also contains the part of the brain that is responsible for movement—the motor cortex. Similar to the general coordination of the sensory system, motor function has primary, secondary, and tertiary centers. The primary motor cortex (located toward the back of the frontal lobe) is responsible for the basic movement of every part of the body. Slightly in front of this area is the premotor cortex, which is the secondary motor association area. The premotor cortex is involved with the control of more complex, integrated movements. These movements are often associated with goal-oriented behavior such as reaching for a desired object. The attention association area acts as the tertiary motor association area with regard to coordinating highly complex movements. The functions of the attention association area have become so complex, however, with the progressive evolutionary development of the human brain that they actually have transcended mere motor function. Thus, this area has become involved in many types of behaviors and activity, but goal-oriented behavior or even purposive organization of thought always derives from input from the attention association area.

There remains the issue of which part of the brain is the most responsible for focusing attention with regard to the ordering of behaviors within time and space. Here we are referring to the necessity of all organisms to order time and space so that they can properly orient themselves and determine where and how behaviors should be directed. While there is much evidence that the attention association area is the primary mover in this regard, there is equally strong evidence that the orientation association area is intimately involved with focusing attention in terms of the ordering of time and space. Pribram maintains that the temporal and spatial ordering of tasks is disrupted in animals with injuries to the attention association area, primarily if such ordering is usually cued by the animal internally.[34] In contrast, injuries to the orientation association area disrupt the ordering of space and time primarily when they are externally cued.[35] This distinction seems to make sense based on what we already know of these two areas. The orientation association area generates a sense of orientation by receiving external sensory input, while the attention association area relies primarliy on internal input from other brain structures. But this distinction is not clear-cut, and it might be more appropriate to consider the attention association area and orientation association area, together with their rich interconnections, as one functional organ with regard to attention and the ordering of space and time.

In humans, the loss of the ability to concentrate is a characteristic of prefrontal disorders as is the loss of the ability to plan and to orient oneself to future behavior. Several reports have suggested that the attention association area, especially on the right, may function to produce redundancy in otherwise novel sensory space.[36] The production of such redundancy seems to be essential to all attention-related functions of human consciousness because there is otherwise an excess of sensory input. This abundance of sensory input would likely distract a person from any task that is being concentrated on. For example, the attention association area is what allows you to read a book when there are other people around or while the television is on. It helps in pushing all of the sensory stimulation into the background as redundant input and allows you to continue to concentrate on the book. Thus, patients with injuries in the attention association area not only lose the ability to plan and orient themselves to future activity, they also suffer a severe deficit in carrying out complex perceptual and conceptual tasks that require concentration or attention. They find it difficult to complete a lengthy sequence of activity or to organize complex behavior, to integrate sensory input, and to anticipate novelty.

The prefrontal cortex, which contains the attention association area, is also richly interconnected with the limbic system and therefore plays a significant role in the modulation of emotion. Patients with lesions in the prefrontal cortex exhibit flatness of emotion and apathy, and tend to have difficulty controlling emotion. Fuster noted that patients with injury to the attention association area seem to display a "profound indifference" to events and objects in the environment. Moreover, such patients show a "deficiency of an active, intentive element of cognitive function that is essential for pursuing prospective goals."[37] These patients cannot alter their patterns of response once established, and thus they are usually incapable of accomplishing anything beyond their initial pattern of behavior.[38]

Therefore, deficits in the attention association area seem to result in a general loss of global sensory integrative capacity. These patients have problems with respect to controlling, planning, integrating, and monitoring activity and behavior and the effects of that activity.[39] To put it bluntly, a great part of what one sees with injury to the attention association area is a loss of will and an inability to form intention. If any part of the brain can be said to be the seat of the will or of intentionality, it is certainly the attention association area.

The Verbal-Conceptual Association Area
The verbal-conceptual association area sits at the junction of the temporal, parietal, and occipital lobes but technically is in the inferior parietal lobe (or the lower part of the parietal lobe). The verbal-conceptual association area may be the area of the greatest integration of sensory input in the brain. In a sense, it is an association area of association areas, and it maintains rich interconnections with the vision, hearing, and touch association areas. This area also has extensive interconnections with the attention association area, the visual association area, and the other higher-order association areas throughout the neocortex.[40] The verbal-conceptual association area is also responsible for the generation of abstract concepts and relating them to words. It accomplishes this task through rich interconnections with the language center, which is primarily located in the left hemisphere and incorporates much of the temporal lobe and parts of the frontal and parietal lobes. The verbal-conceptual association area is also involved in conceptual comparisons, the ordering of opposites, the naming of objects and categories of objects, and higher-order grammatical and logical operations. As we shall see, this region might be very important in the development of consciousness and the expression of consciousness through language.

THE LIMBIC SYSTEM

We have now considered the four tertiary association areas that we will refer to in our neuropsychological model of the mystical brain as it develops myth, ritual, and religion. We have indicated at times, however, that part of the functional product from the tertiary association areas involves emotional content. We have also considered that the ability to generate emotional value toward various thoughts and objects is derived from the limbic and autonomic nervous systems. Phylogenetically, the structures of the limbic system are ancient. In fact, most animals with central nervous systems have a limbic system even if they have no cerebral cortex for higher-level thinking. Thus, many other species have a limbic system that actually has a similar function to that in humans beings. The limbic system is that part of the brain that generates and modulates our feelings of fear, happiness, sadness, aggressiveness, and love. Since many of these responses, even if they are on a more primitive level, are absolutely necessary to life, it seems appropriate that all animals should require a limbic system in order to interact with the external world. After all, animals must be aggressive to find food (especially predators). They must have some form of affiliative behavior (i.e., primitive love) for there to be offspring, and in higher animals, so that they care for their offspring until they can survive on their own. They also must be able to fear predators and to avoid life-threatening situations.

In human beings, the limbic system has a similar function in terms of modulating and generating emotions.[41] However, as the human neocortex developed, and higher-level thinking became possible, the limbic system became connected to higher-level thoughts. This allows us not only to have complex thoughts but also to assign emotional value to these thoughts. Thus, we may contemplate God, arrive at some conclusion, and back that conclusion with a strong emotional response. In order for our higher-level thoughts to be assigned an affective value, there must be numerous interconnections between the limbic system and the neocortex.

We have already described how the attention association area is intimately linked to the limbic system. There are, however, particular areas within the limbic system that connect with the neocortex and allow for interaction between them. We will be most concerned with four areas in the brain called the hypothalamus, the thalamus, the amygdala, and the hippocampus. Further, we will describe how these structures connect the limbic system and neocortex with the arousal and quiescent systems.

Phylogenetically, the hypothalamus is the most ancient of these structures. The part of the hypothalamus that is closest to the midline represents an extension of the quiescent system into the brain, thus connecting the quiescent system with the rest of the brain.[42] As we have mentioned, the quiescent system is involved with the baseline function of the organism, with vegetative functions, and with a subjective sense of peace and calmness. By contrast, the outer edge of the hypothalamus seems to be an extension of the arousal system into the brain.[43] It is involved with fight-or-flight responses, with sensations of terror or rage, and with the sensation of positive emotions ranging from moderate pleasure to bliss. An important aspect of the emotions generated by the hypothalamus, whether positive or negative, is that they tend to be stimulus bound. This means that they respond to a specific stimulus and then die off quickly when the stimulus is removed.

The amygdala, located in the middle part of the temporal lobe, is evolutionarily more recently developed than the hypothalamus and is preeminent in the control and mediation of all higher-order emotional and motivational functions.[44] It has extensive interconnections with various regions of the neocortex and with subcortical structures through which it is able to monitor and determine which sensory stimuli are of motivational significance to the organism. This includes the ability to discern and express quite subtle social-emotional nuances such as love, affection, friendliness, fear, distrust, and anger. In addition to emotional and motivational functioning, the amygdala is involved in attention, learning, and memory. Like the hypothalamus, the amygdala is divided into a middle part (toward the midline of the brain) and an outer part (away from the midline). Although the function of the amygdala is complex, it is becoming clear that it has primarily an arousal function, particularly in the outer part. It does have some quiescent functions, however. The outer region of the amygdala receives nerve connections that originate from the outer region of the hypothalamus, which in turn is connected to the arousal system. Further evidence of the amygdala's arousal function is the fact that it performs environmental surveillance and maintains attention if something of interest or importance appears.[45]

In a later chapter, we shall see how this orienting function of the amygdala generates a sense of religious awe that can be attached to "marked" ritual gestures, such as bows or signs of the cross, inserted into the flow of slow ritual rhythmicity. These marked ritual elements insert, as it were, a premature arousal stimulation into the smooth stream of slow ritual. Similarly, electrical stimulation of the outer part of the amygdala tends to initiate quick and/or anxious glancing and searching movements of the eyes and head. The organism appears aroused and highly alert as if in expectation of something that is about to happen. Again, this indicates the arousal functioning of the amygdala. Other physiological changes occur as the result of stimulation of the amygdala, including respiration pattern changes and heart rate increases, both of which signify the orienting response in most species.

Once a stimulus of potential interest is detected, the amygdala acts to analyze its emotional-motivational importance and will function to activate other areas of the brain such as the hypothalamus so that appropriate actions may take place. Since the amygdala is richly connected to various sensory association areas as well as the autonomic nervous system, the amygdala facilitates and modulates the transmission of information from various neocortical areas to the autonomic nervous system. However, because of its connections with the neocortex, the amygdala is not stimulus bound in its emotional functions as is the hypothalamus. Therefore, the emotional tone, whether positive or negative, that is generated through the amygdala will tend to persist over time and will diminish only after a long time has passed since the stimulus was encountered. Further, the amygdala modifies the function of the hypothalamus and can subserve the emotions of fear, rage, joy, and compassion.

The final structure of the limbic system that requires discussion is the hippocampus, which is shaped like a telephone receiver and is located slightly behind the amygdala in the temporal lobe. The hippocampus plays a major role in information processing, memory, new learning, cognitive mapping of the environment, attention, and some orienting reactions.[46] In general, these functions serve homeostasis and are primarily, although not solely, quiescent since they help maintain baseline function. The hippocampus is greatly influenced by the amygdala, which in turn monitors and responds to hippocampal activity. The amygdala also acts to relay certain forms of information from the hippocampus to the hypothalamus. Thus, the hippocampus and amygdala complement each other and interact with regard to the focusing of attention and the generation of emotions linked to images, as well as learning and memory.

The hippocampus also modulates the activity in another structure that connects the autonomic nervous system to the neocortex called the thalamus.[47] Since the thalamus is the major sensory relay system to the neocortex, the hippocampus often appears to be able to block information input to various neocortical areas. Whereas the amygdala may enhance information transfer between neocortical regions, the hippocampus usually tends to do the reverse. Thus, these two structures create a push–pull effect in the transfer of information between neocortical regions. Further, since the hippocampus predominantly functions as part of the quiescent system response, it acts in concert with the middle part of the hypothalamus so as to prevent extremes in arousal and thus maintain a state of quiet alertness or quiescence. In this way, the hippocampus does not generate the expression of emotion directly, but acts to modulate both the amygdala and the hypothalamus by means of its interconnections with both. Through neuronal interconnections with the amygdala, the hypothalamus, and the attention association area, the hippocampus can inhibit activity in these areas, thereby preventing emotional extremes. This ability to inhibit the transfer of information from one region to another, in addition to its control over emotional responses, will prove important in generating certain mystical experiences.

There is one other structure that requires brief mention: the reticular activating system. It is called this because its structure looks like a wispy complex of lines (a reticular pattern), sort of like what a tangle of thread would look like.

This tangle of neuronal threads has specific connections, however, as it receives significant input from the outer part of the hypothalamus (i.e., the arousal system) as well as from other limbic structures. Therefore, the reticular activating system has primarily an arousal function and is greatly responsible for the stimulation of the neocortex, producing the state of wakefulness.[48] This is how this system got its full name: it is reticular in shape and is responsible for activating the brain; hence the name "reticular activating system."

DEAFFERENTATION

One other aspect that is crucial to our neuropsychological model of mystical states is the concept of deafferentation. In deafferentation incoming information (or afferents) into a brain structure are "cut off." This cutting off is an actual physiological process, which may be partial or total. Deafferentation can be caused by either physical interruption such as by a destructive tumor or surgery, or by "functional" deafferentation. Perhaps the most investigated form of physical deafferentation involves patients with epilepsy. As noted above, in epilepsy, one part of the brain starts to become overexcited. This excitation can spread throughout the entire hemisphere and then can cross over to excite the other hemisphere. The result is a generalized seizure, which has traditionally been the hallmark of epilepsy. This seizure results from the overexcitation of the entire brain. Sometimes, in severe cases that cannot be helped by medication, patients undergo a "commissurotomy" to cut the connector tracts between the two cerebral hemispheres; this procedure prevents communication between the hemispheres, thereby inhibiting seizure activity. This deafferents them from each other such that neither hemisphere is aware of what the other hemisphere is doing.

Functional deafferentation occurs when inhibitory fibers from a brain structure block transmission of information between two other structures. Thus, impulses from inhibitory fibers can block input into a neural structure. For example, Hoppe has shown that one hemisphere can be prevented from knowing what is occurring in the opposite hemisphere via the inhibitory actions of the frontal lobes.[49] Hoppe called this prevention of interhemispheric communication a "functional commissurotomy." There is similar evidence that intrahemispheric information transmission can be partially or totally blocked by impulses originating in the attention association area. This is accomplished via inhibitory nerve fibers of the hippocampus.[50]

A particularly interesting aspect of deafferentation is what happens when a certain structure is totally deafferented. Normally, all parts of the brain are affected by numerous other parts. Therefore, the function of any structure is determined not only by itself but also by its interaction with many other areas of the brain. If deafferentation of a structure occurs to a significant degree, the neurons within that structure are no longer under the influence of any other parts of the brain and they begin to fire on their own. These deafferented neurons either fire randomly, or, more likely, function according to their own "internal logic."[51] This internal logic derives from the function for which a given structure evolved.

Let us consider an example of how deafferentation may result in generating unusual experiences that may be associated with altered phases of consciousness. Remember that the orientation association area receives information from the sensory areas and generates a sense of space and time. It does this by integrating the senses of touch, sight, and hearing, and creates an overall concept of space. If this structure is totally deafferented so that it receives no input from the outside world, then it cannot form a sense of space and time abstracted from sensory input. It is still trying, however, to generate an orientation in space and time. It is still working by its internal logic. It continues to attempt to generate a sense of space and time even without input from the external world to work on. The result is a sense of no space and no time, or conversely, it might be described as infinite space and infinite time. No matter how it is defined, it is the same sensation. The world's mystical literature is replete with experiences of no space and no time or infinite space and infinite time. Therefore, it appears that total or near-total deafferentation of the orientation association area may be involved in the generation of such mystical states.

WATCHING HOW THE BRAIN WORKS

To measure how the brain functions, neuroscientists have used several different methods. By measuring electrical activity in the brain, they have been able to locate areas of the brain that are associated with certain functions. For example, a person may be asked to repeatedly tap his left hand. While the person is doing this, electrodes surrounding the brain pick up electrical changes that can be isolated to a particular structure (this procedure is called electroencephalography, or EEG, which literally means graphing the electrical activity of the brain). Computers have been used to give three-dimensional images of this electrical activity so that brain function can be better localized. The ability to pinpoint the electrical activity is not enough to resolve small brain structures.

Newer brain-imaging methods have been developed in the past three decades and have improved resolution and accuracy for identifying structures in the brain. Computerized tomography (often called CT or CAT, computerized axial tomography) uses X rays to generate a three-dimensional image of the brain. CT scans have been used in medicine to study a large variety of problems, including brain tumors and strokes. Magnetic resonance imaging (MRI) uses magnetic fields and computers to generate images of the human brain. MRI has the advantage over most other imaging modalities of a high resolution of two to three millimeters (about the thickness of two pennies stacked together). Thus, MRI can be used to study parts of the brain that are only a few millimeters across. MRI has also been very useful in the study of strokes, tumors, and other neurological disorders.

The field of nuclear medicine has two imaging tools that have been extensively used for studying the function of the brain: single photon emission computed tomography (SPECT) and positron emission tomography (PET). SPECT requires the injection of a small amount of a radioactive isotope that emits a single photon of light (hence the name). The photons are detected by a camera and then converted into a three-dimensional representation of the brain by a computer. PET is similar except that the isotope emits a positron (an antielectron), which emits two photons when it encounters an electron. These emitted photons can then be detected by a camera and converted into an image. Of course the science behind these techniques is complicated, but the important thing to remember is that MRI and CT give anatomical images, images of the structures themselves. SPECT and PET yield functional images (more recently, MRI has also been used for functional imaging). They are considered functional because the isotopes that are injected work like natural substances that normally occur in the brain. For example, some isotopes act like water (which follows the path of blood to the brain), some act like glucose (which is used by the brain for energy), and some act like neurotransmitters (the chemicals that allow nerve cells, or neurons, to communicate with each other).

The purpose for describing these brain-imaging methods is that when someone is asked to perform a specific task, like tapping her left hand, there should be changes in the area of the brain responsible for doing that task. This is exactly what has been observed in many studies over the past three decades.

As we consider our model of various human thoughts and behaviors, we will rely on a number of studies that have demonstrated how certain areas of the brain function. Further, we will attempt to integrate the results of these studies into a coherent model of brain function. Another field includes brain stimulation studies. Electrical stimulation of the right amygdala has been found to produce vivid visual hallucinations, out-of-body sensations, déjà vu, and numerous types of illusions. Stimulation of the right hippocampus has been associated with the production of the sensation of déjà vu, automatic memory recall, and dreamlike hallucinations. In fact, hallucinations seem to occur most frequently following stimulation of the hippocampus in comparison to stimulation of any other part of the brain. In general, moderate electrical stimulation of the hippocampus produces EEG changes often associated with dreaming, daydreaming, or dreamlike hallucinations. We maintain that such moderate stimulation of the hippocampus might be achieved not only by internal electrical activation but also by the external effects of certain types of rhythmic ritual. This might explain how ritual can produce trance states or dreamlike hallucinations. More intense stimulation of the hippocampus, as well as the effect of drugs such as LSD, tends to produce EEG changes in both the hippocampus and the amygdala. These EEG changes are associated with the generation of vivid or hyperlucid (extremely vivid) hallucinations. We believe that similar, intense hippocampal stimulation may also be caused by rhythmic ritual of long duration and strong intensity. This is the way in which ritual may cause hyperlucid experiences. Overall, it appears that the amygdala, hippocampus, and neocortex of the temporal lobe are highly involved in the production of vivid hallucinatory experiences. Further, it seems likely that these structures are involved in visionary mystical experiences, although their functioning in these cases must be understood to arise within an integrated and extremely complex web of neural structures and their interconnections.

IS BRAIN IMAGING USEFUL IN THE STUDY OF RELIGION AND THEOLOGY?

We have reviewed some relevant studies of brain activity and have considered the function of the brain in general. The question that now arises is why information from brain-imaging studies might be relevant to the study of theology. We mentioned in the introduction that the primary goal of theology is the study of how human beings interact with God. To accomplish this, one must certainly study how human beings experience religion and how they respond to the vast array of experiences from the mystical chill of awe in a forest or in an empty cathedral at sunset, through profound unitary states, all the way to the *unio mystica* or void consciousness.

We have also suggested that, as far as we can determine, all human experience eventually enters human awareness via the function of the brain. It certainly seems reasonable to reach the conclusion that the brain is the structure that gives all of us our thoughts, feelings, and experiences. But is there any empirical support for such an argument? This question will be important, especially in considering religion, because the concept of the human soul is often invoked as being an element of human nature through which human beings interact with a higher being or state of being. We have argued that even if there is a soul, our experience of whatever we mean by "soul" must pass through the brain. The question again is how we can show that the brain is what mediates all of our experiences.

This is where imaging studies lend a strong degree of empirical support. An extensive number of studies have explored almost all of the basic components of human behavior and experience. Thus, people have studied how the brain reacts when each of the five senses are stimulated. The results have indicated the parts of the brain responsible for interpreting smells, sights, sounds, tastes, and touches. Other parts of the brain have been activated while doing some type of motor activity. There is a part of the brain responsible for moving everything from the entire body to the little finger. Some parts of the brain are activated during mathematical problem solving, or during language tasks, or while observing faces, or while experiencing pain.

The conclusion to be drawn from this huge database of studies is that, at least for now, it seems that no matter what happens to us or what we do, there is a part of the brain that becomes activated. Furthermore, studies of patients with strokes or brain tumors have shown that when a part of the brain is destroyed, then that person no longer can do or experience the things that are mediated by that brain part. Thus, the brain appears not only to react to everything that happens to us, but is eminently responsible for everything that we do or experience. In this way, studies of brain function help to show that our initial statement seems valid—that it is the brain by which all of our thoughts, feelings, and experiences are derived.

In approaching theology, it seems that any human religious or ritual experience is necessarily modulated by the brain. In fact, we have already begun studies to show the activity in the brain during profound meditation (we will discuss this research in a later chapter). Therefore, it seems most important to consider the functioning of the brain in relation to how human beings experience religion and God. We have begun to take the first steps toward this new perspective on theology. This study of neurotheology is based on how the brain and mind function in order to generate and experience myths, ritual, religious, and mystical phenomena. Furthermore, neurotheology attempts to explain how the mind and brain function to interpret, codify, and rationalize such experiences into logical cognitive systems. But even more interestingly, we must ask, and attempt to answer, the question: Can neurotheology and our understanding of the mystical mind and brain form the basis for a universal metatheology?

Chapter Three

The Basis for the Mystical Mind

We have now developed a general understanding of how the human brain works on a neurophysiological level. We have also seen that, in general, certain brain structures or networks of structures are responsible for certain mental activities. These functions include, among others, an orientation in space and time, the generation of ideas, the verbalization of ideas, and the generation of emotional responses. Our purpose is to present the brain and mind in a more holistic manner, however, as opposed to a simple aggregation of specific areas with specific functions. Furthermore, our discussion up to now only gives a glimpse of how the brain and mind may function in a mystical manner. We must consider how the mind functions to give us our more complex thoughts and feelings. We must also begin to relate the functions of the mind and brain to mystical and religious concepts and, ultimately, to theology.

In order to understand how the brain functions as a whole, we have first described how the parts work individually. Now that this has been accomplished, we can begin to describe a holistic neurophysiological model for the generation of mystical states, religious rituals, near-death experiences, culture, and consciousness itself. This model will incorporate the combined and integrated function of all of the parts of the brain. In fact, one might argue that the whole is greater than the sum of its parts in the sense that when individual parts of the brain work, they can perform certain specific functions, but as a whole they can create incredible experiences and phenomena that cannot occur with any of the parts individually.

The mind is the name for the intangible realities that the brain produces. Therefore, thinking, logic, art, emotions, and intentions all fall into the realm of the mind. Of importance is the question of whether the mind can somehow be separated from the brain. If one wished to take a dualistic approach, one could state that it is theoretically possible to determine the precise neural activity that creates a thought, such activity being seen as distinct from the thought it generates. Thus, if we had a sensitive enough machine, we could detect the neural events that work to yield an epiphenomenal reality, that is, a particular thought. This is a bit disconcerting and certainly not holistic. While there might be some theoretical validity to such a notion, thoughts and feelings are so complex that they can only be generated by the highly complex and integrated working of hundreds of thousands of neurons. Thus, regardless of whether it is theoretically possible to ascertain the specific neuronal activity involved in a given thought or behavior, it is practically impossible both now and in the forseeable future. But when we go from a single thought to consider the neuronal basis of mind in its entirety, the situation becomes almost infinitely complex, requiring us to see the brain as a whole of the neurophysiological substrate for an individual mind.

WHY CALL THE MIND AND BRAIN MYSTICAL?

Part of the purpose of this chapter is to lead to the concept of the mystical mind. First, however, we must define what we mean by the concept of a mystical mind. In the context of our discussion, the notion of the mystical mind and the mystical brain is twofold. In the first place, the idea that the brain and the mind are mystical suggests that the function of the brain and mind can lead to mystical experiences. We will consider the details of how this occurs in a later chapter, but it is necessary here at least to acknowledge that this is part of the overall intent of this book. The implication is that the brain and the mind either generate mystical states or allow us to experience mystical states. Differentiating whether the brain and mind actually cause mystical phenomena or are merely the necessary occasion for them is most difficult. The former implies that mystical phenomena are completely caused and contained within the functions of the brain and the mind. The latter requires that mystical phenomena exist "out there" in the external world, which can then be experienced by human beings through the brain and mind.

We have argued in the past that the most problematic aspect of this issue is that the only way in which to solve this problem is somehow to get out of the function of our brain and mind, since, as far as we know, everything about the world, both internal and external, comes to us through the brain. Thus, it is difficult from an epistemological perspective to determine the true reality of any phenomenon, whether it be mystical or ordinary in nature. We will consider in a later chapter the epistemological issues regarding the brain and the mind, but suffice it to say that one cannot be certain whether or not mystical phenomena, or any other phenomena, are generated by the brain and mind, or experienced by them. On the other hand, this question may not necessitate an answer at this time. Regardless of the true nature of mystical phenomena, it is the brain and mind that inform us of them and take us to them. Therefore, to be consistent, our model of how the brain and mind function to generate our experience of mystical phenomena does not rely on there being an external mystical object or being. One simply has to alter the interpretation of the function of the mind and brain. For example, if deafferentation of the orientation association area yields a sense of no space and no time, it matters little if the deafferentation causes the state of no space and no time or allows us to enter this state that already exists "out there." This subtle difference requires a more rigorous epistemological approach than is appropriate here, and we will take up this issue in a subsequent chapter using the perspective of neuroepistemology. Further, we shall then consider how the concepts of reality and neuroepistemology relate to the development of a neurotheology.

We have indicated that part of the reason for considering the brain and mind as mystical derives from their ability to generate or experience mystical phenomena. We also mentioned, however, that there is a second reason for considering the brain and mind as mystical. In mystical states, there is usually a diminution, or even a complete lack, of differentiation between objects. In this way, there is a breakdown of opposites such as good and evil, justice and injustice, and God and humanity. All things tend toward a unified undifferentiated oneness. Curiously, there is a similar phenomenon in physics in the area of quantum mechanics. Specifically, there is a breakdown in the duality between waves and particles. At the level of the electron, it is difficult to distinguish that which is a wave and that which is a particle. The double slit experiments beautifully demonstrate this dual behavior of the electron. This experiment is performed by passing a beam of electrons through two narrow slits in a screen. When a device is placed behind the slits to determine the end placement of each electron, the result is an interference pattern in which there are alternating areas of increased electrons. This same type of pattern is observed by waves that pass through narrow slits. The reason for this pattern is that the wave (which has peaks and troughs) is essentially split by the slits. The result is that there are some places in which two peaks get added together, resulting in an area of increased intensity, and others where a peak and a trough cancel each other out, resulting in an area of zero intensity. Since these areas alternate, the result is alternating bright and dark areas. If one observes the electrons as they pass through the slits, however, a given electron will be observed going through either one or the other slit. This would result not in an interference pattern but in an image of the two slits. Thus, depending on how the measurement is made, the electron can sometimes appear to act as a wave and sometimes as a particle. The question then is, Is the electron a wave or a particle? The only possible and logically consistent answer is that the electron must be regarded as both a wave and a particle. In other words, it has both wave and particle properties. Thus, the wave and particle are not two separate things, but are really two different ways of looking at the same thing. The wave-particle metaphor may be useful for understanding what is experienced during mystical states. Pairs of opposites such as good and evil are suddenly understood as being two different ways of looking at the same thing. The dualities are broken down, and the opposites are unified in a single nature.

But what if this is also true of the mind and the brain? We have already discussed how the brain functions and how it is structured. The mind represents the more intangible functional aspects of the brain. The brain simply refers to the more structural, physiological, and "objective" aspects of neural activity, and the mind refers to the more functional, psychological, and "subjective" aspects of neural activity. Thus, one might argue that there can be no brain without mind and no mind without brain. They are merely two different ways of looking at the same thing. To reject one and not the other is simply not possible. In fact, it might be more accurate to speak of a mind/brain rather than of a separated mind and brain. It is the mind/brain that is another way of saying either the "mystical brain" or the "mystical mind." After all, the notion of either a mystical brain or a mystical mind must necessarily incorporate the other. Thus, for the remainder of this book, the terms *mystical mind* and *mystical brain* will be essentially equivalent to the mind/brain. The mind/brain is perhaps a more scientific way of saying mystical mind. Anytime that we consider one particular aspect of the mind/brain for simplicity of description, we will refer to the particular part. As we originally mentioned, however, we must always remember that the mind/brain reality is the reality whenever we focus on a more reductionist approach to either the mind or the brain.

Since we have already described the brain component of the mind/brain in some detail, it is now necessary to explore the mind component. Once both aspects of the mind/brain are described, we can then begin a more thorough exploration of the mystical mind.

COGNITIVE OPERATORS

Prior to considering the global functioning of the mind, we must consider the primary functional components of the mind, which we have referred to as cognitive operators.[1] These operators are specific functions that specific parts of the brain perform as part of the mind. Cognitive operators are essentially analogous to the operators used in mathematics. In mathematics, operators can be looked upon as the means by which mathematical elements are related to one another.

For example, plus (+), minus (-), multiplication (×), and division (÷) signs are all operators. Respectively, they tell us to add, subtract, multiply, and divide numbers. For example, if we take the case 3 × 5, we understand that we are to multiply the number 3 by the number 5. Another way of saying this is that the × tells us to relate the 3 and the 5 by multiplying them. It is also important to mention that, in this case, 3 and 5 are the inputs of the operator ×. This is because 3 and 5 are put into the operator ×. The result, 15, is the output.

The mind has cognitive operators that work in a similar manner to the mathematical operators. However, cognitive operators have sensory perception, thoughts, and emotions as input in contrast to the mathematical operators. Further, the mind functions on these inputs in much more complicated ways than do the simple mathematical operators. Thus, in our attempt to integrate the brain and mind as a single functional complex, we need to expand on the concept of cognitive operators. The functioning of the cognitive operators is what produces a sense of "mind." The brain structures and neurons that work to generate the functions of the operators are part of the overall structure and function of the brain. Thus, brain function results in the function of the cognitive operators and therefore results in the function of the mind.

In considering the cognitive operators, it is helpful to break them down into their basic functions. This allows for an easier understanding of the operators. It appears that these cognitive operators function in a similar manner in the minds of all people. This is an important point. It has been remarked that virtually all brains, at least on a gross anatomical level, look very similar. Studies have shown a remarkable similarity in the location of various functions of the brain in all human beings. Functions such as language, vision, movement, and thought tend to be localized to the same general areas regardless of whom we are examining. For example, the language center in all people resides in the temporal lobe, particularly in the left hemisphere. This being the case, it would seem logical that the brain structures responsible for the cognitive operators should be in similar locations in each person's brain. Furthermore, we suggest that these facts imply that the basic functions or operators are likely to be preprogrammed into the brain. In fact, studies of infants suggest that a number of operators may begin to function prior to the development of more complex thoughts. This preprogramming is undoubtedly accomplished by our genetic makeup. In other words, the functions of the operators are in our genes. This notion was first proposed in the theory of biogenetic structuralism, which we mentioned earlier. The concept of cognitive operators is another area in which we encounter the genetic basis of human behavior.

We will describe seven primary cognitive operators that comprise the most basic functions of the mind. These functions allow the mind to think, feel, experience, order, and interpret the universe. Thus, each operator represents a specific function of the mind. The mind, in its totality, includes all of these operators. It should be noted that there may be other operators that function within the mind. The following seven operators, however, appear to be the most fundamental in the function of the mind:

1. The holistic operator
2. The reductionist operator
3. The causal operator
4. The abstractive operator
5. The binary operator
6. The quantitative operator
7. The emotional value operator

In its basic form, the holistic operator allows us to view reality as a whole or as a gestalt. In other words, this operator helps to give us the big picture so that we can experience a given situation in a more global context. A number of experiments involving both animals and human beings have indicated that the parietal lobe in the nondominant hemisphere is intimately involved in the perception of spatial relations. More specifically, the perceptions generated by this area are of a holistic or gestalt nature. Thus, we have proposed that the holistic operator likely resides in the parietal lobe in the nondominant hemisphere.[2] It is also interesting to note that this area sits almost directly opposite the area in the dominant hemisphere that is involved in the performance of various logical-grammatical operations. In particular, the parietal lobe on the dominant side is capable of the perception of opposites and the ability to select one object over another. Thus, the right parietal lobe is involved in a holistic approach to things and the left parietal lobe is involved in more reductionist and analytic processes.

Examples in which we might utilize the holistic operator include various scientific studies of how a group of objects or organisms function as a single unit. For example, holistic medicine implies the study of how all of the individual body parts function together to maintain health. In religion, the holistic operator might allow us to apprehend the unity of God or the oneness of the universe. Regardless of the particular object or group of objects involved, whenever one considers or perceives the global or unitary perspective of things, one is employing the holistic operator.

The reductionist operator functions in the opposite manner to that of the holistic operator. The reductionist operator allows us to look at the whole picture and break it down into an analysis of individual parts. As we have mentioned, the reductionist operator probably resides primarily in the left parietal lobe and is connected to the sensory modalities of sight, hearing, touch, and so forth, as well as to our language center.[3] This operator is probably the one that gives us our scientific, logical, and mathematical approach to studying the universe. It is through these disciplines that we break down the world into small parts that can be controlled and studied. The important point is that in order to develop the most accurate understanding of the universe, one must combine the holistic and the reductionist approaches. In this way we can see not only how an individual part functions but also how that part affects the global system, and finally how the global system affects each of the individual parts. Thus, both the holistic operator and the reductionist operator are crucial to the mind's ability to understand the universe in its totality.

The causal operator permits reality to be viewed in terms of causal sequences. This particular operator seems to have played a significant role in the development of human science, philosophy, and particularly religion. The causal operator is believed to result from the connections between the left frontal lobe and the left orientation association area.[4] Patients who have strokes or tumors in either of these two areas have serious deficits in causal thinking: they have difficulty determining the reason why something happened. In its basic function, the causal operator tends to impart a sense of causality on all of the events that we observe. Thus, this operator forces us to question why we are here, why something works the way it does, and what created the universe. In all of these, and in every other instance, we want to know the cause that lies behind every event that we experience. Thus, we would suggest that it is the mind or brain itself that is designed to seek out causality. Our brain functions in such a way that it tries to find the cause of all of the things it experiences. If this is the case, then it is a biological necessity for us to seek out causality. In fact, we might call this the causal imperative. Furthermore, there is evidence that our drive to determine causality may be present even as early as infancy. Recent studies of infants show that they react strongly to events that appear to break the natural laws of causality. For example, infants pay attention longer (suggesting that they are intrigued by an unusual event) when watching a large ball fall through a small hole compared to watching a small ball fall through a large hole. This also supports the notion that this function of the mind and brain is genetically hardwired in all human beings.

As we mentioned, the causal operator may lie at the very heart of much of our scientific investigation, philosophical speculation, and religious beliefs. After all, science always strives to determine how and why the various things in the universe work the way they do. Philosophy, too, tries to uncover the causes that guide the universe and human behavior. Throughout history, philosophers have struggled with the idea of causality—what causes what and what might have no cause. This causal imperative has often led to the development of myth formation and, in particular, religious beliefs.[5] Religions, in general, offer an answer as to what ultimately causes things to happen in this universe—power sources, gods, and, in the monotheistic religions, God. In order to explain how God originated, monotheistic religions necessarily conclude that God is the ultimate uncaused cause of all things. This is the only manner in which we can satisfy the causal imperative that forces us to pose the question as to why God exists. In fact, we might suggest that the causal operator is crucial to our understanding of the concept of God. For if we search hard enough for causes, we eventually work our way back to some first cause that appears not to be caused by anything else. It is this first, and ultimate, cause that many religions call God. This conclusion alleviates our urge generated by the causal imperative.

The abstractive operator permits the formation of general concepts from the perception of individual facts. For example, it permits a person to place the perceptions of a golden retriever, a poodle, and a dalmatian into a single conceptual category. This category can then be plugged into the speech center of the brain and can be given an auditory, written, and pronounceable name—"dog" in English. The abstractive operator is not directly responsible for the linguistic entities called nouns or naming words. Rather, it is responsible for the formation of abstract concepts, derived from the perception of various singular objects, upon which such linguistic naming depends. Thus, all general concepts or ideas underlying much of language are derived from the abstractive operator.

On a more complex level, the abstractive operator allows us to put two facts together and create the abstract concept that these two facts might be linked. Any idea that is based on some factual evidence, but is not proved to be factual itself, is generated by the abstractive operator. Thus, scientific theories, philosophical assumptions, and religious beliefs can all fall into the realm of the abstractive operator. Ideas involving areas such as mathematics, government, justice, culture, and family are all under the influence of the abstractive operator. In many ways, the abstractive operator is responsible for generating most of our higher-level ideas. The reason that the abstractive operator can perform these functions is that it receives input from the association areas of the various sensory modalities. Thus, the abstractive operator is derived from an association area of association areas and it can therefore generate classes of objects that are vastly more inclusive than any classification system that is possible within a given sensory modality.

The abstractive operator likely resides in the inferior portion of the parietal lobe in the left hemisphere.[6] Lesions of the parietal lobe, which also houses the orientation association area and the reductionist operator, have also been found to prevent a person from comparing objects.[7] Therefore, such statements as "larger than," "smaller than," "better than," and so on become impossible for patients with these lesions. It appears that the inferior parietal lobe on the dominant side not only may underlie conceptualization but may be responsible for the human proclivity for abstract antinomous or binary thinking, which underlies the basic structure of myth. Interestingly, lesions in the inferior parietal lobule also prevent patients from being able to name the opposite of any word presented to them. This area is thus the seat of another operator—the binary operator.[8]

The binary operator allows us to extract meaning from the external world by ordering abstract elements into dyads. A dyad is a group of two elements that are opposed to each other in their meaning. Therefore, dyads include good and evil, right and wrong, justice and injustice, happy and sad, and heaven and hell. It is important to note that each opposite in the dyad, in some ways, derives its meaning from its contrast with the other opposite. In this sense, the opposites do not stand completely on their own, but require each other in order to define themselves individually. This is particularly true since opposites are verbal descriptions of objects. For example, in physics, there are positively and negatively charged particles. There is no absolute meaning of "positive" and "negative," however; they are defined only in relation to the other so that a particle is positive only if it is not negative, and vice versa. The important point is that these dyads are one of the mind's most important ways of ordering the universe, and they do not represent an absolute function.

The binary operator is particularly important in the generation of myth.[9] There are examples too numerous to mention in myth and religion in which opposites are set against each other (e.g., good versus evil). More important, the dynamics of myth almost always involve the resolution of whatever opposites comprise the myth structure. This resolution often involves a being of power (gods, demons, God, etc.) who somehow contains the opposites and thus brings them together. By creating a myth, we understand why good things happen to bad people and why bad things happen to good people. Myths also can develop the notion that the opposites that we see are actually illusions, a notion that comprise part of the ideologies of Buddhism and Hinduism. Thus, for example, the opposites that we see in the world—good and evil, self and nonself, compassion and cruelty, and so on—are only our perception or misperception of the world. The goal of meditative philosophies is to break down opposites and arrive at a place where there are no opposites—where evil and good become one and where self and nonself become one. Thus, the binary operator plays a very important role in the generation of our mental picture of reality. In a later chapter, we will explore in more detail the relation of the binary operator as well as the other operators to the generation of myths.

The quantitative operator permits the abstraction of quantity from the perception of various elements. The part of the brain that functions as the quantitative operator is in the general area of the inferior parietal lobe and is situated near the anatomical areas underlying the binary and the abstractive operators.[10] This makes sense since the latter two operators have components that are also involved in the function of the quantitative operator. It seems that from a very young age we are capable of counting or quantifying things. In fact, recent studies have indicated that infants only several months old are able to understand basic mathematical concepts such as addition and subtraction.[11] We use this quantitative ability to help us order objects according to some numbering system or else by estimation of amount. More significantly, this operator is what has allowed human beings to develop the concepts of mathematics. It is clear that our ability to count things is critical to our survival. Throughout our life, we must continually be aware of quantities around us. We need to quantify time, distance, how much work we have to do, and how many people are around us. Even in past civilizations, the studies of mathematics, measurement, and time were often focal points of their cultures and religions.

The emotional value operator permits us to assign a particular emotional value to various elements of perception and cognition.[12] This is highly significant in terms of the development of culture, society, and belief systems. The other operators previously mentioned give us specific ways of ordering the external world. They allow us to infer cause, quantity, or unity in the elements that comprise the universe or else to order them in oppositional dyads. These are merely ways of interpreting what we experience, however. None of the other operators allows us to respond and evaluate our perceptions. This is the role of the emotional value operator: it works on all of our perceptions and thoughts to generate feelings about them. Thus, the emotional value operator tells us how we feel about all of the information obtained by the holistic, reductionist, causal, abstractive, binary, and quantitative operators. Then, based on this feeling, we can use the other operators to act upon our feelings.

The emotional value operator may require the most complex brain function of any of the operators. Because it has to place emotional value on the responses of all the operators, the emotional value operator must somehow be tied into all of them. Neuroscientists have clearly shown that the limbic system is the seat of our emotions and our emotional drives. It is the limbic system that causes our feelings of happiness, sadness, love, and fear. Interestingly, the limbic system is also one of the earliest evolved parts of the mammalian brain. This makes sense because it seems likely that, from an evolutionary view, all animals must be able to respond with some type of value operation to various elements in their environment. Otherwise, there would be nothing that would drive a bear to protect her cubs or cause an animal to run from a predator. While it is difficult to determine with any certainty the emotions of animals, it seems that they must have some type of value response that tells them what to avoid and what to be drawn to. Whether these responses imply the emotions of fear and love as humans know them is, however, difficult to discern. It is also difficult to assess precisely what the limbic function is in other animals. Suffice it to say that all animals must at least be able to derive an operational value from their experiences even if there is no emotional response similar in form to that of human beings. In human beings and in other animals, the limbic system is clearly involved in such responses as aggression and sexual behavior. It modulates these emotions by means of the autonomic nervous system (i.e., the arousal and quiescent systems). Thus, when an animal feels aggressive, it is because its arousal system is activated by the limbic system.

As the primate brain developed, and especially in human beings, the limbic system acquired more varied and subtle emotional responses. This allowed for the development of our full emotional repertoire. It should be mentioned that this evolutionary development of emotions from the more primitive emotions of aggression and sexual behavior lends some support to the concepts developed by Sigmund Freud, who theorized that our emotions and psychological development are based, in large part, on our most primitive emotions.

We have described how the emotions arise from the limbic system, but we have also indicated that these emotions must be ascribed to all of our higher brain functioning. Studies have suggested that the hippocampus and the amygdala serve to modulate emotions, but they also connect to the higher cortical areas where the cognitive operators exercise their functions. Thus, it seems probable that the amygdala and hippocampus function as the mediating structures between the limbic system and the cortex. In fact, there are a vast number of neural connections between the limbic system and the cerebral cortex. In this way, thoughts and experiences are transmitted from the cortex (the home of the other cognitive operators) to the limbic system, where they are given their emotional value. From here, the emotional value operator allows us to interpret our experiences and generate appropriate behavioral responses.

The cognitive operators represent the way that the mind functions on all input into the brain. This input includes sensory input, thoughts, and emotions. The mind can analyze and interpret this input and, based on that understanding, generate a response. It is within the brain that all of these operators originate, but as we mentioned previously, the brain must be considered as a whole, and certainly, each of the cognitive operators requires the entire brain in order to be fully expressed. For example, we have already referred to the right parietal lobe as the part of the brain that is primarily responsible for generating the function of the holistic operator, whereas it is our left parietal lobe that is responsible for generating the function of the reductionist operator. But both operators require many other parts of the brain in order to create thoughts, cognitions, emotions, and eventually behaviors. With the genesis of behaviors as output from the mind and brain there completes a loop of interaction in which the external world impacts upon the brain, the brain interprets this input, and then produces a behavior in response to the original input.

THE EMPIRIC MODIFICATION CYCLE

Here is where we need to consider another very important aspect of the inter-action between the mind/brain complex and the outside world. Specifically, we have presented a model that shows how the mind/brain is set up to respond to the external world. We have described how the brain works to receive input from the world, interpret that input, and apply emotional value to the input and its interpretation. From here, the mind/brain must determine what output should be sent as a response. Much of the model we have presented of the mind/brain has dealt with how the brain is set up to respond to a given input, but the question remains as to how the brain adjusts to the continuous flow of input. Furthermore, how does the brain adjust to new inputs that are signifi-cantly different from the ongoing model of the world contained within the mind/brain and upon which behavior is usually predicated? How does the brain generate new behaviors and responses to this input? And how is the mind/brain's model of the world changed to incorporate this new information so that the internalized model may more closely represent what is "out there"? We call this cycle of experiencing new inputs, understanding the meaning of these inputs, developing a response to these inputs, and generating new behav-iors to these inputs the empiric modification cycle (EMC).[13] And this process ultimately modifies or changes the internalized worldview of the organism.

The EMC is a crucial characteristic of the mind/brain function: it is what allows us to adapt our behaviors and ourselves to the world around us. Thus, we approach each new experience based on our previous experiential and behavioral repertoire. Then, based on a given new experience, the mind/brain develops new behaviors that help us adapt to the experience. In this way, we are always changing, always incorporating new experiences, and always devel-oping new behaviors. But how and why does this EMC actually occur? If we consider our actions and thoughts as part of the mind/brain function, then we should be able to derive the mechanism of the EMC from how the mind and brain work.

To begin with, there is strong evolutionary pressure for the mind/brain to develop a system by which it continually monitors and adjusts to the external world. The reason for this is that evolution is based on an animal's adaptability to a given environment. Adaptability is determined by an animal's ability to sur-vive and reproduce so as to perpetuate the species. Thus, evolution allows for the development of characteristics that enhance an animal's survivability and its ability to reproduce. Hence, the brain should develop so that any animal can learn new information that is helpful for its survival. This includes learning information about prey and predators, about the terrain, and about various dangers to be avoided. Perhaps more important, the brain must allow an animal to interact with other members of its species in order to allow mating to occur as well as to allow for the animals to live in groups. Thus, the brain needs some mechanism by which it processes input from the external world so that it can adapt its behavior in such a way that it maximizes its survivability and ability to reproduce. The better an animal's mind/brain can adapt to various novel inputs from the external environment, the more likely it is that the patterns of brain activity will evolve into the genetic structure of that animal. If this is true, then human beings have developed a highly adaptive mechanism in their brain for processing input and altering their behavior to maximize their survivability. This pattern of behavior is what we have called the EMC.

It seems reasonable that all animals have some type of EMC since all animals must be able to respond to the external environment. The EMC of various animals ranges in complexity from very simple to the highly complex neuronal system that has evolved in human beings. Thus, the EMC in humans has evolved from the more primitive EMC of other animals. It is also conceivable that there is room for further adaptation with regard to the EMC's ability to respond to the environment.

We should mention that the use of the word *cycle* in the name empiric modification cycle is important since it is a continuous cycle of receiving input, producing output, observing how that output alters the external world by receiving new input, and producing new output in return. Thus, the EMC functions in a rhythmic manner. There is a rhythm of input and output between the external world and the internal world. This rhythm is what determines our behaviors and how the internal and external worlds change. For human beings, this rhythm is modulated by the EMC, and therefore, in the end, our individual and group behaviors arise out of the rhythm generated by means of the EMC.

Now that we have considered the reason why there is an EMC, we can hypothesize where in the brain the EMC resides. Since the human EMC encompasses a complex set of functions, it is reasonable that it incorporates a large portion of the human brain. In order to achieve its function, the EMC must be comprised of the parts of the brain responsible for receiving input from the external world, processing that input into meaningful concepts, determining an emotional response to these inputs, and then formulating a behavior to those inputs. If the EMC functions properly, the behaviors that are generated should help the animal in its survival and reproduction. This would require that the interpretation of input be as accurate a representation of the external world as possible or that the behaviors correlate highly with improved adaptability in the external world. If the brain did not formulate a reasonably accurate picture of the external world, then that person or animal would probably have significant difficulty in adapting to the external world. For example, if an animal's brain did not recognize another animal as a predator, then the animal would soon be lunch. In fact, any danger that cannot be recognized as such would lead to a most maladaptive and unfortunate malfunctioning of the EMC. Likewise, if a species of animal were unable to recognize its mate, then that species would undoubtedly have great difficulty in reproducing. Obviously, this too would be maladaptive.

In terms of the actual parts of the brain involved in the EMC, we have already described that the primary sensory areas receive input from the external world. The input then goes to the secondary and tertiary association areas (particularly the cognitive operators) for the input to be processed. This implies that all of these sensory areas, as well as the tertiary association areas that help to process the input, are involved in the function of the EMC. The limbic system and the autonomic nervous system are also involved in the EMC since these parts of the brain allow the emotional value operator to evaluate various inputs. Once this is done, the parts of the brain that initiate action and thought take over to generate a behavioral response to that input. These areas are undoubtedly located in the frontal lobe, which includes both the attention association area (which directs action) and the premotor and motor cortex (which are involved in controlling muscle movement). There are also areas in the inferior parietal lobe involved in the function of the abstractive operator that contribute to formulating concepts and ideas about input from the external world. This may help us respond with verbalizations as well as active behaviors. Thus, it appears that many parts of the brain are necessary for the overall functioning of the EMC.

As we have noted, the interpretation and internal representation of sensory input must be reasonably accurate in comparison to what really is out there for the EMC to function adaptively. Furthermore, the EMC must function so that the patterns of behavior generated in response to various inputs make sense. For example, even if we recognize that the cliff might be dangerous, we must still make sure that we walk away from it rather than jump off. If our EMC generated the behavior of jumping off high places, then it would not be well adapted to the external world.

This also may explain why there seems to be such specific cognitive operators. If these operators are to be adaptive, it is likely that the representation that they generate of the external world corresponds closely to what is actually there in the external world. Thus, we would argue that we have a causal operator because things in the external world have aspects remarkably similar to what we subjectively experience as causes. The reason that we have a reductionist operator is that things in the external world have aspects similar to our sense of whole things that are composed of smaller parts. All of the cognitive operators likely correspond fairly well to what is actually in the external world. The objects and functions of the external environment have particular characteristics that must be identified, interpreted, and responded to. Over time, some behaviors that are developed become programmed into the gene pool of the species. This leads to the notions of prepared learning and prepared behaviors.

PHOBIAS AND PREPARED LEARNING

Prepared learning implies that there are some behaviors that we are genetically prepared to learn easily because they are particularly adaptive to the environment. In fact, it may be more accurate to state that prepared learning is based on behaviors that developed early in an animal's evolution. This allows us to recognize the cliff as being dangerous the first time we see it and does not require us to explore what will happen if we jump off. A specific example of such prepared learning in human beings is phobias, from which many people suffer.

The nature of phobias may be elucidated by considering our neurophysiological model of the mind/brain. Phobias have generally been defined as persistent, excessive, and irrational fears of specific objects or situations. We must question, however, whether these fears truly are irrational and excessive in light of their possible evolutionary basis. By this we mean that the "negative" alignment that a person might have toward the object of his or her phobia might be reflected in the evolutionary advantage of avoiding that object. For example, a common phobia is a fear of heights. This seems perfectly rational given the potential danger that heights can present. This being the case, it would make sense that we should fear heights because it is adaptive to avoid them.

Thus, it appears that phobias may result from evolutionarily "prepared" responses that have somehow become excessive. It is interesting to observe the relationship of evolution to the development of normal fear responses and of phobias. M. E. P. Seligman writes:

> A neglected fact about phobias is that, by and large, they comprise a relatively non-arbitrary and limited set of objects: agoraphobia, fear of specific animals, insect phobia, fear of heights, and fear of the dark, etc. All these are relatively common phobias. And only rarely, if ever, do we have pajama phobias, grass phobias, electric-outlet phobias, hammer phobias, even though these things are likely to be associated with trauma in our world. The set of potentially phobic events may be non-arbitrary: Events related to the survival of the human species through the long course of evolution.[14]

This description of phobias makes sense from an evolutionary point of view since more recently developed hazards tend never to become the object of phobias whereas age-old fears do. Thus, the basic negative alignment to objects of phobias probably required millions of years of human evolution. The remaining question is why this negative alignment has become excessive to the point of becoming a phobia. It is possible that the difficulty may be the result of an improper alignment of the self with the phobic object. Specifically, the attention association area might become excessively activated so that all focus turns toward the phobic stimulus evoking an unusually strong fear response within the emotional value operator.

In further considering the origin of phobias, it may be that they are more easily focused upon because of the prepared learning mentioned above. Seligman states that "phobias are highly prepared to be learned by humans, and, like other highly prepared relationships, they are selective and resistant to extinction, learned even with degraded input, and probably are non-cognitive."[15] Thus, it seems likely that phobias derive from behavior that has been "preprogrammed" into the neurophysiology of the brain. This may originally be accessed by the attention association area when the stimulus is present. If there is excessive focusing on the object, however, there may be an amplification of the fear of that object. The result is that the person becomes almost immobilized whenever the stimulus is encountered. It is also interesting to hypothesize that the reason not all people have phobias is that as society has evolved, the object of the phobias eventually became less worrisome. In that way, phobias have slowly been extinguished because they no longer are required for selective advantage. The vestiges may persist and arise in those people with phobias, however.

THE PRIMARY CIRCUIT

We have said that there needs to be a rhythm between the outside world and the inside world of the mind/brain. In human beings, this occurs through the function of the EMC. For this to occur at all, there must be a mechanism that allows for the reception of input into the brain, an analysis, and then a transmission of output from the brain. For these three things to occur, the parts of the brain responsible for these functions must necessarily be connected to each other. Thus, there must be some global connection of neurons that allows for input, analysis, and output so that these functions can occur in the right order and allow for adaptation to occur. We have already considered the neurophysiology that forms the basis of the EMC, but we will now expand upon this concept to incorporate the more global functioning of the mind/brain.

We suggest that the mind/brain is set up in such a way that there is one primary working circuit. We will call this the primary circuit, or, when incorporated into a psychological perspective, the primary ego circuit. This circuit comprises our sensory input areas, our input analysis areas, and our output processing areas. This circuit is obviously complex. After all, it must allow for the reception of sensory input from all five modalities—sight, hearing, taste, touch, and smell. The most complex part of the circuit is probably the input analysis since this includes memory of past experiences, emotional input, cultural norms, logic, and any other parts of the mind/brain that we bring to our analysis of sensory input. This analysis then feeds into another region of the brain that is responsible for generating behaviors. This sometimes generates learned behaviors from previous experience, but may allow for the synthesis of new behaviors in an attempt to do something more adaptive.

We believe that it is also the primary circuit that is involved in the development of consciousness. For us to generate consciousness, we must somehow project ourselves outward, which we may do through our behaviors, our language, or even internally by "talking to ourselves." This final way is important since it is an internal projection of our self within our own mind/brain. This output is then perceived by our senses as new input, which in turn is analyzed and identified as self. The more this self is projected outward, the more we are able to perceive its existence. All of this projecting and perceiving occurs within the confines of the primary circuit. Specifically, the mind/brain is aware that it is projecting something. If this projection correlates with the input, then we state that the input must have come from us and we identify that input as originally being generated by our self. This self is distinguished from the rest of the outside world because we do not identify all input as coming from our self. Any input that does not specifically correlate with our output is considered to be from something outside of the self.

In fact, there seems to be a self-resonance that is required for the development of consciousness. As the cycle continues, things such as memory, past emotions, and behaviors all become incorporated into what we perceive to be our self. This notion of resonance or rhythm appears to be important in the development of our own consciousness. It is likely a fundamental need of animals to recognize self from nonself at least in some form since this lies at the heart of behaviors such as finding food, mating, and avoiding danger. Note that this probably does not constitute consciousness, which is a bit more complex. But awareness of the self may be the rudimentary basis of consciousness.

There are two possible circumstances in which there would be a fundamental defect in the perception of self. First, if everything is perceived as self, then the organism would never eat, try to mate, or avoid any danger because it obviously would have no reason to do this. If the organism ate, it would be eating itself. In such a case, all dangers would be perceived only as an extension of self and would not need to be avoided. Second, the organism would have similar difficulties if it had the opposite perception such that nothing is the self. In this case, there is no self to feed, no self to take care of, and no self to live. Thus, this ability to resonate with oneself to develop an awareness of self as distinct from nonself is highly adaptive and absolutely necessary for survival. Conversely, a serious problem with the sense of self may be virtually incompatible with life. This explains why the brain might be set up to allow for such a resonance via its primary circuit.

This primary circuit is most likely preprogrammed so that some semblance of it exists almost as soon as the mind/brain is working. Thus, even infants appear to have a primary circuit that responds to outside stimuli and fashions responses in an attempt to maintain survival. The primary circuit is what senses hunger, generates a crying response, and expresses happiness once it senses food being provided. As the child develops, this primary circuit becomes more deeply established as the neural pathways that maintain the circuit are used more and more. It is known that the more a neuronal circuit is used, the more stable and permanent the connections become. Thus, the self-aware consciousness becomes more and more permanent the longer the resonance between the outside world and the mind/brain continues.

Of course, the mind/brain does not contain only the primary circuit. It contains many, perhaps millions, of other circuits of varying complexity and content. Some of these secondary circuits may underlie only one thought. Others might underlie a huge array of emotions, thoughts, and behaviors. These secondary circuits are usually not immediately accessible to the primary circuit, however. This does not mean that they do not receive input from the outside world, but they most likely do not receive the same quantity and quality of the input that the primary circuit receives. Furthermore, while these secondary circuits might be able to analyze input and generate behaviors, these behaviors are not manifested (at least directly) as part of the primary behavior of the organism because they are shut out by the primary circuit.

This is an important point since there are two requirements for maintaining the primary circuit. One requirement is constantly to support the function of the primary circuit. This occurs by the circuit continuously resonating with the outside world in order to maintain consciousness. The second requirement is to prevent other circuits from becoming too significant with regard to the primary circuit. If secondary circuits invade the primary circuit to an excessive extent, then the consciousness of that person would actually undergo a change. This may be exactly what occurs in people with schizophrenia. They can no longer distinguish themselves clearly from the outside world because many of their secondary pathways are accessible to the primary circuit. This allows them to think that hallucinated voices they hear come from external reality or allows them to think that the television is speaking directly to them. We all hear the television talking at us, but most of us realize that it is not talking *to* us. This is because our primary circuit allows us to distinguish what is happening around us from what is happening to us. Patients with schizophrenia cannot make this distinction.

There are other manifestations of secondary circuits invading the primary circuit. For example, many psychologists and psychiatrists speak of the subconscious mind. This is that part of the mind/brain that houses many thoughts and feelings that we do not normally access. The subconscious mind/brain may contain experiences or feelings that occurred during childhood and are now long forgotten in consciousness. The subconscious is not completely separated from consciousness, however, since these underlying feelings and experiences often affect how we behave. In fact, in many instances, psychologists and psychiatrists will try to bring out or access the subconscious mind/brain in order to determine why a person might be behaving in an atypical manner. For example, a person may have an unusual fear of dogs for reasons she is not aware of consciously. But, by trying to reach the subconscious mind, the psychologist might find that the person was attacked by a dog when she was two years old. Even though there is no direct connection between the subconscious experience and the conscious mind, the former clearly can affect the latter in less direct ways. In this example, the subconscious manifests itself in the form of an emotional response.

This brings us to another example that strongly supports the notion of primary and secondary circuits in the mind/brain—split-brain research.[16] While we have mentioned these experiments in an earlier chapter, their results are particularly important in our understanding of consciousness and how a primary circuit might interact with other circuits. In patients with severe epilepsy or seizure disorders, sometimes the only therapy is to surgically cut the connector tracts between the two hemispheres. This prevents the seizure activity in one hemisphere from spreading to the other hemisphere. Interestingly, this creates a split brain in which both hemispheres can function in relative isolation from one another. This is distinctly different from the normal brain since the connector tracts are usually important in conveying information from one hemisphere to the other. In our model, these connector tracts are responsible for including structures from both hemispheres in the primary circuit.

Many experiments have been performed using these patients with surgically isolated hemispheres to determine how the two hemispheres interact. What makes this possible is that both hemispheres receive sensory input from the outside world. The right hemisphere receives input that enters on the left side of the body and the left hemisphere receives input from the right side of the body. The classic experiment is when a subject is shown a figure of an object, for example, a hammer, to each hemisphere. If it is shown so that the input goes only to the left hemisphere, where the language center is, then the person can verbally state that he has seen a hammer. If the hammer is shown only to the right hemisphere, he cannot verbally describe that he has seen a hammer. Furthermore, he appears to have no conscious awareness that he has seen a hammer. But, if you ask the subject to draw what he saw, he can draw a hammer. He can also pick out a hammer from a group of objects if he is asked to pick out the object that he has seen even though he does not know why he chose the hammer. Clearly, some part of the person's mind/brain has seen the hammer, and he can somehow express that awareness, but not in a conscious way.

The split-brain experiments show that if the two hemispheres are not connected into a single circuit—that is, they cannot communicate with each other—there exist essentially two major circuits. Only the circuit connected to the language center, however, seems to result in conscious awareness. This supports the notion that there is always a single primary circuit that is connected with the outside world and allows for consciousness to occur. Any circuit that is not connected to the primary circuit does not enter directly into consciousness. Hence, in split-brain patients, the right-hemisphere functions do not enter into consciousness directly since they are not connected to the left hemisphere. The functions of the right hemisphere can enter consciousness indirectly given that the person can draw a hammer and then realize that he must have seen a hammer. Nonetheless, the person still has no awareness of the original perception of the hammer.

The two hemispheres can talk with each other on another level that does not require the connector tracts: they can also communicate with each other via the limbic system through the thalamus, hypothalamus, and the autonomic nervous system. For example, if a male split-brain subject is shown a picture of a naked woman so that the input enters the right hemisphere, he will not be able to verbalize what he has seen because the right hemisphere has no language center. He may blush when he sees the picture, though, because the right hemisphere can generate emotional responses via the limbic system. In turn, these emotional responses can be felt by the left hemisphere and a vague sexual response to something may be sensed. Thus, he may be aware that he is blushing even though consciously he does not know why specifically. In this way, emotions can be felt and communicated between hemispheres even if the original reason for the emotion is not communicated to the primary circuit.

Another interesting example of secondary circuits not easily joining the primary circuit can be found in people with something called blindsight.[17] In these people, a stroke or tumor causes damage to the nerve fibers running between the secondary association areas and the visual association area. These people will tell you that they are completely blind. They have no conscious awareness of being able to see. They can even pass lie-detector tests confirming their "total blindness," but they have the ability to walk through a room without bumping into any furniture. Thus, part of their brain can "see" and make sure that they avoid walking into any object. But the part of the brain responsible for conscious awareness of vision is not connected to the part of the brain responsible for the primary and unconscious aspects of seeing. In this example, we can discern that the problem is that a circuit that is normally part of the primary circuit is no longer connected. Hence, there is no longer any conscious awareness of this circuit of sight. What is also important to realize in this example is that the secondary circuit does interact with the outside world just as the primary circuit does. It is simply that it has become disconnected from the primary circuit, and so it no longer is perceived as part of normal consciousness. The point is that there are probably many other secondary circuits that contribute to our behaviors even though we may not consciously be aware of them.

There is another important aspect of the maintenance of the primary circuit. While the primary circuit is being positively reinforced, the secondary systems often need to be suppressed. There is clear evidence of inhibitory neurons and fibers throughout the brain. In fact, we referred to them earlier in our discussion of deafferentiation. For deafferentation to occur, there must be inhibitory fibers that suppress information input by suppressing excitation in other neurons. We would suggest that a large amount of energy must be expended by the brain in order to keep secondary circuits from overwhelming the primary circuit. As noted, the decrease in a person's ability to suppress secondary circuits might result in psychotic states in which visions, voices, and bizarre thoughts readily enter consciousness.

THE BRAIN AND CONSCIOUSNESS

The final part of this chapter will go beyond our theoretical discourse about how consciousness occurs and try to arrive at an understanding of the actual parts of the brain involved in the generation of consciousness. We feel that this is best done by remembering the theoretical requirements for consciousness and then apply them to what we know about the various brain structures that we have considered before. Clearly, the most important thing is to try to determine the parts of the brain that make up our primary consciousness circuit. It is important to note that not all of these parts of the brain may make up the primary circuit in all individuals. However, we are proposing an overview of the most likely structural organization that results in consciousness. Also, the primary circuit is just that—a circuit. As such it does not have a specific beginning and end. For simplicity, we will begin with the parts of the brain involved in projecting ourselves outward, then consider the parts involved in receiving input, and conclude with the parts involved in analyzing that input in order to determine that we are ourselves.

Several brain structures are involved in projecting ourselves outward. These include the areas of the brain involved in directing motor function so that we may move ourselves through the outside world. Movement of our legs and arms, movement of our head, and the creation of gestures such as facial expressions and body position that reflect what we are thinking and feeling are all part of our projection. The other primary part of our brain's ability to project itself outward is the language center. We have mentioned that language may be the most efficient way of projecting ourselves outward. Language clearly has become our most commonly used method of expressing our ideas and emotions. Therefore, the motor part of the brain and the language center are very important components in the development of consciousness.

The second component of consciousness is sensory input from the outside world, which includes the body. And for consciousness, this is necessary to perceive the self that we have projected outward. This would imply the need for all of the primary and secondary sensory areas. Thus, the areas in the brain responsible for taste, smell, hearing, touch, and sight should be a part of the primary circuit. There are also body sensors that determine the position of parts of the body that also make up the input part of consciousness. All of these sensory areas in the brain are connected to the outside world and allow the mind/brain and consciousness to create a loop between the internal and external worlds. These areas eventually tie into the tertiary association areas that are responsible for the analysis of the input.

The tertiary association areas form the part of the primary circuit involved in the analysis of the input since these areas involve connections with the limbic system, which helps determine emotional responses to various stimuli. Thus, the limbic system as well as its connections to the arousal and quiescent systems are part of the primary circuit. The parts of the brain that house the functions of the cognitive operators also must be tied into the primary circuit so that appropriate quantitative and qualitative analysis of input can occur. Also, the amygdala and hippocampus are essential parts of the primary circuit because they are involved in memory and hence help in referencing new experiences. These two areas also are connected with almost every other part of the brain, including other parts of the limbic system, and therefore help in much of the higher-level analysis of input. Perhaps at the top of this analysis hierarchy is the part of the brain within the orientation association area that distinguishes self from nonself. This part of the brain can take all of the input and determine what correlates with the part of the mind/brain that was originally projected outward. It is through this area that the loop of consciousness is completed.

Finally, the analytic areas of the brain are tied into the outward-projecting parts such as the motor area and the language center so that new behaviors can be generated based on all of the previous experiences and emotions. Because the attention association area is part of the motor system and also has connections to the language center, this area is probably important to the primary circuit. Therefore, the attention association area helps tie analyzed input into the outward-projecting parts and hence derive new behaviors from prior experience. All in all, this area plays a significant role in completing and maintaining the primary circuit of consciousness.

One final part of the entire circuit of consciousness is the area of the brain responsible for suppressing the secondary pathways and thus maintaining the primary circuit. This area is most likely the attention association area (which we have already included in the generation of consciousness) since it is the area that helps us focus attention. To that end, this area suppresses other intruding thoughts and feelings so that we may focus on current activity. We already have evidence that the attention association area can inhibit many other fibers through its connections with the thalamus, the amygdala, and the hippocampus, and it therefore seems to be connected with many of the other structural elements of the primary circuit. By being connected to many other parts of the primary circuit, in addition to having the ability to inhibit neuronal activity from other parts of the brain, the attention association area may be the most important part of the brain that helps maintain the integrity of function of the primary circuit by suppressing secondary circuits.

INTELLIGENCE AND THE MYSTICAL MIND

There is another aspect of the mind/brain that deserves inspection before considering how theology and eventually neurotheology arise. This is the notion of intelligence. Intelligence is a difficult concept to define, although we often use the term to refer to someone's mental abilities. But what exactly do we mean when we say that someone is intelligent? What is it that makes someone more intelligent, and is it possible to increase our own intelligence? In order to answer these questions, we must again focus on the structure and function of the mind/brain.

We have attempted to describe higher cognitive functions as an integrated system of cognitive operators. Indeed, the brain seems to function as a series of systems embedded within other systems. There are small parts of the brain that interact and work with other small parts to form a system. These smaller systems connect to larger areas of the brain to form larger systems of neurons. Eventually, all of the parts function together to form the mind/brain. This type of "nesting neurosystems" approach to brain functioning is increasingly being accepted by neurophysiologists and neuropsychologists as the following observation makes clear.

The systems approach for understanding brain functioning has recently won considerable recognition. Mental processes are believed to require complex interacting networks that chemically stimulate participating brain structures. Parts of the brain responsible for producing behaviors become interdependent, forming a communicative chain of connected subsystems. These interacting structural groups can be widely distributed throughout the brain. Injuries to any single part can cause dysfunction of the entire network. However, because the systems are not confined to narrow boundaries, lesions in differing locations can create either similar or very different disturbances within a single system.[18] Such an understanding of the function of cognitive operators as neural networks is essential to our understanding of intelligence.

Intelligence is an attribute that is eminently amenable to analysis based on the evolutionary development of the mystical mind. Although it is almost impossible to give a totally satisfactory definition of intelligence, we will define intelligence as the ability to learn, to solve problems, and to deal with new or unanticipated situations. We further propose that intelligence can best be divided on the basis of neurophysiological criteria into three parts: (1) abstract objective intelligence, (2) creative or intuitive intelligence, and (3) social intelligence.

Abstract objective intelligence consists predominantly of extracting meaning from reality by generating concepts, by juxtaposing or comparing one element with another in the form of opposites, and by the perception of efficient causality operating between perceived or conceptualized elements of cognition. In simpler terms, abstract objective intelligence is what we often call intelligence in general parlance. It is the type of intelligence that tests reasonably well and that school tends to focus on. The neural network subserving this type of intelligence likely consists of parts of the frontal lobe (particularly the attention association area) and the inferior parietal lobe and their interconnections. It is interesting to note that it is these brain areas, which have evolved and developed most recently in human beings, that clearly exhibit a great deal of this type of intelligence compared with any other species. Although abstract objective intelligence also requires the inclusion of other brain structures, the network just noted underlies its essential components.

A systems approach also suggests that it is not necessarily the number of neurons that one has, but rather the way in which they are connected, that helps determine intelligence. In other words, what makes someone intelligent is how complex and how well integrated the individual subsystems in the brain are put together. Pure complexity is not enough to create abstract objective intelligence, however, since the complexity must occur in ways that generate thoughts that allow for adaptability to the external world.

Intuitive or creative intelligence refers to the ability to solve a problem, usually presented by and to the language center of the left hemisphere, which cannot be solved by the usual rational operations of the left hemisphere. We have theorized that the verbal formulation of an original problem by the left (or dominant) hemisphere crosses the connector tracts of the corpus callosum and the anterior and posterior commissures and is encoded into what we call the gestalt language of the right (or nondominant) hemisphere. By the gestalt language we mean that the right hemisphere, which does not contain the formal language center, nonetheless has a system by which it can encode and consider things. Furthermore, it is clear that the gestalt language of the right hemisphere is visual or imaginative, not verbal. Thus, the right hemisphere has a way of generalizing ideas and concepts and considering them in the form of visual objects. The right hemisphere takes the information that has been sent to it by the left hemisphere and then scans both the external environment and its own memory banks for an analogous "problem gestalt." This problem gestalt can be so similar to the solution to the original problem that it contains elements that are the actual solution to the problem. This yields the "solution gestalt" to the problem gestalt and hence to the original problem. In terms of the origin of this process in the mind/brain, it seems likely, given that the process is not a conscious one, that the scanning procedure of both the external and internal environment and memory banks takes place in secondary association areas. Once the unconscious scanning has discovered an appropriate solution gestalt, it is communicated to the person by a brief assertion of the unity of the original problem with the solution gestalt. This is accomplished in part by the right orientation association area, which can generate a sense of wholeness, in this case referring to the relationship between the original problem and the solution gestalt of the right hemisphere. Because the orientation association area is heavily connected to the limbic system, there can be a concomitant increased activity in the limbic system. We believe that the rush associated with arriving at the answer to a problem causes, through this activation of the limbic system, what has been referred to as the "eureka phenomenon." The solution is then sent back across the connecting structures and decoded into verbal elements by the language center of the dominant hemisphere. Admittedly, little is known of the precise networks and structures involved in the process of creative intelligence. The overall process just described, however, does gives us a general notion of the underlying neurophysiology. It should also be mentioned that there appears to be a rhythm between the left and right hemispheres of the brain such that together they arrive at an answer to a given problem. When the answer is attained, there is a type of resonance between the two hemispheres in which the problem gestalt and the solution gestalt are united and the eureka phenomenon occurs.

There is also artistic creativity, which may not necessarily require the left hemisphere with its language center. In this type of intelligence, the problem is originally developed in the right hemisphere and is then modified according to the various problem gestalts available to the right hemisphere. If this occurs entirely in the right hemisphere, the artist may have difficulty expressing or even understanding these creative events on a cognitive or verbal level. In this case, the only resolution is through music or art or some form of nonverbal communication. Thus, by producing music or works of art, the language of the right hemisphere can be accessed directly. In artistic expressions such as poetry or writing, the creativity requires both hemispheres even though the problem gestalt may arise originally in the right hemisphere.

More is known about the neurophysiological basis of social intelligence than about the other types of intelligence. Social intelligence requires a multitude of abilities to interact with other organisms. Therefore, an organism must determine the relationship between predators and nonpredators, conspecifics and nonconspecifics; the relationship of other conspecifics to each other and to the self in terms of hierarchy—the ability to perceive alliances and enmity among individual conspecifics or groups of conspecifics; the ability to read the emotional state of conspecifics; and the ability to cooperate appropriately with group conspecifics toward social ends. Obviously we do not have a complete map of any animal's, much less a human being's, social intelligence system. We do, however, understand a number of important elements upon which social intelligence is predicated.

Even though the brain may generate and regulate social behaviors, social interactions also alter the function of the brain (via the empiric modification cycle). Taylor and Cadet propose that social behaviors such as play and sexual activity are not only related to socialization needs, but also influence the development of the brain itself.[19] It is for this reason that animals raised in enriched environments show superior learning as well as a higher number of nerve cells in their brains. In addition, the brains of animals raised in enriched environments have more complex interconnections between the neurons in their brain than those of animals raised in less rewarding environments.[20] Other investigators have corroborated these results and have shown that animals raised in an enriched environment have greater perceptual and social problem-solving skills.[21] Thus, the social environment has a direct impact on the neuronal structures and interconnections in the brain.

A number of areas of the brain are involved in social intelligence and more generally in social behavior. In fact, when one considers the complexity of social interaction, one can see a need for the functioning of many of the cognitive operators. Animals too employ many areas of the brain for the generation of their social behavior; the thalamus, the attention association area, and the temporal lobes are involved in the network subserving social behavior. It appears, however, that the amygdala is the principal focus of this network and perhaps the most important structure underlying social intelligence in both animals and man. Among mammals in general, bilateral destruction of the amygdala markedly interferes with the capacity to determine and identify the emotional and motivational meaning of externally occurring events. The animal becomes unable to discern social-emotional nuances conveyed by conspecifics or to choose the behavior that is appropriate in a particular social context.[22] Animals with bilateral amygdalar lesions have reduced aggressiveness, fearfulness, competitiveness, dominance, and social interest.[23]

This condition can be so profound that animals seem to have great difficulty discerning the meaning or recognizing the significance of common objects, a condition sometimes referred to as psychic blindness when it occurs in humans. Such animals can see and interact with their environment, but they respond in an emotionally blunted manner and seem unable to recognize what they experience. Adult humans with this syndrome become like infants who similarly are without a fully functional amygdala (this part of the brain is not fully developed until later in infancy). Thus, they will engage in extreme oral behavior, indiscriminately placing various objects into their mouth regardless of their appropriateness. There is also a repetitive quality to this behavior. Once they put an object down they seem to have forgotten that they have just explored it, and will immediately pick it up and place it again in their mouth as if it were a completely unfamiliar object.

Although superficially this is exploratory behavior, there is a failure to learn, to remember, to discern motivational significance, to habituate with repeated contact, or to discriminate between appropriate and inappropriate stimuli. Thus, when the amygdala has been removed bilaterally, the organism reverts to the most basic and primitive modes of interaction such that everything that is seen and touched is placed in the mouth.[24] This condition pervades all aspects of higher-level social-emotional functioning, including the ability to interact appropriately with loved ones. Among primates who have undergone bilateral removal of the amygdala, once they are released from captivity and allowed to return to their social group, they no longer respond to emotional or social nuances. They act as if they have no comprehension of what is expected of them or what others intend to convey, even when the behavior is friendly and concerned. In fact, studies have shown that adult primates with bilateral amygdala lesions prefer total isolation to group interaction.

Another area of the brain that we will call the social inhibiting area (neuroanatomically, the septal nuclei, which sit on top of the hypothalamus) is responsible for the critical function of modulating and inhibiting the function of the amygdala. In contrast to lesions in the amygdala, lesions in this area produce a dramatic and persistent increase in social cohesiveness. This occurs because the normal inhibition of the amygdala by the social inhibiting area no longer exists. Thus, the animal is released from the primary social functions of the amygdala.[25]

After complete bilateral destruction of the social inhibiting area in animals, the drive for social contact appears to be irresistible, and the animal makes persistent attempts to be in physical contact with living beings, even with species quite unlike their own. For example, rats with lesions in the social inhibiting area would inevitably choose to be in a cage with a cat rather than be in an empty cage. The rat will even attempt to huddle with and crawl on this normally feared creature. If a group of animals with lesions in the social inhibiting area are placed together, extreme huddling results. So intense is this need for contact comfort that if other animals are not available they will seek out blocks of wood, old rags, bare wire frames, and even walls.

Among human beings with disturbances in the social inhibiting area, a behavior referred to as "stickiness" is observed. These individuals make repeated, prolonged, and often inappropriate contact with anyone who is available or who happens to be nearby. Such patients seem to have little concern regarding the feelings of others or how interested they might be in interacting. Indeed, they do not readily take a hint and are very difficult to get rid of.

Attachment behavior during infancy is now generally understood to result from the differential maturational rates of the amygdala and the social inhibiting area. Broadly considered, the various parts of the limbic system mature at different times. Thus, certain behaviors and capacities appear at different periods, overlie previous capacities, become differentiated, and can become suppressed or eliminated. Since the development of the amygdala precedes that of the social inhibiting area, social–emotional activities mediated by the amygdala are expressed in an uninhibited fashion in early infancy. The influences of the social inhibiting area are absent due to functional immaturity, and thus the infant (animal or human) demonstrates indiscriminate contact seeking or attachment behavior. As the infant grows older, the social inhibiting area develops and more mature social interactions begin to emerge.

Crucial parts of the social intelligence network involve the reciprocal interconnections between the amygdala and the attention association area and between the amygdala and the visual association area in the right hemisphere. Possibly due to the visual and spatial complexity of the human face, the right hemisphere has been shown to be dominant in the perception and recognition of familiar and unfamiliar faces.[26] Whether the face of a friend or that of a stranger, the superiority of the right hemisphere for facial recognition is augmented by the additional display of facial emotion.[27] Not only is the right hemisphere predominant in perceiving facial emotion, regardless of the emotion conveyed, but faces are judged to be more intensely emotional when viewed exclusively by the right hemisphere.[28] Thus, there can be no question that the right hemisphere is dominant for the perception and recognition of faces and facial emotion.

Likewise, the left side of the face (which is controlled by the right hemisphere) has been found to be more emotionally expressive and also to be perceived as more intensely emotional.[29] When the right hemisphere is damaged, and most particularly the visual association area, a severe disturbance in the ability to recognize the faces of friends, loved ones or pets results.[30] Some patients with this condition are unable to recognize their own face in a mirror.

Of critical importance to social intelligence is the fact that lesions of the visual association area result in extreme difficulty recognizing, distinguishing, and differentiating facial emotions.[31] Thus, these patients are unable to recognize what others are feeling as conveyed by facial expression. This creates for them a great handicap for responding appropriately in social situations. We must emphasize that the visual association area of the brain is reciprocally interconnected with the amygdala and is consequently an integral part of the social intelligence network.

The significance of the entire mind/brain function is clear in terms of intelligence regardless of whether it is abstract, objective, creative, or social. The study of intelligence is a useful method for understanding the overall function of the mystical mind.

SUMMARY

In this chapter we have attempted to give an account of the neural networks and neural operators that form the basis of the functioning of the brain and result in the functioning of the mind. In our model, the mind and the brain are essentially two different ways of looking at the same thing, the brain representing the structural aspects of the mind, and the mind representing the functional aspects of the brain. They each affect the other and are effected by the other in the rhythmic process of the empiric modification cycle. Further, we can see how the mind and brain can generate intelligence, including abstract intelligence, intuitive or creative intelligence, and social intelligence.

THE NEXT STEP

In this first part, we have explored the workings of the human mind and brain and how they function together. We have started from the basic functioning of the brain and applied it to the complex workings of the mind. We have hinted at how the mind/brain may function in a mystical manner, but have yet to find the fully constellated "mystical mind." This is the reason that we have called this part of the book "Prelude to the Mystical Mind." In part 2 we will expand upon the functioning of the mind/brain to find out why human beings generate myths and perform rituals. These protoreligious elements will help us form the basis for the development of the mystical mind. We will then consider detailed models for the generation of mystical phenomena. These mystical phenomena can span a spectrum of experiences from brief, "lesser" mystical states to the highly advanced states of meditation and contemplation. We will also consider the significance of spontaneous mystical states such as the near-death experience and how they relate to the mystical mind. This understanding of the mystical mind will then clear the way for an understanding of the paradox of pure consciousness or absolute unitary being and for the development of a neurotheology that we will explore in the final part of this book.

Part Two

The Mystical Mind

Chapter Four

Why the Mind Creates Myth

In developing the background of the concept of mystical mind, we can now use our understanding of mind/brain functioning to explore the structuring and transformation of myth. Specifically, we propose that the generation of myth can be traced to the functioning of the cognitive operators. Mythmaking, as well as other cognitive processes, is seen as a behavior arising from the evolution and integration of certain parts of the brain. Human ceremonial ritual, as well, will be considered as the culmination of a long phylogenetic evolutionary process. Finally, the mechanism by which ritual is used to resolve the antinomies of myth structure will be explored in this chapter.

We would suggest that the generation of myth, its structure and transformations, as well as the resolution of the myth problem through ceremonial ritual are derived from the functioning of neural structures (i.e., the cognitive operators). These structures evolved and became progressively elaborated because of the adaptive advantage they conferred on their bearers. We will present a model that derives the nature and necessity of myth formation from certain operators as well as from the neurobiology underlying the transformations of the surface structure of myths. Finally, we will present a model based on recent neurophysiological research that explains the resolution of mythic antinomies by the integration of ritual behavior into myths.

The purpose of exploring myth formation and transformation is that myths form the basis of religions. Myths are stories that purport to explain ultimate aspects of reality either in terms of efficient causality (creation or foundational myths) or in terms of final causality (salvation or apocalyptic myths) or in terms of both. Therefore, to understand the neuropsychological basis of myth formation is to begin to understand the basis of religion and ultimately of theology.

More important, we will see later that the neuropsychological model that helps describe myth formation is compatible with models of higher forms of religious experiences such as those that occur during meditation and other mystical states. In this way, we begin to observe the functioning of the mystical mind.

COGNITIVE STRUCTURES

We have already considered the functioning of the cognitive operators in detail. The result of the functioning of the cognitive operators is "cognitive structures," which simply refer to the subjective manifestations of ways in which reality is organized by the operators. In other words, depending on which operator is functioning, the world is perceived in terms of synthetic unity, abstract causal relationships, relationships of binary opposition, and so on. In ordinary, day-to-day cognitive functioning, all these operators function together, each relating its function to that of the others in order to construct meaning from experience and create a coherent view of the world. Thus, the mind/brain normally operates as a functional unit. The predominant function of any single operator to the exclusion of the others is a rare event, although, as we shall see, it is not impossible. Here we will explore how a specific aspect of the functioning of the cognitive operators leads to the generation of myth.

The cognitive operators allow us to propose that the most sophisticated mathematical, logical, or grammatical operation can ultimately be reduced to the simplest spatial and spatiotemporal analysis. These fundamental spatiotemporal operations can be understood as an evolutionary elaboration of the more gestalt operation of the nondominant hemisphere of the brain. It is generally the nondominant hemisphere that has been shown to be responsible for abstraction and the development of three-dimensional spatial relations. Temporal sequencing is primarily a left hemispheric function that is integrated into the spatial organization of the right hemisphere by means of the connector tracts. The overall integration of these spatiotemporal functions occurs primarily in the orientation association areas.

We would also argue that the apparent multiplicity of relationships between elements of a cognitive structure such as a myth theme can be reduced to a relatively small list of ultimately basic analytic relationships, including inside-outside, above-below, left-right, in front-behind, all-nothing, before-after, and simultaneous-sequential.[1] These relatively few basic spatiotemporal relationships can be enriched by combining them with affective or emotional tone and elaborated by adding other cognitive and experiential data. Thus, within is usually identified with good and without with bad, above with good and below with bad, right with good and left with bad, in front with good and behind with bad, all with good and nothing with bad, and so on. These emotional responses certainly are not absolute and the reverse of any of them may occur.

It is interesting, however, to reflect on how common, if not universal, are the relationships just mentioned. In other words, the same relationships are found in many cultures throughout the world. We feel there is a reason for this common association that involves issues of simple preservation and hence evolutionary significance. For example, above is usually safer than below because one can look out for predators more easily when one is situated high up rather than when the predator is situated higher. The result is that above is considered good whereas below, which may be more dangerous, is considered bad. For similar reasons, within is usually safer than without, and therefore, the former is considered to be good. Nevertheless we must reiterate that these associations are not absolute and that the reverse associations can theoretically occur and occasionally, in fact, do occur.

It is difficult to list all of the possible complex relationships that can exist between elements processed by the cognitive operators. Therefore, we have chosen to attempt to reduce them to a handful of simple spatiotemporal relationships. We feel it can be practically demonstrated that all complex relationships (whether they be mathematical, local, or grammatical) can be reduced to either one or a combination of the basic spatiotemporal relationships we have just considered, with one exception: affective or emotional relationships.

Affective relationships represent emotional states of crucial importance to our understanding of and response to the world. In one way or another, they enter into all of our moral and value judgments and underlie the emotional impact of myths. On the most basic level these affective relationships can be resolved into whether a stimulus is positive or negative for an organism's survival. Simply put, that which provides either immediate or delayed gratification is good; that which the organism experiences as unpleasurable or not conducive to survival is bad. As with the spatiotemporal relationships, the basic affective relationships can be elaborated into a number of subtle feeling states and can be related to perception and cognition in various ways. The neurophysiological substrate for these affective-cognitive-perceptual linkages is the connections between various limbic structures and the secondary sensory association areas (in the case of perceptions) or tertiary association areas, especially the inferior parietal lobule (in the case of cognitions).

Thus far we have attempted to delineate the basic classes of relationships—spatial, temporal, and affective—that occur between elements processed by the cognitive operators. Within our overall neuropsychological model, we have proposed an evolutionary basis for such relationships. Furthermore, these affective-cognitive-perceptual relationships most probably form the basis of myth structure. All this brings us to the problem of the transformation of affective-cognitive-perceptual structures (e.g., myths). The transformation of cognitive structures presents the rearrangement of the relationships of cognitive elements and underlies the various mutations of the surface forms of myths. The reason why this is important is that there is a significant amount of anthropological evidence that the various myths, worldwide, that underlie religions and religious behavior can be grouped into thematic classes. Some anthropologists, particularly those with Lévi-Straussian leanings, maintain that the various myths within a class are transformations of each other and represent various surface structures of one deep structure. We feel that there is much truth to such an analysis, but, if it is true, an account must be given of the neuropsychology and the neurophysiology that underlie transformations.

THE NEUROBIOLOGY OF TRANSFORMATIONS

The neuropsychological basis of transformations within a structural system is one that has received little or no attention by structuralists whether they be anthropologists (e.g., Claude Lévi-Strauss), linguists (e.g., Noam Chomsky), or even developmental psychologists (e.g., Jean Piaget). Developmental psychologists have suggested the most comprehensive meaning of transformation that involves more complex cognitive structures such as myth themes (in which are embedded potential models of the world) evolving from simpler structures. More specifically, developmental psychology is viewed as the progressive elaboration of a series of nesting structures of increasing complexity.

The relationship of the more complex to the less complex structures involves several rules of transformation. These rules include

1. a possible alteration or substitution of one element for another;
2. the addition of new elements of content which were not previously present in the simpler structures; and
3. specific rules of reorganization of all the elements of content such as is conveyed in the Lévi-Straussian understanding of transformation.[2]

Such a complex system of transformation allows for the classical Piagetian model of nesting structures, which often has been described as the form of the simpler structure becoming the content of the more complex. Recent evidence suggests that the human capacity to organize data in terms of nesting or hierarchical structures may involve the part of the inferior frontal lobe known as Broca's area.[3] It has been known for some time that the syntactic structure of language is organized by this area of the brain, and it has been presumed that the nesting structures that generate language (i.e., in Chomsky's model) likewise reside in this area.

What is exciting about this new evidence is that it seems to indicate that the inferior frontal area in the dominant hemisphere may be generally responsible for the organization of thought into hierarchical structures (not just for linguistic organization). Such a structural system may be referred to as "semiclosed" to emphasize that such configurations of elements are highly stable neural and cognitive systems, not easily changed, but not absolutely and permanently fixed in either an ontogenetic or a phylogenetic sense, as the Lévi-Straussian structure would seem to imply.

Of course, the major question that needs to be answered in order to understand myth formation and myth structure is, Under what circumstances does the surface manifestation of a structure (or myth) undergo a transformation? Considering the work of Lévi-Strauss as well as a number of cognitive psychologists, it seems that structures such as myths are composed primarily of relationships between dyads of cognitive elements. These relationships set one element against another for semantic clarity. Further, the relationships *themselves* can be grouped into dyads involving the opposing of spatial, temporal, or affective relationships we have considered above, such as up-down, left-right, before-after, and good-bad.[4]

One of the ways in which the work of cognitive psychologists and of anthropologists such as Lévi-Strauss can be made to make neurophysiological sense is if we postulate that it is inherent within the machinery of the brain to relate the cognitive elements of a structure (again in this case a myth) in this dualistic manner. In this way, for every pair of cognitive elements related by one aspect of a relationship such as *up* at least one other pair must be related by the opposite relationship such as *down*.[5] Furthermore, one must postulate that these relations occur in such a way that if the elements related by *up* are changed so that they are now related by *down,* then at least some of the elements formerly related by *down* must now become related by *up*—unless, of course, the reciprocal change would result in nonsense. Note that, according to this "postulate of reciprocal change," such change is operative only when it involves a new surface structure that has meaning. Certain combinations can obviously involve nonsense. It would appear at this point that we are invoking the subjective entity of meaning to be the constraint within which basic neurophysiological processes operate. If this were true, then the phenomenon would be dependent upon the epiphenomenon, and we would be reduced to absolute idealism.

On the contrary, we would suggest that those relationships between cognitive elements of a structure that we consider meaningful possess the quality of meaningfulness simply because they are the subjective manifestations of inherently stable relationships within the mind/brain's structure. The reason for such relationships' stability probably resides in various configurations' being evolutionarily adaptive and thus conducive to survival. It is only in this physicalist sense of the word *meaning* that we will say that meaning imposes constraints upon the postulate of reciprocal change during a transformation.

Thus, any given cognitive (or social) structure is limited to the number of its possible transformations, not by the theoretical total number of permutations generated by the postulate of reciprocal change, but rather to a number that represents a subset of that total set of possible transformations. This subset contains those transformations that have subjective meaningfulness or, in terms of evolution, have adaptive properties and represent a high degree of isomorphism with the external world. Specifically, this meaningfulness must be considered in the context of the primary circuit, since it is this circuit that establishes the empiric modification cycle, and thus, is intimately involved in the determination of adaptability.

Any given surface structure of relationships among elements of a semantic field such as a myth is present and stable simply because it is adaptive psychophysiologically for an individual or social group. It must be that the external world contains within it a certain degree of stability or unchangeability. After all, if there were no stability, it would be almost impossible for anything to exist, since existence itself is defined by a certain degree of permanence. For an organism to adapt to the external world, it would likely have some mechanism by which it can learn and familiarize itself with its environment. By "getting used to" its environment, an organism would gain an adaptive advantage by increasing its capacity to function more and more efficiently within its environment. Of course, the external world is also continuously changing. Thus, an organism must be able to adjust to changes in its environment in order to remain adaptive. If the organism is prone to change excessively, however, then it will lose its existence as that particular type of animal and will either evolve into a new organism or become extinct.

It is this rhythm between permanence and changeability that defines that which is adaptive. This rhythm between permanence and impermanence will also be relevant later in our consideration of religion and theology. The important point here is that the environment ultimately imposes the constraints that define exactly which surface manifestation of a deep structure will survive, either cognitively or socially, at any given time. It is change in the environment, ultimately, that causes a disconfirmation of a given surface structure (or actual myth) as representing the "real world" and that permits a change in one or more relationships between cognitive elements. Once one change takes place, the entire system becomes rearranged according to the postulate of reciprocal change; a number of possible configurations are generated until one that is more adaptive to the circumstances becomes fixed (either for the individual or for a group).

A related comment involves the theory of mazeway resynthesis postulated by Anthony Wallace.[6] What he is essentially describing is the rearrangement of relationships between multiple dyads (usually under the influence of intense limbic arousal) of a structure involving the relationship of the individual to the universe as a whole. Thus, mazeway resynthesis can be seen as a transformation of the most encompassing superordinate cognitive structure under conditions of intense stress. Essentially, it is a total reorganization of the self. It is a testimony to the stability of cognitive structures that only the most severe stresses, the most intense states of limbic arousal, are able to facilitate the transformation of such important superordinate structures as the self.

RESOLUTION OF THE MYTH PROBLEM COGNITIVELY AND RITUALLY

We have previously described a myth as performing two distinct but related functions. First, a myth presents a problem of ultimate concern to a society. This problem is always presented in antinomous form in the surface structure, that is, in terms of juxtaposed opposites such as life-death, good-evil, or heaven-hell.[7] Second, once the existential problem is presented in the myth, it is solved by some resolution or unification of the seemingly irreconcilable opposites that constitute the problem. Usually the myth problem is resolved cognitively within the myth itself by a unitary symbol. But the problem presented in the myth is generally not just a cognitive one but a deeply felt existential problem of the society that generates the myth. Thus, a deeply felt, experienced resolution usually occurs only when the myth is enacted in ritual form. In chapter 5 we will consider the effects of ritual in detail. For the moment, it is sufficient to state that, properly performed ritual, in and of itself, produces a powerful unitary sense. When the ritual is enacting or "incarnating" the myth, this sense of union or oneness is applied by the mind to the major antinomies of the myth. When the ritual enactment works, the sense of resolution of the myth problem is vividly experienced by the participants of the ritual, and the resolution of otherwise irreconcilable opposites becomes an experienced fact. The symbolic resolution by way of a unifying symbol is usually far less satisfying than the existential solution to the myth problem when the myth is enacted in ritual behavior. We will begin a more detailed presentation of the nature of ceremonial ritual at the end of this chapter, especially as it relates to myth. A more general consideration of human ceremonial ritual will be presented in chapter 5.

The ability to structure a mythic problem and its resolution involves the cognitive operators we have discussed. The abstractive, causal, binary, and holistic operators have a key role in the formation and resolution of myths. To begin with, myths are created using named categories of objects, which we call concepts or ideas. These concepts and ideas, which may be derived through the function of the abstract operator, serve as the elements of the surface structure of the myth. Myths, like all other rational thoughts, also involve causal sequences of events. The development of causality is clearly a function of the causal operator. Myths involve the orientation of the universe into multiple dyads of polar opposites, an orientation generated by the binary operator. The resolution of the problem presented by these antinomies is accomplished most effectively by a unification of the opposites presented in the original problem. This resolution, therefore, appears to employ the holistic operator to unify the opposing sides of the myth.

We would suggest that the most efficient and powerful method of resolving myths occurs during ritual, but in order to understand why this is the case, we need to consider the development of the mythic problem and the mythic resolution in more detail.

THE MYTHIC PROBLEM

Human beings have no choice but to construct myths to explain their world.[8] The reason for this necessity is that as long as there remain unanswerable questions, the cognitive operators necessarily perform their functions even if they must generate gods, demons, or other "power sources" to do so: we must develop myths in order to find at least temporary solutions. Both explanatory and motivational stories (myths) are thus necessarily generated by the brain. Myths may be social in nature, or they may be individual in the form of dreams, daydreams, and other fantasy aspects of the individual person. Even science and the scientific method are a special type of myth that helps human beings explain the universe. Nevertheless, as long as human beings are aware of the contingency of their existence in the face of what often appears to be a capricious universe, they must construct myths to orient themselves within that universe. As we have stated, this constructive orientation is inherent in the obligatory functioning of the neural structures or operators we have described. We have referred to this as the cognitive imperative since it is a necessary behavior, most likely based on its evolutionary adaptiveness to use our mind/brain to order the universe into meaningful patterns.[9] Because it is highly unlikely that human beings will ever know the first cause of every strip of reality observed, it seems that we will always generate gods, powers, and other entities as first causes to explain what we observe. Indeed, we cannot do otherwise.

Myth problems, therefore, are structured either socially or individually, according to the analytic and verbal mode of consciousness that exists in the dominant (or left) hemisphere. Myth problems classify unexplained aspects of reality in terms of antinomies or polar opposites such as good-evil and change-permanence, and in terms of causal explanatory sequences.

Thus far, we have only presented the outline of a neuropsychological model explaining the mechanism (based on the cognitive operators) and the necessity (based on the cognitive imperative) for structuring input from the external world into causal sequences and mythic antinomies, that is, into dyadic structures of concern to humanity. The second aspect of myth is to unify these opposites to resolve the problem.

The Mythic Solution

Examples of mythic solutions to the god-human antinomy are a solar hero, a Christ figure, or divine kingship. Similarly, good and evil might be unified into a single entity such as absolute good that encompasses both good and evil. From the neuropsychological perspective, these resolutions are caused by a subtle shift in cognitive dominance from the dominant (left) hemisphere to the nondominant (right) hemisphere of the brain. The cognitive functions we have been considering up to now—conceptualization, abstraction, causal thinking, and antinomous thought—represent the evolution of the dominant hemisphere's function. As we have noted, it is the nondominant hemisphere that generates the perception of sensory input as a whole rather than as a string of associated discrete elements. We propose that the cognitive unification of logically irreconcilable opposites presented in the myth structure (such as god and human in a solar hero or a Christ figure) represents a shift of predominating influence from the left hemisphere to a predominant influence of the right hemisphere, which allows the antinomies to be perceived in a more unitary or integrated mode.

Thus, for example, the concepts of a Christ figure or a solar hero represent cognitive solutions within the myth to the problem presented by the basically antinomous myth structure. Although this is undoubtedly so, we feel that classical structuralists have tended to overemphasize the resolution in terms of the internal dialectic of structures. We contend that the only resolutions that are psychologically powerful to both individuals and groups are those that have an aspect of existential reality. Further, we will attempt to show that such a powerfully emotional resolution arises most effectively from myth embedded within ritual and rarely from a cognitive fusion of antinomies alone. It may be, however, that cognitive fusion is a necessary precursor in human religious ritual.

The Ritual Resolution

Religious ritual aims at existentially uniting opposites in an effort to achieve some form of control over what appears to be an essentially unpredictable universe. The ultimate union of opposites is that of a vulnerable humanity with a powerful, possibly omnipotent, force. In other words, we propose that humanity and some "superhuman" power are the ultimate poles of mythic structure. Furthermore, it is this polarity that is the fundamental problem ritual must resolve existentially.

Juxtaposed with this fundamental antinomy are other correlated opposites, which also must be resolved. These secondary opposites are dependent on the specific purpose of the myth and often require solving before the basic god-human antinomy can be resolved. Opposites such as heaven-hell, sky-earth, good-bad, left-right, strong-weak, as well as an almost endless series of other polarities, recur frequently in myths. But, before we consider how ritual allows such a powerfully affective union of mythic opposites, let us first consider why it is that human beings tend to act out their myths at all.

There is some evidence that whatever is present in one neural system tends to be present in other neural systems, even if its manifestation in other systems is inhibited. For example, it has been known for some time that whatever is heard tends to be repeated within the mind/brain. In normally functioning individuals the actual physical repetition of whatever is heard is inhibited by mechanisms within the frontal lobe, leaving only an internal repetition. If the frontal lobe inhibitory mechanism is released, however, as occurs in certain pathological states, the phenomenon of echolalia occurs in which individuals obligatorily repeat whatever they hear. Likewise, there is an inbuilt tendency for the mind/brain to have a representation in the motor area of whatever movement, usually by another human, appears in the visual system. This representation is ordinarily inhibited except in a few pathological conditions in which the patient exhibits echopraxia. In this condition, a person necessarily performs any action he or she sees. The auditory-motor connection is seen in the rare condition of latah in which patients obligatorily obey whatever they hear.[10]

The cognitive-verbal-motor connection is significant when considering the development of ritual behavior. The motor manifestation of cognitive-verbal expression is ordinarily inhibited as occurs in the other systems mentioned earlier, but it tends to break through in normal individuals when we "talk with our hands." We propose that there is a powerful inbuilt mechanism that drives us to "act out" our thoughts. This may be the case because of the evolutionary advantage of using our increased intelligence and cognition to modify our outward behaviors. Thus, our motor behaviors could be adjusted more easily and quickly than those of other animals who did not have the same cognitive capacity. In the end, changing our actions based on our cognitions may have improved our chances of survival.

It is because of the reciprocal representation of the content of the major neural systems that human beings are naturally disposed to act out their myths. Myths are not acted out by ordinary motor behavior but by rhythmic motor activity. Humans reach far into their evolutionary past and graft an ancient motor behavior onto the product of their neocortex, that is, onto myth. Why should we do so? The answer lies in the consideration of the nature of ritual behavior itself.

Ritual Behavior

We define ritual behavior as a sequence of behavior that:

1. is structured or patterned;
2. is rhythmic and repetitive (to some degree at least), that is, tends to recur in the same or nearly the same form with some regularity;
3. acts to synchronize affective, perceptual-cognitive, and motor processes within the central nervous system of individual participants; and
4. most particularly, synchronizes these processes among the various individual participants.

The last component refers only to rituals performed in groups and not to individual ritual such as that often associated with meditation. We have mentioned that individual rituals satisfy the first three criteria. The fourth component is slightly different for individual ritual compared to group ritual. Individual ritual helps synchronize the participant with some higher form of being, whether that be the rest of the world, the universe, or God. For now, we will concern ourselves with components of group ritual and the synchronization that occurs between individuals involved in group ritual.

A number of animal studies have shown that there is something about the repetitive or rhythmic emanation of signals from a conspecific which generates a high degree of arousal in the limbic system of the brain.[11] With respect to this rhythmic quality of ritual, Konrad Lorenz notes: "The display of animals during threat and courtship furnishes an abundance of examples, and so does the culturally developed ceremonial of humans. The deans of the university walked into the hall with a 'measured step'; pitch, rhythm and loudness of the Catholic priests chanting during mass are all strictly regulated by liturgical prescription. The unambiguity of the communication is also increased by its frequent repetition. Rhythmical repetition of the same movement is so characteristic of very many rituals, both instinctive and cultural, that it is hardly necessary to describe examples."[12]

Other researchers have shown that such repetitive auditory and visual stimuli can drive neuronal rhythms in the brain and eventually produce an intensely pleasurable, ineffable experience in humans.[13] Furthermore, such repetitive stimuli can bring about simultaneous intense discharge from both the human arousal and quiescent systems.[14] When one considers the evidence taken from the literature on animal studies together with the limited studies that have been performed with humans, one can infer that there is something about repetitive rhythmic stimuli that may, under the proper conditions, bring about the unusual neural state consisting of simultaneous high discharge of both the arousal and the quiescent system.

As we have mentioned in chapter 2, normally either the arousal or the quiescent system predominates, and the excitation of one system normally inhibits the other. In the special case of prolonged rhythmic stimuli, it appears that the simultaneous strong discharge of both parts of the autonomic nervous system creates a state that consists not only of a pleasurable sensation but, also, under proper conditions, a sense of union with conspecifics and a blurring of cognitive boundaries. We suggest that such driving of the autonomic nervous system by rhythmic stimuli powerfully activates the holistic operator, allowing various degrees of gestalt perception. This occurs through deafferentation of the orientation association area with concomitant functioning of the holistic operator. The simplest paradigm to explain the situation in humans is the feeling of union that occurs during orgasm. During orgasm, as during other states we shall consider later, there is intense simultaneous discharge from both autonomic subsystems.

Hence, we are postulating that the various ecstasy states, which can be produced in humans after exposure to rhythmic auditory, visual, or tactile stimuli, produce a feeling of union with other conspecifics participating in that ritual. In fact, the oneness of all participants is the theme running through the myth of most human rituals. It is probably also the sense of oneness and the vagueness of boundaries, which are experienced at certain "nodal points" in ritual to allow for a given symbol (i.e., a religious symbol) to be experienced as that for which it stands. This fusion of symbols and their referents at various points in human religious ritual is undoubtedly accomplished by the underlying feeling of oneness that occurs when a particular ritual triggers the holistic operator. Although it is very difficult to extrapolate from humans to animals, it is probable that some sort of analogous affective state is produced by rhythmic, repeated ritual behavior in other species. This state may vary in intensity, but it always has the effect at least of unifying conspecifics.

Thus, it seems that rhythmic or repetitive behavior synchronizes the limbic discharges (i.e., the affective states) of a group of conspecifics. It can generate a level of arousal that is both pleasurable and reasonably uniform among the individuals so that necessary group action is facilitated. Rhythmic activity likely causes these effects, in part, by its ability to function as a form of communication. The position of many ethologists is that rhythmicity evolved in lower animal species as a primary form of communication. Rhythmicity also evolved an autonomous effect of its own, however, separate from its communication function. Lorenz states: "Both instinctive and cultural rituals become independent motivations of behavior by creating new ends or goals toward which the organisms strive for their own sake. It is in their character of independent motivating factors that rituals transcend their original function of communication and become able to perform their equally important secondary tasks of controlling aggression and of forming a bond among certain individuals."[15]

THE NEUROPSYCHOLOGY OF RITUAL

How does all of this happen from the neuropsychological perspective? In humans we have proposed that, concomitant with the simultaneous stimulation of the lower aspects of both the arousal and the quiescent system, the extensions of these systems into the brain cause both hemispheres of the brain to function simultaneously. Cognitively, this is manifested by the presentation of polar opposites by the analytic or left hemisphere (i.e., the presentation of a problem to be solved in terms of the myth structure) and the simultaneous experience of their union through the activation of the holistic operator, whose function is derived from the orientation association area in the right hemisphere. This could explain the often reported experience of the resolution of unexplainable paradoxes by individuals during certain meditation states or during states induced by ritual behavior. In previous works we have often referred to the similarity or even identity of meditation and ritual in terms of the resolution of opposites. The neuropsychological identity rests in the final activation of the holistic operator in generating the unitary experience that reconciles opposites. It should be obvious that the overall neuropsychological mechanisms underlying meditation, on the one hand, and ritual, on the other, are actually quite different except in the last stage. Meditation is what we have called a top-down mechanism and ritual is a bottom-up mechanism. Both will be considered in more detail in chapter 5. For now, suffice it to say that meditation, as well as effective ritual, can, and usually does, produce the powerful subjective experience of the integration of opposites.

In one of the few experiments carried out in any kind of controlled manner on the experiences of meditation, A. J. Deikman notes that one of the phenomena common to all subjects is what appears to be simultaneity of conflicting perceptions during relatively advanced meditation states: "The subjects' reports indicated that they experienced conflicting perception. For example, in the third session, subject B stated, about the vase, 'it certainly filled my visual field' but a few minutes later stated 'it didn't fill the field by any means.' In the seventh session referring to the landscape he commented, '. . . a great deal of agitation . . . but it isn't agitating . . . it's . . . pleasurable.' In general, subjects found it very difficult to describe their feelings and perceptions during the meditation periods—'it's very hard to put into words,' was a frequent comment. This difficulty seemed due in part to the difficulty in describing their experience without contradictions."[16]

Thus, during certain meditation or ritual states, logical paradoxes or the awareness of polar opposites may appear simultaneously, both as antinomies and as unified wholes. This experience is coupled with an intensely affective, oceanic, or blissful experience. During intense meditative experiences, the experience of the union of opposites is expanded to the experience of the total union of self and other. In the *unio mystica* of the Christian tradition, the experience of the union of opposites, or *conjunctio oppositorum,* is expanded to the experience of the union of the self with God.

Ritual itself is always performed in order to solve a problem presented by and to the verbal analytic part of the mind/brain. The problem may be between good and evil, life and death, or the disparity between God and humanity. The problem may be as simple as the disparity between human beings and a capricious rain god or as subtle as the disparity between humanity's existential contingent state and the state of an all-knowing, all-powerful, unchangeable ground of being. In any case, the problem is presented in the analytic mode, which involves excitation of the arousal components of the brain.

Like all other animals, human beings must cope with any given environmental situation by means of a motor behavior. This motor behavior goes back far into our evolutionary past. It is usually a repetitive motor activity with visual, auditory, and other sensory feedback. This rhythmic stimulation strongly drives the arousal system. With prayers and chanting, the arousal system may be driven in two ways. The myth's meaning may be presented within the ritual prayer, thereby exciting the cognitive arousal functions of the left or analytic hemisphere. The rhythmicity of the prayer or chant drives the ergotropic system independent of the meaning of words. If the ritual is effective, the arousal system becomes highly activated, resulting in the previously mentioned spillover phenomenon. This causes excitation of the quiescent system and activation of the holistic operator.

This unusual physiological state produces other aesthetic-cognitive effects besides a sense of the union of opposites. Many religious traditions indicate that such states yield not only a feeling of union with a greater force or power but also an intense awareness that death is not to be feared and a sense of harmony of the individual with the universe. This sense of harmony with the universe may be the human cognitive extrapolation from the more primitive sense of union with other conspecifics that ritual behavior generates in prehuman animals. Thus, we can see how ritual has evolved from the behaviors of primitive animals to the most complex human religious rituals.

Although our higher cognition may have evolved as a very practical, adaptive, problem-solving process, it carried with it—indeed, it requires—the formation of myths that present problems for which the ancient rhythmic motor behaviors help generate solutions. In other words, when ritual works (and it by no means works all the time), it powerfully relieves our existential anxiety. Furthermore, when ritual is most powerful, it relieves us of the fear of death and places us in a sense of harmony with the universe. Ritual allows individual humans to become incorporated into myth and, conversely, allows for the very incarnation of myth. One can see why so powerful a behavior has persisted throughout the ages and is likely to persist for some time to come.

Chapter Five

Ritual, Liturgy, and the Mind

As we delve into the mystical mind and its relationship to theology, the first stop is a basic form of mysticism. Ritual and liturgy help bring mysticism and spirituality to the masses in a manner impossible by meditation. Meditation is an individualistic approach to mysticism and to a sense of some higher order of the universe. Even though meditation may be practiced in groups, it is usually the individual who actually benefits from the experience. Furthermore, meditation is designed to bring the individual toward some more exalted state of reality even if it is practiced as a group. Ritual, on the other hand, is usually practiced within a group and, to that end, helps to bring the members of that group into a sense of corporate unity.

We have mentioned that an analysis of both ritual and meditation reveals that the two practices are similar in kind, if not in intensity, along two dimensions: (1) intermittent emotional discharges involving the subjective sensation of awe, peace, tranquillity, or ecstasy, and (2) varying degrees of unitary experience or feelings of oneness, correlating with the emotional discharges just described. Further, this second dimension often generates a decreased awareness of the boundaries between the subject and other individuals (generating a sense of community), between the subject and external inanimate objects, between the subject and any putative supernatural beings, and indeed, at the extreme, the abolition of all boundaries of discrete being leading to brief states of absolute unitary being (AUB).

Human ceremonial ritual is best understood as a morally neutral technology that, depending on the myth in which it is embedded, can either promote or minimize particular aspects of a society and promote or minimize overall aggressive behavior. Thus, if a myth that achieves its incarnation in a ritual defines the unitary experience that the myth generates as applying only to the tribe, then the result is only the unification of the tribe. It is true that aggression within the tribe has been minimized or eliminated by the unifying experience generated by the particular ritual. However, this fact may only serve to emphasize the special cohesiveness of the tribe vis-à-vis other tribes. The result may be an increase in overall aggression when considered on a more global scale (specifically, intertribal rather than intratribal). The myth and its embodying ritual may, of course, apply to all members of a religion, a nation-state, an ideology, all of humanity, or all of reality. As one increases the scope of what is included in the myth within which the unitary experience is generated, the amount of overall aggressive behavior decreases.

The states that can be produced during ceremonial and religious ritual seem to overlap with some of the unitary states generated by various meditative practices. It is probably not too strong a statement that human ceremonial ritual provides the "common man" access to some modified form of mystical experience. This by no means implies that the mystic is impervious to the effects of ceremonial ritual. In fact, precisely because of their intense unitary experiences arising from meditation, mystics may be more affected by ceremonial ritual than the average person. Given the historical success of ceremonial ritual, at its most effective, it appears to be an incredibly powerful technology, whether used for good or for evil purposes. Further, because of its essentially social nature, it tends to have immeasurably greater social significance than meditation or contemplation. Even though meditation or contemplation may produce more intense and more extended unitary states compared to the relatively brief flashes generated by ritual, the former nevertheless are solitary experiences. They may be of immense significance to the individual. Indeed, the significance of meditative states may be of a genuinely transcendent nature, but they are not essentially social experiences, although they may have social consequences.

Over the past several decades, we and others have gradually been working toward the development of a neuropsychological model of unitary experience that would encompass ritual, meditation, and contemplation within one theoretical framework.[1] In order to accomplish this, we must consider that ritual and meditation both can generate a number of states along a continuum of unitary states. We will call this the unitary continuum, and the concept refers to all states of human experience as they relate to a sense of unification or connection with other things. These states begin with the least holistic, which is essentially baseline, daily living. This includes our interactions with others, eating, sleeping, and working. In this state, however, we tend to approach each of these activities as if it is only ourselves performing the activity. There is very little sense of a greater organization of our reality. In states related to ceremonial ritual there is a sense of union with the others involved in the ritual. As we have described, this allows for a sense of community or group unity that allows all members to experience a connection with the rest of the group. As we proceed along the unitary continuum, we can eventually find profound mystical states in which there is a sense of unity, not to others in a group, but to the universe as a whole, and even to apparently transcendent reality.

It is our hope that, within the model presented in this book, this entire spectrum of human experience, from a very reductionistic to a very holistic perspective, will be understood as resulting from the human brain and the human mind. But, to do this requires the human brain to be able to function at various levels of activation as well as to relate these different levels to different subjective senses of reality. In this chapter, we will consider the experience of traditional ceremonial rituals and determine how these rituals may affect the mind/brain, and how the mind/brain may have brought us to the development of such ritual.

THE NEUROPHYSIOLOGY
OF THE UNITARY CONTINUUM

We have already considered important functions of the mind/brain with respect to the experience of various states along the unitary continuum, without calling attention to the ordering of these states along that continuum. Specifically, we have considered the arousal/quiescent states of the brain. These were the hyperarousal state, the hyperarousal state with quiescent breakthrough, the hyperquiescent state, the hyperquiescent state with arousal breakthrough, and the state of mutual maximal activation of the arousal and quiescent systems.

Based on these states alone, one can see how there could be a continuum of human experience. For example, if there is a high quiescent drive such as during the playing of a slow, rhythmic song, one may experience a deeper and deeper serenity of the experience. One may eventually achieve a state of total bliss that would be considered the state of maximal excitation of the quiescent system. This state may lead to intermittent breakthroughs of the arousal system causing heightened awareness of the quiescent state itself. Eventually, one might achieve consistent activation of both the quiescent and the arousal systems. A person may experience a similar progression of states as she enters a hyperarousal state, possibly leading to quiescent breakthrough. These states allow for the emotional aspect of the unitary continuum. By this we mean that the unitary continuum consists not only of the experience of unity but also of the emotional response to that unity. Thus, as one progresses to greater and greater states of unity, one attains more extreme emotional responses associated with those states.

The unitary continuum goes from the roughly fifty–fifty diversity/unity perception of baseline reality, through states of increasing perception of unity over diversity, to the perception of absolute unity characteristic of absolute unitary being. An example of some of the important nodal points along this continuum would be the following: baseline reality; aesthetic experiences such as the appreciation of a sunset or a symphony; the intense feeling of romantic love in which "it's bigger than both of us"; the numinous experience of reality often through a dream or vision of a divine being or of a mandala; cosmic consciousness as described by Richard Maurice Bucke in which there is a profound sense or "knowledge" of a deep unity underlying discrete reality, but with individual things being perceived as individual; various progressively intense trance states during which there is a blurring of the boundaries of individual things; all the way to the state in which there is no perception of spatial or temporal boundaries whatsoever, accompanied by the experience of absolute unity, devoid of content and with even the self–other obliterated. Thus, AUB may be considered the ultimate trance state. It has interesting and important characteristics that apply to it alone, however, and we will consider these when we elaborate upon AUB.

We maintain that the aspect of mind/brain function that allows for the ability to move along the unitary continuum is the progressive deafferentation of the orientation association area. Remember that as input into the orientation association area is blocked (deafferentation), the person will gradually lose the ability to orient him- or herself within the usual frame of reference that is based on the five senses. As the deafferentation becomes greater, the person experiences a movement from a baseline orientation in external reality to a more intense sense of unity with the rest of the world and an increasing loss of a sense of self and other. This results in the ability to lose individuality and to experience a sense of absorption into the object of focus or into the universe in general. For example, if we are listening to a slow, rhythmic song, we might eventually feel absorbed into the rhythm of the music. This can lead to total absorption into an object of focus in which we feel as if we have truly become one with that object. Finally, in absolute unitary being, we experience not only the breakdown of the self–other dichotomy, but the object that we are absorbed into is also broken down, resulting in an experience of unity with all things.

In this chapter we will consider in more detail the types of states that occupy the unitary continuum as outlined. We will look at various types of ceremonial ritual and see how they can generate increasing senses of unity and can create what have been referred to as "lesser" mystical states. In the next chapter we will proceed beyond the "mini mystical states" of effective ritual experiences of human beings into the realm of true mystical experiences and the neurophsyiology underlying them.

SLOW VERSUS RAPID RITUAL

We are now in a position to see how the rhythmicity of human ceremonial ritual can produce various states along the unitary continuum. What is particularly important is that ritual behavior can elicit various states along the unitary
continuum from a "bottom-up" approach. The bottom-up approach indicates
that the initial neural stimulation is with the autonomic nervous system (either
sympathetic/arousal or parasympathetic/quiescent) and proceeds to stimulation
of progressively higher structures in the brain stem, midbrain, and cerebral
cortex. This is opposed to the "top-down" approach of meditation, during
which the initial neural activity is within the cortex, proceeding to activation
of progressively lower structures, culminating finally in the activation of the
autonomic nervous system. Ritual clearly demonstrates the bottom-up
approach to alternate phases of consciousness. Thus, the rhythmic quality of ritual eventually leads to different states through activation of various brain structures by means of either the arousal or the quiescent system. The top-down
mechanism that we will later see occurs during meditation generates different
states of consciousness by cognitive activity in the brain's cerebral cortex that
eventually activates the arousal and the quiescent system.

In order to explore in more detail how ritual behavior can generate various
states along the unitary continuum, we will begin with the four defining characteristics of ritual behavior described in the previous chapter; namely, that ritual
is a sequence of behavior that (1) is structured or patterned, (2) is rhythmic and
repetitive, (3) acts to synchronize affective, perceptual-cognitive, and motor
processes to generate powerful unifying experiences within the individual, and
(4) synchronizes these processes among the various individual participants creating a strong sense of group unity. With the exception of the cognitive elements
mentioned, these defining characteristics of ritual are perfectly general and can
refer to animals as well as humans.

We have noted the initial quiescent drive of "slow" rhythmic rituals like
Christian or Shinto liturgy. We must also consider the mechanism of "rapid" rituals such as Sufi dancing, the Umbanda of Brazil, or voodoo frenzy, among
many others. Although slow external rhythms can manifest as quiescent dominance, an imposition of rapid external rhythm represents a dominance of the
arousal system. Using our model, one can see a bottom-up process with rapid
external rhythms driving the arousal system. We hypothesize that rapid external rhythmic drivers would eventually lead to a release of hippocampal inhibition on arousal centers in the brain. This would result in an increased arousal
drive via the amygdala to the cortex. This process continues until maximal
arousal occurs, which, as mentioned before, leads to spillover and quiescent
breakthrough. The initial quiescent breakthrough would result in a change in

the activation of the hippocampus, which is highly correlated with trance or dreamlike states.[2] In these states, there is a profound sense of both internal harmony and union with external ritual participants. These states of quiescent breakthrough allow the hippocampus and the orientation association area to generate a powerful unitary experience. We will explore this model of activation in detail in the next chapter, but now we are considering the basic components of that model.

Slow ritual can achieve the same effect simply and directly by activating the quiescent drive without first going through the intense "flow" experience of hyperarousal drive and subsequent quiescent spillover. In both cases, however, the result is brief unitary states. However brief they may be, if these states are experienced as being profound, there obtains not only a sense of union of the ritual participants but also a sense of the union of opposites presented in the myth that the ritual incarnates. Problems of life and death, good and evil, quest and attainment, God and human being, that are presented in mythic form, can be perceived to be resolved in the powerful unitary experience of a hyperarousal state with quiescent breakthrough or in a hyperquiescent state directly.

It is our sense from the descriptive literature that human ceremonial ritual does not usually go beyond this point. If the arousal activity is maintained at high intensity, however, and if the quiescent breakthrough can be maintained at a slow and gradual increase, then theoretically one could move into a state of hippocampal activity known to be associated with hyperlucid hallucinations and mystical visions.[3] Hallucinations and mystical visions are occasionally reported to occur in particularly physically vigorous and protracted rituals. It seems that this state would be especially unstable because it is difficult to maintain the vigorous activity required to drive the arousal system in the face of quiescent breakthrough. Thus, this state is often likely to deflate to baseline conditions once the rigorous activity is stopped. It is nonetheless theoretically possible for the quiescent breakthrough to increase to a point of maximal stimulation of the quiescent system. If this condition should occur, then the maximal stimulation of both arousal and quiescent systems should yield the state of absolute unitary being that will be described later in detail. We feel that it is improbable, however, that the state of AUB can be maintained for any length of time in the presence of the physical activity necessary to maintain the rhythmicity of ritual.

In addition to the direct effect of rhythmicity, there are other neuropsychological components of ceremonial ritual that we believe can clearly augment the effect of rhythmicity. Human ceremonial ritual, which typically activates the quiescent system, often incorporates "marked" actions. Thus, any action such as a prostration, a slow bow, the slow and deliberately excursive movement of the arms and hands, or any other action that by its form or meaning draws attention to itself as different from ordinary baseline actions produces an orienting response by the amygdala. Remember that the amygdala performs environmental surveillance and can direct attention toward something of interest in the environment. In animals, electrical stimulation of the amygdala initially produces sustained attention and orienting reactions. If the stimulation continues, fear and/or anger reactions are elicited. When some degree of fear follows the attention response, the pupils dilate and the animal will cringe or withdraw, all of which are functions of the arousal system. We propose that during human ceremonial ritual, the amygdala, which helps fix our attention, is more than normally responsive to specifically marked ritual actions. This tends to produce sustained attention and orienting reactions accompanied by a mild fear response, which, in this context, may be responsible for what humans call "religious awe." Thus, marked actions may cause brief arousal breakthroughs (although not true eruption from maximal stimulation) during the hyperquiescent state of slow ritual.

In addition to the amygdalar response to ritually marked actions, we should also mention, at least in passing, the effect of the sense of smell as an arousal driver. The middle part of the amygdala receives fibers from the olfactory tract, which comprises the neurons for the sense of smell or olfaction. During times when we experience a strong smell, there is concomitant activation of the amygdala.[4] It would seem, then, that the use of incense or other fragrances might cause direct stimulation of the amygdala, subsequently augmenting the general arousal drive by means of marked ritual actions. This also enhances activation of the arousal system and facilitates the development of a hyperarousal state either during rapid ritual or to facilitate arousal breakthrough during slow ritual.

We would suggest that all of these systems—rapid rhythmicity, marked ritual actions, and olfactory drive—can result in powerfully reinforced arousal stimulation, which can ultimately lead to quiescent breakthrough (in addition to causing arousal breakthrough during slow ritual). It should be noted that this intense arousal stimulation almost certainly includes activity of areas of the brain such as the hypothalamus, resulting in positive psychological states varying from mildly pleasant to ecstatic. We believe that human ceremonial ritual taps into the same overall neuropsychological mechanisms that meditation and contemplation tap into, at least with respect to the production of unitary states. We will consider the more specific pathways involved in meditation in the next chapter. There are, of course, significant differences between ritual and meditation, but that there is also significant overlap should by now be obvious.

We have termed the mini mystical states or feelings associated with ritual "lesser mystical states," to distinguish them from the great states often generated by intense meditation. Lesser mystical states are not necessarily ritual related, however. Occasionally, they arise from meditation, but often they occur spontaneously. We will consider such lesser mystical states here, however, because they frequently occur within the context of ritual.

LESSER MYSTICAL STATES

In the context of what we have mentioned about the functions of the tertiary sensory association areas, and the arousal and quiescent systems, it is now possible to gain some preliminary insight into the genesis of what we might term lesser, although extremely powerful, mystical states or religious experiences. For example the experience which Carl Jung and others refer to as "numinosity" can be described as a combination of the experience of both fear and exaltation usually described as religious awe, and almost always associated with religious symbols, sacred images, or "archetypal" symbols.[5] When this occurs as a result of meditation it probably begins with the meditator's intending or willing to focus intensely on the stream of images as they come into and leave consciousness. We would suggest that this subjective state of the free flow of consciousness is probably attained when the attention association areas causes a deafferentation of the visual association area. The interaction of the visual association area and the amygdala and hippocampus can result in eliciting visions and hyperlucid hallucinations. Without modulating input into the visual association area subsequent to deafferentation, the images from the visual association area's memory areas flow according to their own internal logic. They appear sometimes as simple representations of external reality, sometimes as monsters or gods composed of fragments of other images, and sometimes they appear as "archetypal" symbols. If Jungian archetypes do in fact exist, it is probably through deafferentation of the visual association area that they rise to consciousness. Thus, the attention association area would stimulate the orientation association area to attend to, not any one object generated by the visual association area, but the total functioning, or the "imaginal flow," of the visual association area as a deafferented unity. Such free-flowing activity of this area, in conjunction with activity in the amygdala and hippocampus (which are located close by), would powerfully stimulate the limbic system in specific ways. It might stimulate some parts of the hypothalamus (via the hippocampus and amygdala) to generate a mild to moderate fear response. At the same time it might stimulate other parts of the hypothalamus (also via the hippocampus and amygdala) to generate a feeling of exaltation.

We suggest that in lesser religious states, we are not dealing with a system of maximal simultaneous arousal and quiescent stimulation as with the genesis of AUB. Rather, we are probably dealing with mild to moderate stimulation of certain neuronal circuits (of the lateral hypothalamus) that generate a mild to moderate fear accompanied by a sense of exaltation. This, then, is the complex often referred to as religious awe, probably because this unusual combination of emotions is generally associated with symbols or constructs generated by the visual association area and identified as religious.

Rudolph Otto's *mysterium tremendum et fascinosum* is the sense of the mighty and wholly other "cause of all" filling the world, and the subject experiences it as a mysterious and awesome presence. In our model, when this occurs as an effect of meditation or ritual, we are probably dealing with the deafferentation of those neural circuits within the verbal–conceptual association area, which is usually responsible for the sense of causality in our ordinary processing of sensory input, and which we have termed the causal operator. Deafferentation of the causal operator would result in a subjective sense of reified causality since these structures presumably act as an operator on sensory input and do not contain memory banks themselves. As with the deafferented visual association area, which results in the sense of numinosity, the deafferented causal operator generates the subjective sense of the great cause coupled with the same limbic discharges that make up the sense of religious awe.

We must note here that the sense of the *mysterium tremendum* and the sense of numinosity can also occur spontaneously, without meditation, and even in persons with no history or knowledge of meditation. We would hypothesize that the immediate and proximate triggers are what we have presented in our model; deafferentation of the visual association area in the case of numinosity, and deafferentation of the causal operator in the case of the *mysterium tremendum*. It is a subject for future empirical investigation as to what stimuli, external or internal, short of meditative concentration, can trigger such sudden deafferentation and limbic stimulation.

We suspect that *spontaneous* intense religious experiences, and perhaps near-death experiences, not generated by intended meditative practices, begin with an unusually high stimulation of hypothalamic or limbic structures. Whether these unusual trigger states occur because of an accumulation of certain life experiences or from other causes is as yet totally unknown. We strongly suspect, however, that the same reverberating circuits, discussed in chapter 6, are set off, but this time spontaneously from the bottom up, as it were, instead of from the top down as with intended meditation.

This chapter does not claim to present a comprehensive model for the great variety of religious experiences generated by ritual. But the principle of selective stimulation and deafferentation of various brain structures accompanied by various patterns and degrees of intensity of limbic (or emotional) stimulation may hold the key to explaining most, if not all, religious experiences, whether generated by ritual, by meditation, or spontaneously.

IMPROVING RITUAL AND LITURGY

In previous works, we have discussed the general applicability of this model of human ceremonial ritual across cultures. Here, however, we will consider some of its implications for religion in Western culture. We would like to consider an interesting question about what the neurophysiology of ritual may have to do with current liturgical practice. Most of us are familiar with the liturgy in our church or synagogue. Christmas, Easter, Rosh Hashana, Passover, or any other holiday has a liturgy that consists of specific prayers, songs, and stories that are put together in such a way as to provide a consistent, spiritual event. Thus, the telling of the Christmas story with its concomitant Christmas songs is different from the story surrounding Easter. The different aspects of the liturgies give each holiday and hence each ritual its own meaning. Some prayers, songs, and stories, however, may be performed at every ceremony, since they refer to some primary tenet of the religion. These might consist of prayers or songs that praise God or refer to God's infinite power. The universal elements of a given religion's liturgy help make all of the ceremonial rituals part of the religion in general. Thus, Christmas and Easter exist not on their own but within the general context of Christianity.

In order for liturgy to work effectively, it must carry many rhythmic components. On a fundamental level, liturgy must strike a rhythm between the theology of the religion in general and the significance of an individual story (i.e., a portion of the basic myth). If we had exactly the same ceremony for each holiday, then we would not be able to distinguish the holidays from each other. On the other hand, if there were no unifying themes that pervaded all holidays and ceremonies, then we would lose site of the religion itself. An example of this rhythm can be found in Judaism, in which each holiday has specific stories and themes in order to express a particular component of Judaism. However, the Shemah is said at every ceremony in the Jewish religion. This is because the Shemah represents the primary tenet of all of Judaism: "Hear, O Israel, the Lord is our God, the Lord is One. Praise be thou O Lord, Ruler of the Universe, to whom all praise is due, now and Forever." This prayer expresses what distinguished Judaism from all other religions in the ancient world, an insistent and uncompromising monotheism. Further, this prayer has been preserved and repeated for thousands of years.

This brings us to the next rhythmic aspect of liturgy. The arrangement of various religious rituals as well as the tenets of a given religion must be set in a rhythm between permanence and impermanence. Religions tend to have a specific set of laws and rituals that remain fixed over time. This creates the overall sense of the religion, defines its boundaries, and allows for the religion to maintain a consistency that everyone can follow, and the more universal and invariant are the many aspects of a religion, the easier it is for people to follow. Religions exist, however, within the framework of changing times, technologies, politics, and diverse adherents. In order for a religion to remain viable, it must have a certain degree of flexibility with respect to changing times and changing attitudes. For example, many religions have had to struggle with the issue of women's role in society. In modern Western society, women have had an increasing role in the business world, in education, and in government, among many other aspects of society. Most of the world's religions, in their original forms, did not consider women as having these types of roles. Thus, if a religion does not allow women to have a job, then the religion will have great difficulty existing within a society in which most women have jobs. The only way to avoid losing its strength as a religion is to alter, at least somewhat, its position regarding women. This might be done by finding a way to allow women to work. The only problem with such changes is that if there are too many, the religion may begin to lose itself. In other words, the religion will begin to lose the characteristics that define it as that particular religion.

What religions must necessarily do is find a rhythm between permanence and impermanence. The appropriate rhythm would allow the religion to adapt to the changing times and attitudes so that what are considered the primary or essential tenets can be preserved. Thus, a religion may need to allow women to work so that women continue to adhere to it, but the religion would undoubtedly maintain its statements regarding core issues such as the nature of God or the most apporpriate way to live one's life. The same may be true of actual liturgical practices in that ceremonies must maintain certain fairly permanent characteristics in order to preserve and pass on the significance of a specific holiday such as Christmas. For example, one could not remove the story of a humble birth in a manger without losing an essential part of the Christmas story. On the other hand, if a particular ritual originally was practiced for ten days, it may be more practical in today's world to relate the main parts of the ritual in a shorter period of time. Another example might be a story's being told in the original liturgical language. If that story is brought to another culture, then it would make sense to change the language so that the new audience can understand the story *within* the rhythmic flow of the liturgy rather than as a sort of addendum to it. Insistence that the story be told in the original language would necessitate various awkward strategies for translation, all of which would interrupt, in one way or another, the rhythmicity of the ritual, inevitably resulting in a diminished effect.

The final rhythmic aspect of liturgy involves the liturgy itself. As we have described earlier, various songs, hymns, chants, or prayers can all drive the arousal or quiescent systems. If we hear slow, rhythmic organ music, we may develop a sense of peace and tranquillity. If certain stories or ideas are narrated or sung during this time, then they will be associated with overwhelming peaceful emotions. For example, during a slow rhythmic chant, a narration about the love God feels for us might leave us with the sense of overwhelming peace and an all-encompassing, powerful love. Alternatively, the song or chant itself may supply the words or story to be interpreted in this quiescent way.

We have proposed that the excitation of the arousal system is related to feelings of awe. Thus, interjecting certain rituals that stimulate an arousal response during a ceremony may occasion a sense of the awe, or even fear, of God. The arousal system seems to be activated by such things as marked actions, incense, stories, chants, or prayers. It also might be activated in the presence of an underlying quiescent state to incorporate a sense of unity in addition to a sense of awe.

In the end, a liturgical sequence that employs both aspects of arousal and of quiescence—some rapid songs, some slow hymns; some words of love, some words of fear; stories of glory, stories with morals; prayers exalting God and prayers asking for help—will allow for the participants to experience religion in the most powerful way. They will experience the profound peace of the love of God, fear and awe of the power of God, and a strong sense of what is right and moral. If a ritual has just the right rhythms, however, then the participants may briefly experience something a step further. If the arousal and quiescent systems are activated during ritual, then they may experience a brief breakdown of the self-other dichotomy. This breakdown will be interpreted within the theology and stories of the religion, and this powerful experience will give the participants a sense of unity with each other because they are all taking part in the same ritual. Furthermore, the participants may have a sense of being more intensely united to God or to whatever the religious object of prayer or sacrifice may be. This liturgical sense of unity can allow everyone (not just monks or mystics) a chance at moving across the unitary continuum to experience the mystical—a sense of unity with God, with the universe, or with whatever is "ultimate."

FUTURE LITURGY

One of the questions posed by our analysis concerns the significance of this model of brain activity during ritual to the development of future liturgy. To begin with, it is important to realize that we are not trying to reduce religion to a simplistic firing of neurons. We are merely trying to explain how the human mind generates and responds to ritual and how this helps our mind experience religion and God. The religious leaders of the past who developed our current liturgical practices were obviously unaware of the neurophysiological effects of the rituals. They only realized that what they were doing was leaving people with certain feelings about God or religion. As time went on, there is no doubt that the rituals evolved as specialists realized that some parts had "better" effects than others. Thus, if a given hymn or chant was found to give participants a strong sense of awe, that hymn would be played the next time such an effect was desired instead of other, less effective ones.

Most likely, the impact of various parts of liturgy was determined by inter-actions between those creating the liturgy (i.e., priests or rabbis) and the par-ticipants. These interactions may have been formally planned discussions or informally arising from the reaction of participants and congregants. Studies into the practice of ritual by liturgists also helped them determine the important ele-ments. Then, based on these reflections and studies, new liturgical sequences were developed and tried. It seems likely that there was a gradual selection process that helped human ritual progress to its current state. This selection may even be culturally analogous to physical evolution. As more effective (i.e., more adaptive) parts of ritual were discovered, they were included in the ritual, and less effective parts were excluded. With regard to permanence and imperma-nence, however, such changes always had to preserve the religion's basic tenets within the ritual so that the religion could maintain its identity and vitality.

In the future, it might be argued that there may be a more "scientific" approach to developing ritual. As we have said, the early liturgists had no back-ground in neurophysiology to be aware of why the rituals they were creating had the emotional impact that they did. Liturgists quickly developed a sense of the rhythm needed for their rituals, however. Now that we have a theoretical framework for how ritual works, perhaps we could develop ritual specifically designed to affect either the quiescent or the arousal system, depending on the purpose of the ritual. If we are trying to give the participants a sense of awe, then we need to activate the arousal system with music and words. Then, by directing the excitation of the arousal system toward God, we might elicit a sense of awe in the presence of God. Conversely, if we are telling of the immense love that God has for us and of God's infinite goodness, then a ritual that directs our quiescent system toward God may help give people this sense. Further, if we are trying to achieve a sense of unity with God or the universe, then we must construct a liturgy that incorporates both arousal and quiescent components.

CONCLUSION

In this chapter we have attempted to explain how ritual and liturgy work to produce various religious experiences from a neurophysiological perspective. It seems that the rhythmic qualities of ritual are very important in generating the various experiences we derive from them. We may experience the peace, tran-quillity, and unity of a hyperquiescent state or we might find ourselves welling up with feelings of awe during a hyperarousal state. Regardless of what rhythms are used and how they are used, a systematic study of rhythmicity and the flow of ritualistic actions is important in understanding how ceremonial ritual can affect all of us. Further, since many of the same circuits in the brain are likely responsible for experiences during ritual as well as for experiences during advanced states of meditation and altered phases of consciousness, we are now situated to move on to a consideration of these topics.

Chapter Six

The Mind, Meditation, and Mysticism

We are now poised to delve more deeply into a neurophysiological analysis of the mystical mind. We will apply a more specific description of the neurophysiological model, which we have been developing to help in the understanding of intense religious and spiritual experiences. There is clearly a wide variety of deeply religious, or mystical, experiences ranging from the sense of the "wholly other" of the divine being to absolute unitary being (AUB), various forms of which are present in Western mystical traditions, but which in one way or another are central to Eastern religions such as Buddhism and Hinduism. Some authors maintain that not only do mystical experiences differ in terms of the language of the culture in which they are embedded, but their very content is altered by the cultural experience the mystic brings to them. All of this presents a rather confused picture about what, if anything, mystical experiences may have in common across cultures and from person to person.

We propose that a neuropsychological analysis of mysticism, altered states of consciousness, and the experience of the divine can bring some order out of the "culturo-logical" confusion. We will therefore present in this chapter a theoretical model that will contain the general neuropsychological principles that we have already been considering, thus permitting an analysis of any kind of mystical experience. Several other investigators have recently proposed models to explain spiritual states and have attributed such states to activity in the limbic system and other cortical structures.[1] These proposals parallel the development of our model. We feel, however, that our model is more comprehensive even though it contains certain aspects that are similar to the other models.

To simplify the description of our model, we will focus on the meditative approach to AUB. As noted above, AUB is a state in which the subject loses all awareness of discrete limited being and of the passage of time, and even experiences an obliteration of the self–other dichotomy. In previous works, we have presented evidence that if AUB is experienced, accompanied by blissful positive affect, it is usually interpreted as the *unio mystica,* or the experience of God.[2] If it is associated with neutral or tranquil affect, it is more frequently interpreted impersonally as the void or Nirvana of Buddhism, or as the Absolute of various philosophical disciplines.

The approach to both of these states can be described as either passive or active meditation. The passive approach involves simply trying to clear one's mind of all thoughts. Nothing in particular becomes the focus of attention. In other words, attention is focused nowhere. Thus, people simply allow themselves to be completely open to whatever happens and, in this sense, passively waits for absolute unitary being. The second approach is one in which people actively focus their attention on some object. This object could be an image, a figure, a person, a sound, or a word. As they focus attention in this way, they begin to experience a loss of a sense of self and can ultimately enter AUB. This chapter outlines the possible neurophysiological mechanisms by which these two basic types of meditation lead to extremely profound mystical experiences.

PASSIVE MEDITATION: THE *VIA NEGATIVA*

We are now ready to consider passive meditation and the state of absolute unitary being that may arise from the patient and persistent pursuit of what was known in the Middle Ages as the *via negativa.* Figure 6.1 is a schematic representation of the neural events that, we propose, occurs with this kind of meditation. One starts in the right attention association area with the will or intent to clear the mind of thoughts and words. As we have noted, this may result in a partial deafferentation of the right orientation association area, which is mediated by the right thalamus. This partial deafferentation of the orientation association area consists of the blocking of input from the verbal-conceptual association area as well as from specific sensory modalities.[3] Thus, there is the attempt not to pay attention to direct sensory input. Further disattention probably generates further deafferentation of the right orientation association area from the sensory areas and from the verbal-conceptual association area. It is only a partial deafferenation at this point because the inhibitory effects slowly build during the meditation. Thus, there is greater and greater inhibition of input, or deafferentiation, as the meditation deepens.

This partial deafferentation of the right orientation association area likely results in stimulation of the right hippocampus by means of the very rich interconnections between the orientation association area and the hippocampus.[4] If, in addition, there is simultaneous direct stimulation of the right hippocampus

FIGURE 6.1
Schematic Mechanism of the *Via Negativa*

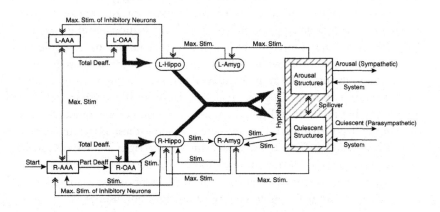

AAA = Attention Association Area
OAA = Orientation Association Area
VAA = Visual Association Area

———▷ initial neural paths forming a recurrent loop of progressively increasing intensity prior to spillover
———⇉ neural paths of maximal stimulation between spillover and the experience of AUB
━━━▶ neural paths following AUB

from the right attention association area, then the right hippocampus ultimately stimulates the quiescent centers of the right amygdala.[5] After the stimulation of the right amygdala reaches a certain threshold it will stimulate the quiescent part of the hypothalamus with a resultant stimulation of the peripheral quiescent system. This stimulation results in the subjective sensation first of relaxation, and eventually, of a more and more profound quiescence.

Not only is it likely that the right attention association area directly stimulates the right hippocampus, but, at every step along the way, stimulation may be reinforced by "leapfrogging" around various structures via numerous neural projections that bypass certain structures going directly to others.[6] Thus, the right hippocampus stimulates the amygdala, which in turn powerfully stimulates the quiescent parts of the hypothalamus; but the right hippocampus also projects fibers directly to the quiescent parts of the hypothalamus, resulting in a marked recruitment of stimulation. So, we should keep this double and even triple leapfrogging stimulation effect in mind as we run through our model's schematic pathway.

In any case, a reverberating circuit is formed, most simply defined by impulses originating in the right attention association area, going to the right orientation association area, to the right hippocampus, to the right amygdala, to the quiescent parts of the hypothalamus, and then back to the right amygdala, to the right hippocampus, and back to the right attention association area directly. Impulses go around and around this circuit, recruiting greater neural activity. The system is accelerated by ever more impulses originating in the right attention association area by continued "willed" meditation, resulting in a progressive increase in the intensity of neural discharge until a maximum level is reached in the quiescent system, which results in spillover and instantaneous maximal stimulation of the arousal system as has been shown to occur in third-stage autonomic tuning. This maximal stimulation of both systems results in ecstatic and blissful feelings through intense stimulation of the quiescent structures in the hypothalamus. Likewise, there is an almost instantaneous maximal feedback stimulation from the hypothalamus to the right and left amygdalas, then to the right and left hippocampi and on to the right and left attention association areas. Maximal stimulation of both attention association areas is powerfully and mutually reinforced by stimulating impulses passing directly between the right and left attention association areas, in both directions, via fibers passing through the interhemispheric connector tracts. The maximal stimulation of both attention association areas should almost instantly result in total deafferentation of both the left and right orientation association areas.[7]

As noted earlier, the right orientation association area is concerned with generating a sense of space and spatial coordinates in which to orient incoming stimuli. The total deafferentation of the orientation association area cannot result in unusual or unmodulated visions, sounds, or tactile sensations because it has no memory banks with previously stored sensations. Rather, its total deafferentation can only result in an absolute subjective sensation of pure space. But space has no conventional meaning except as a matrix in which to relate objects. We propose, therefore, that pure space arising from total deafferentation of the right orientation association area is subjectively experienced as absolute unity or wholeness.

At the same instant that the right orientation association area is totally deafferented, the left orientation association area is likewise totally deafferented. We have previously presented evidence that the left orientation association area may be intimately involved with the maintenance of the self-other or the self-world dichotomy. We propose that the total deafferentation of the left orientation association area results in the obliteration of the self-other dichotomy at precisely the same moment that the deafferentation of the right orientation association area is associated with a sense of absolute transcendent wholeness. All the events from the moment of spillover in the hypothalamus with resultant maximal firing of both the arousal and the quiescent system to the total deafferentation of both the right and the left orientation association area may occur so rapidly as to be experienced by the subject as instantaneous. We believe that this results in the subject's attainment of a state of rapturous transcendence and absolute wholeness that conveys such overwhelming power and strength that the subject has the sense of experiencing absolute reality. This is the state of absolute unitary being. Indeed, so ineffable is this state that for those who experience it, even the memory of it carries a sense of greater reality than the reality of our everyday world (as reported by a number of experiencers interviewed by us as well as reported in the world's mystical liturature). The first part of the schematic drawing (Figure 6.1), beginning with the will or intent to obliterate thoughts from the mind up to the moment of spillover in the hypothalamus (which involves the reverberating circuit described above), may take days, weeks, months, or even years of regular disciplined meditation to develop (the time necessary depends on the aptitude of the subject). The events represented by the rest of this schematic drawing subsequent to the moment of spillover are automatic and occur almost instantaneously.

There is still one further step before achieving the final stage of meditation. As shown in Figure 6.1, the arrows go from both the right and left orientation association area back to the hypothalamus. This is possible because, in this model, although both the right and left orientation association areas have had all input blocked, they still can send output to other parts of the brain. In other words, although no impulses can get into these structures, impulses can get out. The impulses arising from the totally deafferented right and left orientation association areas pass through fiber tracts primarily to the hippocampi but also to other limbic structures. We believe that these impulses determine the steady state of the limbic system during the period of AUB. They either reinforce the initial ecstasy by ultimately reinforcing the arousal hypothalamic discharge, or they switch balance from ecstasy to a deep and profound quiescence by allowing the quiescent hypothalamic structures to regain dominance. If the first case occurs, not only is AUB experienced initially as ecstasy but the ecstasy is maintained throughout the remaining period of meditation. If the second case occurs, then, after the initial moments of ecstasy, AUB is experienced as a deep quiescent void or Nirvana. We suggest that the first case tends to be interpreted (after the fact) personally, as the immediate experience of, or union with, God. In the second case, the experience of AUB tends to be interpreted impersonally, as the peace and emptiness of the absolute ground of being. What is not clear is which variables result in one or the other affective state becoming stabilized during the AUB experience. It seems to be the case that most mature meditators who practice the *via negativa* tend to end up in the quiescent experience of AUB which in our model represents the quiescent state. Likewise, it is true that those who practice the *via positiva* (to be described below) by intensely concentrating on an object or idea tend to end up with the ecstatic experience of AUB, which we would suggest is an arousal state. So it may be that one ends up more or less according to the general mode in which one starts out. But this is by no means always true, and there seem to be many exceptions. Perhaps the socioculturally determined belief system of the meditator has something to do with the outcome as well. In any case, much research needs to be done into why certain mystics experience AUB as active and personal while others experience it as passive and impersonal.

ACTIVE MEDITATION: THE *VIA POSITIVA*

Figure 6.2 represents the hypothesized mechanism of active or absorptive meditation also known as the *via positiva*. It is only the events up to the point of hypothalamic spillover that are significantly different from those depicted in Figure 6.1. After the point of hypothalamic spillover the events of both passive and active meditation are almost identical, with one significant exception to be considered later. The *via positiva* begins by the subject's willing or intending not to clear his mind but to focus either on a mental image or on an external physical object. Sometimes the image is a religious symbol, the meaning of which carries powerful emotional overtones that help stimulate the limbic system. But the object of meditation need not necessarily be a religious symbol. It could be something as mundane as a stone or a chair.

The simplest case is when one chooses to focus upon a visual object of meditation in the external world with eyes open. In our model, impulses pass from the right attention association area of the willing or intending subject to the right orientation association area. Note that in this case the impulses are facilitatory and stimulating and not inhibitory or deafferenting, as they were in the *via negativa*. It is the right orientation association area that fixes an image presented by the visual association area. If the meditator's eyes are open and the image originates in the retina, it is passed back through the visual system to the primary visual area in the occipital lobe and then to the secondary visual association areas where it acquires essential associations; from there it passes to the visual association area, where it receives its most complex associations. The image is then fixed and attended to by the right orientation association area.

If the subject intends to call forth an image from memory, whether it be an image of a physical object, a religious symbol, a past memory, or whatever, this would be effected by stimulatory impulses running from the right attention association area directly to the right visual association area.[8] This is the first step if the image is not originating within the field of vision. Subsequently, the right attention association area stimulates the right orientation association area to fix the image and attend to it in a steady, highly focused manner. In any case, we postulate that continuous fixation on the image presented by the right visual

FIGURE 6.2
Schematic Mechanism of the *Via Positiva*

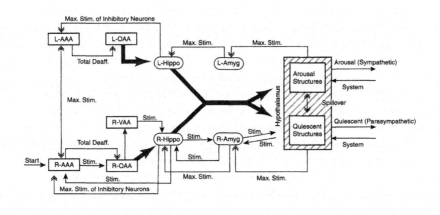

AAA = Attention Association Area
OAA = Orientation Association Area
VAA = Visual Association Area

———▶ initial neural paths forming a recurrent loop of progressively increasing intensity prior to spillover
———▶ neural paths of maximal stimulation between spillover and the experience of AUB
━━━▶ neural paths following AUB

association area begins to stimulate the right hippocampus, which in turn stimulates the right amygdala, which in turn stimulates the arousal parts of the hypothalamus, generating a mildly pleasant sensation (although initial rhythmic repitition may elicit a quiescent response). Impulses then pass back to the right amygdala and hippocampus, gathering intensity as they go along. This then feeds back to the right attention association area, reinforcing the whole system with progressively intense concentration upon the object. Thus, a reverberating loop is established, similar to that in the *via negativa*.

In our model, the circuit continues to reverberate and to augment in intensity until the stimulation of the arousal parts of the hypothalamus becomes maximal, creating a "spillover" such that maximal stimulation of the quiescent parts of the hypothalamus occurs simultaneously with the ongoing maximal stimulation of the arousal system. At this point, there would be maximal stimulation feedback through the limbic structures to the left and right attention association areas. As in figure 6.1, this results in instantaneous maximal stimulation of the left attention association area with immediate total deafferentation of the left orientation association area. The situation on the right, however, is somewhat different in the case of active meditation. Although from the moment of spillover there is also maximal limbic stimulation of the right attention association area inhibitory system, one notes that there is already an ongoing and powerful stimulation system (*not* deafferenting) from the right attention association area to the right orientation association area, which has been reinforced by a constant feedback loop until the moment of spillover.

Therefore, the inhibition generated by the attention association area must fight against a preexistent, and very strong, facilitatory or stimulating system that is generated by fixating and focusing upon an object. Since the meditating subject is still intending to focus in an ever more concentrated way on the object of meditation, this system continues to be reinforced even in the presence of ecstatic feelings generated within the limbic system and a progressively stronger assertion of the inhibitory deafferenting system. Throughout the period of time when there is conflict on the right between facilitatory and inhibitory mechanisms, there has been total instantaneous deafferentation of the left orientation association area. Thus, the self–other dichotomy has been obliterated during a period of time, perhaps fairly long, when the image still remains a focus of meditation. We would suggest that this is the period of time when subjecst feel absorbed into the object or describe themselves as becoming one with the object. This period of meditation upon the object, during which the subject becomes one with the image, the symbol, or the event, may be relatively long.

The length of time depends upon the determination of the meditator to continue fixating upon the object and thus to reinforce the facilitatory stimulating system in opposition to the maximal stimulation from the limbic system of the inhibitory nuclei of the right attention association area. Sooner or later, in the face of maximal arousal and quiescent discharge, either the meditators surrenders or possibly even against their will, the inhibitory influences take over and total deafferentation of the right orientation association area occurs. Since the left orientation association area has already been totally deafferented, the self–other dichotomy has been obliterated for some time. Thus, the end point of the *via positiva* then becomes the end point of the *via negativa*, namely, maximal stimulation of the arousal and quiescent systems with total deafferentation of the right and left orientation association areas, creating the experience of absolute unitary being. The period of time from spillover to the final assertion of dominance of the inhibitory neurons in the right attention association area is the period of absorption of the meditators into the object of meditation.

LESSER MYSTICAL STATES REVISITED

Now that we have considered in greater detail the neurophysiological model of the mystical experiences of absorption and AUB, we can return to our analysis of lesser mystical experiences to determine if there is any relationship that can be found between mystical states and everyday religion. An interesting question is, How are lesser mystical experiences interpreted by the experiencer, especially in relation to religion? Clearly, in AUB there can be no distinction between what is experienced by different individuals, even from totally different cultures. There may be significant differences in how these experiences are described and interpreted, particularly since they are usually related in terms of the specific cultural and societal milieu from which the experiencer comes. We maintain, however, that the actual experience of AUB in itself is necessarily the same for any individual who experiences it. This is necessary from a neurophysiological as well as a philosophical perspective. It is necessarily experienced as an infinite, unified, and totally undifferentiated state.

Lesser mystical states such as hyperlucid visions, trances, and senses of religious awe present a different problem. In these states, the full neurophysiological substrate described for AUB does not occur. For example, there may not be a total deafferentation of both orientation association areas or there may be slight changes in the activity of the limbic system. Other aspects of the AUB model may also be slightly different in lesser mystical states. Furthermore, various lesser mystical states may not only be described in different terms, but are likely based on somewhat different neurophysiological substrates. Therefore, different lesser mystical states are, in fact, experienced differently.

This may also have significant implications in terms of how lesser mystical states are incorporated into religious myth and, eventually, theology. Part of the problem is that it is difficult for an outside observer to distinguish a state of AUB from a lesser mystical state because both will be subject to inadequate linguistic description that will make them appear fragmented and less unitary or holistic. This is precisely why mystical states are termed "ineffable." The universal experience from many cultures is that language is incapable of adequately capturing these states. This is because, unlike most human "higher cortical" experiences, language elements are not integral to mystical states. Neurophysiologically, it seems that the language centers are generally bypassed in the generation of mystical experiences. Thus, language elements are at best peripheral to the core experiences. If linguistic precision cannot be relied upon to differentiate between certain mystical states, how can they be distinguished? Our answer is that the only totally reliable method of differentiation is by their underlying neurophysiology.

It seems that any lesser mystical state will necessarily prevent the entirety of the AUB neurophysiological model from occurring. Since the model requires a complex circuitry of interconnecting neural fibers, perhaps the most important distinction between lesser mystical states and AUB is that the final part, consisting of total deafferentation of the right and left orientation areas, should not occur. One or the other might be totally deafferented, but neither will be totally deafferented at the same time. If this is true, then the primary distinguishing characteristic of lesser mystical states compared to AUB should be a lack of total undifferentiation. In other words, lesser mystical states should be associated with some degree of multiplicity of elements within a unitary matrix. This also will have implications later in terms of how these states are incorporated into the body of a religion. Suffice it to say at this time that lesser mystical states are associated with different neurophysiological states with the particular distinction that they contain at least some degree of fragmentation.

PROOF OF THIS MODEL

In presenting this theoretical model of the neurophysiological mechanisms underlying various mystical or religious states, we have attempted to integrate current data regarding our understanding of brain functioning. This model expands upon these data, however, in order to explain the phenomenology of such experiences. It is certainly possible that in the future we will be able to add to this model. For example, there may be other areas of the brain involved in the meditation process, including a structure called the cingulate gyrus, which is involved in attention tasks and other higher-order thought processes, and the reticular activating system, which is involved in stimulating various parts of the brain during thought. There is not enough research to be able to better define their role now. There may also be parts of this model which will be proven to be incorrect, but we hope that most of the basic aspects of this model will be confirmed. Some of this confirmation exists already in the work of others who have implicated the frontal lobes, the limbic system, and the thalamus as having an important role in mystical and religious experiences.[9] It is important to understand, however, that simply the ability to describe mystical states from a neurophysiological perspective, whether this model proves accurate in all respects or not, is an important step in understanding how the human brain relates to religious experience.

To prove this model in its entirety will be difficult since it is rare that actual mystical or religious experiences occur at a predictable enough time and place to study them. The only possible way would be to study people who are well practiced in meditation and to study them while they actually meditate. We have previously mentioned that there are some remarkable technologies that might allow us to study the brain during meditation. We have performed preliminary studies using a technique called single photon emission computed tomography (SPECT) to image brain activity during meditation.[10] Our initial results give strong support to the model we present here. In this study we measured blood flow to the brain that is increased in areas that have increased activation and decreased in areas that have diminished activity. We used highly practiced meditators in the art of Tibetan Buddhist meditation. Their technique resembles the approach of the *via positiva* in that the meditator focuses on a particular object or image. The meditators were imaged during a resting state, considered to be baseline wakefulness, and were imaged again at their peak of meditation. The two images were compared to determine what areas had increased or decreased activity.

We found that there was increased blood flow to the attention association areas. This coincides with the notion of increasing concentration that arises during meditation. There was decreased blood flow in the area near the orientation association area on both sides, specifically on the left. This would seem to reflect deafferenation of these areas, which we believe causes a breakdown of the self-other dichotomy and results in a sense of wholeness and unity. There were other areas that were also altered during the meditation. In particular, the thalamus on both sides had increased blood flow during meditation. Recall that the thalamus is the first relay station between the attention association area and the rest of the brain, including the limbic system. It would make sense that the major relay system would be activated during meditation, since it is likely involved in generating the reverberating circuit with increasing neural activity throughout the circuit.

The results of our preliminary studies, in addition to the results of related studies that have shown increased activity in the frontal lobes during meditation,[11] clearly support our model, but many more studies need to be done to elucidate the neurophysiological mechanisms that underlie mystical experiences. New studies of different types of meditation and looking at more specific areas would be helpful. In addition, other physiological variables such as the effects of the activation of the arousal and quiescent systems would enhance the overall model. Other types of imaging techniques that have better resolution than SPECT, such as positron emission tomography (PET) and magnetic resonance imaging (MRI), might be very useful in following brain function or cerebral blood flow during various phases of meditation.[12] This might allow us to observe the selective stimulation of areas such as the attention association area, the hippocampus, the amygdala, and the hypothalamus as the person proceeds toward maximal stimulation of these structures and actual higher-level mystical experience. The use of PET and MRI, with more traditional measures of electroencephalography and measures of arousal and quiescent tone, might help complete our understanding of the neurological functioning that occurs during mystical or religious experiences.

FINAL CONSIDERATIONS

The reader should be cautioned against using this model in too reductionistic a way. Even if subsequent testing with PET scanning and similar procedures should support the model to the point that it is generally considered to have

been proved correct, either wholly or in important part, it still raises significant neuroepistemological problems. To maintain that the reality of people's
"objective" experience of God is reducible to neurochemical flux, and nothing more, may be equivalent to maintaining that their experience of the
"objective" reality of the sun, the earth, and the air they breathe is reducible
to neurochemical flux. There is a Zen koan[13] in which two monks argue about
the temple flag waving in the wind. One says, "The flag moves." The other says,
"The wind moves." Finally, the Zen master says, "It is not the flag that moves.
It is not the wind that moves. It is your mind that moves." So perhaps we might
argue that it is always the mind that moves, regardless of whether it is experiencing our usual baseline reality or whether it is experiencing God.

The model presented in this book of certain "absolute" esoteric states compared with "baseline" reality brings up questions about the fundamental nature of
subjectivity, objectivity, and consciousness itself. Any attempt to trivialize their
ontological status by naive reductionism might be a serious misinterpretation of
the true nature of these mystical experiences. We are only now embarking upon
a scientific investigation of some of the most powerful experiences humans can
attain. Thus, we should maintain an attitude of humility, rather than presume that
our understanding of neurophysiology can give us an intrinsic knowledge of the
relationship between "reality" and consciousness, whether that consciousness is in
its baseline or in its more esoteric forms.

Chapter Seven

The Near-Death Experience as a Mystical Phenomenon

We have considered mystical experiences derived from ritual and meditation in terms of religion and theology. When considering the function of the mystical mind in terms of theological implications, however, one must also consider other forms of mystical experiences. In particular, one must explore mystical experiences that can be attained spontaneously by anyone, not just by those whose focused goal is to reach some higher state. These more "available" experiences, if they are truly mystical, can have a tremendous impact on our understanding of both religion and theology. The near-death experience (NDE) is one of the most compelling such experiences that human beings can encounter. There are no specific requirements in terms of the person's life; the only thing he or she must do is come close to death. In the Tibetan and Egyptian Books of the Dead, during the European Middle Ages, and to the present day, NDEs have been experienced, written about, and argued about. There is little doubt that many people perceive themselves to have had NDEs. Precisely how and why an NDE occurs has yet to be determined, however.

One group of investigators, after reviewing many explanations of what causes NDEs, has indicated that no explanation is more plausible than another. They also state that "a multidimensional model, which acknowledges psychodynamic and stress processes with attendant neurochemical changes and attributed meanings, may be appropriate."[1] Furthermore, any explanation must include all aspects of the NDE, including the fact that not everyone who is physically near death appears to have an NDE.

In this chapter, we will expand upon our model of the mystical mind to include a possible mechanism for the generation of the NDE. The model reconsiders some aspects of the Jungian archetypal hypothesis and explores how the neural activation of certain archetypes may be involved in the NDE. We will also propose specific neural pathways that might be responsible for the archetypal activation generating the NDE. We hope that our model will explain most, if not all, of the features of the NDE and allow for a better understanding of the NDE as part of the experiential repertoire of human beings.

WHAT IS A NEAR-DEATH EXPERIENCE LIKE?

Prior to considering our neurophysiological model, we must first consider the phenomenology of the NDE. Kenneth Ring and Raymond Moody have both done extensive research on NDEs. They and others have determined the basic characteristics of a "core experience" to be the essential description of the NDE. Ring describes the NDE as "unfolding according to a single pattern almost as though the prospect of death serves to release a stored, common 'program' of feelings, perceptions, and experiences."[2] Other investigators have also observed the universality of the NDE, but indicate that the ability to describe an NDE may be affected by culture or other personal background characteristics. The basic aspects of the core experience as it is generally described are as follows:

1. Ineffability
2. Hearing the news of one's own death
3. Feelings of peace and quiet
4. The noise
5. The dark tunnel
6. Out-of-body experience
7. Meeting others
8. The realm of light
9. The review of life events
10. The border
11. Coming back

These characteristics have been described in detail by numerous investigators, but, not all of these aspects of the core experience occur during each NDE. These aspects are also described slightly differently by different people. Further, the specific characteristics seem to vary, depending on the circumstances of the actual near-death event. There does seem to be a progression that most NDEs follow. The first part of the NDE is usually a sense of peace and tranquillity. According to Ring, virtually all of those who experience an NDE describe feelings of peace and calmness.

The next phase, which occurs in approximately one-third of people who have NDEs, is a sense of being detached from the body. This is usually called an out-of-body experience (OBE). Subjects often describe themselves as being an objective observer, without emotion, during the OBE. They are usually at some vantage point, such as the corner of the ceiling, looking down on the events taking place. They report seeing their own body and hearing and seeing the people surrounding their body trying to administer aid.

Following the OBE, the next stage of an NDE consists of entering a dark "tunnel" or vastness. These "tunnel" experiences are simple and consistent regardless of the experiencer. This tunnel has been described as empty, space, or nothingness, and has been likened to describing the end of the universe. The darkness has usually been described in positive terms, however.

After the "tunnel" experience, subjects may perceive a light toward which they are traveling. This light has been described as golden, brilliant, and of ineffable beauty. The light often takes on a symbolic meaning that, according to Ring, is usually culturally dependent. For example, it is frequently identified as God, heaven, or other spiritual entities, depending on the religious beliefs or culture of the person.

Actually entering into the light is experienced by only a few people who have an NDE. Entering the light appears to be the final stage of the NDE. Nobody who has had an NDE has reported experiencing anything beyond the realm of light. In other words, entering the light is apparently the most transcendent realm attainable during the NDE. The realm of light is associated with descriptions of beautiful music and natural objects as well as the place where "others" are met. Who and what type of beings are encountered is highly dependent on the culture of the person having the NDE. A study of ND experiencers in India showed that they tended to see more religious and sacred figures, while those in the United States tended to see more deceased relatives and friends. It should also be mentioned that there is often a presence associated with the light. This presence is not usually directly perceived, but it is sensed and understood by the experiencer.

The return to life from the NDE was characterized by Kenneth Ring as having three potential components: a life review, an encounter with a presence, or an encounter with deceased loved ones. Many times, the life review is panoramic in that there seems to be a replay, often sequential, of one's entire life in a matter of seconds. The actual decision to return is sometimes that of the experiencer, or else the decision to return is made for the person.

General descriptions of NDEs reveal several consistent characteristics. Most, but not all, persons who have NDEs have the perception of their own imminent death. Somehow, they come to know that they are either dead or on the verge of death. How this happens is not clear. Justine Owen, Emily Cook, and Ian Stevenson have suggested that the awareness of being close to death may be an important factor in the genesis of the NDE.[3] Moody also

indicates that the ND experiencer will often hear a doctor or onlooker pro-
nounce him or her dead.

Interestingly, most ND experiencers feel that their cognitive functions are
clear and sharp. They describe feeling calm, in control, and rational. Further, they
sense a state of "hyperalertness" in which they have heightened visual and auditory sensations in addition to mental clarity. Time and space, however, are usually not perceived in the normal way. There seems to be a slowing or absence
of time, and space is generally perceived as being either infinite or nonexistent.

Perhaps the most difficult aspect of NDEs to explain, at least in terms of currently available scientific methods, are the reports of anomalous or "paranormal"
events. Anomalous events include meeting someone during the NDE who,
unbeknownst to the subject, had recently died. Subjects have reported being
able to relate events that occurred in different rooms of the hospital that they
supposedly visited during their out-of-body phase. Some of these anomalous
events are more difficult to deal with scientifically than others, and certainly all
of these events should be considered with a skeptical eye since anomalous
events during NDEs are rare and are usually presented in anecdotal form. For
example, although some ND experiencers have been able to describe the events
that occurred in other rooms, it is not known how many of these accounts have
eventually proved to be inaccurate. There have also been some reports of prescient abilities in ND experiencers. It is not known, however, exactly what
constituted a validated prescience and how many prescient experiences turned
out to be incorrect. Obviously, our attitude toward the paranormal is skeptical,
both because of the relatively few NDEs that have been reported with paranormal elements and because of the sloppy way in which they have usually been
reported. This fact brings up the question of how paranormal events would
affect our model of mystical experiences if such events were conclusively proved
to be real. The answer is, probably very little. Paradigmatic shifts in science, dramatic as they are, do not affect directly observed or sensed phenomena. They
affect secondary or tertiary inferences from those observations. Thus, the great
paradigmatic shift that occurred with the Copernican revolution in no way
altered the precise observation of planetary movements. What was thrown into
question was something not directly observed, at least in the sixteenth and seventeenth centuries, namely, celestial mechanics. Since neuropsychology, and
indeed most biology, is based on direct observation with very few inferential
leaps, the model presented in this book would be very little changed. Physics
suffers from paradigmatic changes much more than biology. Obviously, an element would have to be added to the model to account for the paranormal elements. For example, if one had a vision of a future event, what would have to
be accounted for would not be the sensory elements. The brain would generate vision just as it always has. The known mechanisms for generating images

in the sensorium would not be violated. What would have to be accounted for would be its futurity. It would be the association of sensory elements *with discontinuous* spatial or temporal elements that would require explanation. An important addendum would have to be made to the current model of neurotheology. But, of course, that would be true of all science. Clearly we are speaking here of the effects on science if paranormal events should be proved to exist. We are very far from such a proof. Many events that people might consider paranormal are not that at all, such as the projection of the "astral" body to the ceiling or the mental rotation of objects in space so that their opposite side can be seen. These phenomena have been briefly discussed in chapter 2. They may seem odd, but they are definitely not paranormal.

Another aspect of NDEs is that, until recently, almost all contemporary accounts of NDEs were reported as being positive experiences. There have always been sporadic reports of terrifying NDEs, however. More recently, a number of investigators have reported hellish or horrifying NDEs with increasing frequency. Foremost among these researchers is Maurice Rawlings, who maintains that not only are hellish NDEs not rare, they are actually quite frequent.[4] Although Rawlings's observations and those of his coworkers are in themselves fairly impressive, his credibility has been questioned because he openly writes as a committed fundamentalist Christian. There is no reason to question his competence as a medical doctor or the honesty of his basic findings, but his insistence on interpreting the meaning of his findings in terms of biblical authority is both unfortunate and alienating to objective scholars.

In addition to the extensive findings of Rawlings, we may add the findings of other investigators who presumably do not have the same religious bias that Rawlings does. Some reports suggest that there may be as much as a fifty-fifty ratio for negative versus positive NDEs. Members of the International Association for Near-Death Studies (IANDS) group at Yale University Medical Center have systematically collected approximately fifty cases of negative NDEs.[5] They have tentatively classified the negative NDEs into three groups. In the first group, the experiencer feels as if he or she is "losing control" of the NDE. For example, some individuals suddenly saw the light in the tunnel "as a reflection of the fires of the gates of hell instead of seeing it as a radiant light." The second group experienced being trapped in a terrifying emptiness, a "great cosmic nothingness." This experience often resulted in profound despair. The third group saw a vision of a hellish place where people were horribly "tortured or tormented."

In addition to these recently reported negative NDEs, there is also evidence from other times and other cultures. Carol Goldsmith Zaleski's comprehensive study of medieval "otherworld journeys" supports the view that the NDE, at least in the Middle Ages, was an integrated experience of both a positive and a negative kind.[6] Typically, the experiencer first encountered a series of hellish visions involving fiendish tortures, dismemberments, the tearing and burning of flesh, and other horrors before they had a glimpse of heavenly glory. Insofar as the "heavenly glory" aspect of the medieval otherworld journey is described, it is structurally remarkably similar to the modern positive NDE. Although the positive termination of the otherworld journey is often present, medieval reporters, or at least transcribers, preferred to dwell at length on the horrible aspects, presumably as a strong motivator for virtuous living. Likewise, the description of the *Chönyid* state in the Tibetan Book of the Dead, if anything, exceeds its European counterparts in the grisly aspects of the negative NDE (the Tibetan Book of the Dead also presents the positive aspects of the NDE). Indeed, many repeated versions of the positive aspects of the NDE are interpreted in terms of Buddhist metaphysics during the days comprising the Bardo states.

Both the medieval and the Asian descriptions involve an integration of the positive and the negative aspects of the NDE. It is not clear why so few of the reported contemporary experiences are integrated, or why the majority of reported contemporary NDEs are of the positive variety. Rawlings seems to feel that at least part of the explanation is a bias in reporting. He maintains that many of the major researchers in this field are members of the "New Age" movement, which, in his view, is well on its way to becoming a religion in itself with profoundly optimistic prejudices. Hellish reports are very unsettling to this optimistic metaphysics. But even Rawlings, with his own opposite religious prejudices, does not feel that this is the only explanation. He notes in passing that, in his experience, the only time that hellish NDEs were present was when there was actual physiological distress and true proximity to death as opposed to the sudden, terrifying perception of probable death without any physiological impairment. Whatever conclusion Rawlings draws from this observation in terms of his own religious prejudice, it is nevertheless an important empirical observation as we shall consider below. Here we must mention one further aspect of the negative NDE. Unlike the positive NDE, which is highly structured, sequential, and even stereotypical in some ways, the negative NDE does not appear to be structured or to have a predictable sequence. Its only predictable quality is that it is horrible and usually terrifying.

Before proceeding to the proposed explanations of the NDE, it is important to note that no investigation has been able to determine the person's actual physical or neurophysiological state while having an NDE. It is difficult to document the physical closeness to death of a patient when he or she is having the NDE. This problem raises many questions about when and how NDEs actually occur. For example, it is uncertain how many people who come physically close to death actually have an NDE. An estimated 25 percent to 50 percent of people who are physically near death have some component of an NDE.

Albert Heim did some of the original research on NDEs and examined the experiences of people who were trapped in avalanches. Interestingly, in a report first published in 1892, Heim found that many people had NDEs without actually being physiologically near death. They only perceived that they were in a life-threatening situation. These people often had no anxiety, despair, or pain, but they usually described a "calm seriousness, profound acceptance, and a dominant mental quickness and sense of surety. The relationships of events and their probable outcomes were overviewed with objective clarity."[7] Others have also reported similar findings in subjects who were in life-threatening situations, but were not actually near death.

As difficult as it is to determine how close to death someone is during an NDE, it has been even more difficult to assess the person's brain state during the experience. Some people may suffer from decreased oxygen to their brain while others may be given various drugs during resuscitation attempts. Still others, as mentioned in Heim's work, were not actually close to death and other studies have indicated that as many as 50 percent of subjects were fully conscious during their NDE. Ring described the relationship between the NDE and the events that led to the near-death state. Specifically, he considered three separate categories: people who had terminal illness, people who had accidents, and people who had attempted suicide. Two patterns arose in this analysis. People who attempted suicide tended not to progress far in their NDE (i.e., they did not reach the light). Ring suggested that the use of drugs, which is the predominant mode of suicide, may have affected brain function and subsequently affected the NDE in people attempting suicide. The other pattern that Ring described was that those who experience an NDE as a result of an accident are more likely to relate a panoramic life review. These findings have also been described by other investigators.

A number of explanations have been postulated for the mechanism underlying the NDE. The problem with developing a satisfactory explanation is that NDEs have many different components and occur in a wide variety of circumstances. Thus, any explanation must be capable of explicating the many aspects of the NDE. Proposed mechanisms include a psychological defense mechanism against one's own death, hallucinations, the involvement of psychotropic substances (endogenous or exogenous), decreased oxygen and blood to the brain, a depersonalization syndrome, temporal lobe seizure-like activity, and hyperactivity of the limbic system. Of course, the final possibility is that there actually is an afterlife. The problem with all of these explanations is that they fail to explain every aspect of the NDE, including both positive and negative NDEs, the remarkable similarity of NDEs, diminished NDEs when psychotropic drugs are administered, NDEs in people in life-threatening situations but not actually near death, OBEs, and even some of the "paranormal" occurrences.

NDEs have also been related to mystical experiences in that the NDE might represent an awakening to a higher spiritual reality. The notion that NDEs represent some type of spontaneous mystical experience is based on the similarity of NDEs to high meditative states. The ability to describe, explain, and model such experiences is what we have done with respect to mystical phenomena in the previous chapters, and what we will consider later in our model of the NDE.

It should also be noted that transcendental experiences (of a higher consciousness) were described by John Lilly and Carl Jung for their own NDEs. Lilly reported that he was aware of guardian angels who were always with him but, he could only experience them when he was in the NDE.[8] Jung stated: "I can describe the experience only as the ecstasy of a nontemporal state in which present, past and future are one. Everything that happens in time had been brought together into a concrete whole. Nothing was distributed over time, nothing could be measured by temporal concepts. . . . One is interwoven into an indescribable whole yet observes it with complete objectivity."[9]

Jung later stated that "the psyche at times functions outside of the spatiotemporal law of causality. This indicates that our conceptions of space and time, and therefore causality also, are incomplete. A complete picture of this world would require the addition of still another dimension; only then could the totality of phenomena be given a unified explanation. . . . I have been convinced that at least a part of our psychic existence is characterized by a relativity of space and time. This relativity seems to increase, in proportion to the distance from [normal] consciousness, to an absolute condition of timelessness and spacelessness."[10] This description can apply both to the NDE and to experiences of practitioners of the meditative philosophies.

IS THE NEAR-DEATH EXPERIENCE A PREPROGRAMMED FUNCTION?

In this chapter, we are proposing a model for NDEs that is both reductionistic and, at the same time, capable of preserving the possibility of transcendent meaning. Such a model consists of a neuroevolutionary understanding of the Jungian archetypal hypothesis. To anticipate our conclusions, we propose that the total possible NDE represents the activation (or partial activation) of two archetypes—the archetype of dissolution and the archetype of transcendent integration (these are our terms, not Jung's). The archetype of dissolution (often including themes of torture and punishment) refers to the termination and disintegration of the self, specifically with regard to a person's individual death. The archetype of transcendent integration (often including elements of bliss and reward) refers to the transformation of the self into a holistic universal structure.

Jung considered archetypes in general to be the most primitive form of stable imaginal/conceptual cognition:

> Among these inherited psychic factors, there is a special class which is not confined either to family or to race. These are the universal dispositions of the mind, and they are to be understood as analogous to Plato's forms *(eidola)* in accordance with which the mind organizes its contents. One could also describe these forms as *categories,* analogous to the logical categories which are always and everywhere present as the basic postulates of reason. Only in the case of our "forms," we are not dealing with categories of reason but with categories of the *imagination.* As the products of imagination are always in essence visual, their forms must, from the outset, have the character of images and moreover of *typical* images, which is why, following St. Augustine, I call them "archetypes."[11]

In another place in his "Commentary on the Tibetan Book of the Dead," Jung notes: "So far as I know, there is no inheritance of individual pre-natal, or pre-uterine memories, but there are undoubtedly inherited archetypes, which are, however, devoid of content, because to begin with, they contain no personal experiences. They only emerge into consciousness when personal experiences have rendered them visible."[12]

In an allusion to what we would call the primitive neuroevolutionary character of the archetypes (probably arising from the paleocortex and early development of the neocortex), Jung goes on:

> The original structural components of the psyche are no less surprising in uniformity than are those of the visible body. The archetypes are, so to speak, organs of the prerational psyche. They are eternally inherited forms and ideas which have at first no specific content. Their specific content only appears in the course of the individual's life, when personal experience is taken up precisely in these forms. . . . For just as the organs of the body are not mere lumps of indifferent, passive matter, but are dynamic, functional complexes which assert themselves with imperious urgency, so also the archetypes, as organs of the psyche are dynamic, instinctual complexes which determine psychic life to an extraordinary degree. That is why I also call them *dominants* of the unconscious. The layer of unconscious psyche which is made up of these universal dynamic forms, I have termed the *collective unconscious.*[13]

Before considering the NDE as the full or partial activation of the archetypes of dissolution and of transcendent integration, let us first consider whether Jung's archetypal hypothesis can be understood from a neuroevolutionary perspective. Such a reworking seems essential if the archetypal hypothesis is to be taken seriously by a neuropsychologically sophisticated audience and not find its final resting place in the domain of literary and artistic criticism.

Jung maintained that instinctive behaviors were always associated with potential images and feelings of a general and stereotyped nature. The question that needs to be answered is, Is there any evidence aside from the Jungian clinical and cultural data to indicate primitive universal thinking patterns intermediate between the purely unconscious motor response and the complex spectrum of neocortically mediated learning? If so, it seems likely that the brain structures involved in these universal thinking patterns would reside in the evolutionarily older parts of the brain. Such evidence would powerfully support the hypotheses that primitive cognitive organization evolved out of the brain stem, midbrain, and limbic structures. These areas are primarily involved in the modulation of repetitive motor behavior and affect, and with the maintenance of physiological homeostasis. In short, such evidence would strongly support, at least in broad outline, Jung's archetypal hypotheses.

In 1968, an interesting study demonstrated that pigeons learned to peck a lighted key that was paired with the delivery of grain even when pecking the key did not cause the grain to be dispensed.[14] Although somewhat startling in terms of the classical laws of learning, this result failed to produce full appreciation of its significance. This had to await the publication in 1972 of a paper titled "Automaintenance in the Pigeon: Sustained Pecking despite Contingent Non-Reinforcement." This paper reported the results of four experiments conducted as a follow-up to those of Brown and Jenkins. The first experiment showed that pecking was sustained even when pecks turned off the key and thus prevented reinforcements. The second experiment controlled for the possible effects of stimulus change and generalization. The remaining two experiments explored procedures that manipulated the tendency to peck the negatively correlated key, and introduced other response keys that had no scheduled consequences.

It became clear that pecking behavior becomes established and maintained by stimulus-reinforcer relationships independent of any other factors between response and reinforcement. This is simply a technical way of saying that there is something about the stimulus (the lighted key), in and of itself, that reinforces the pecking behavior, whether or not food is dispensed. It may be simply that the lighted key looks like a kernel of corn. The conclusion is that there is a built-in mechanism that markedly facilitates learning to peck a lighted key (or something similar in size and shape).

What has emerged from this work is a recognition that certain behaviors are very easily learned by some species, often even after one trial, whereas other species require the usual or "normal" number of trials to learn the behavior. Furthermore, behaviors for which there is "preparedness" to learn seem to have marked survival value for particular species. Thus, it has been postulated that the similarity of the lighted key to a kernel of corn or grain of some other cereal may be sufficient to activate the prepared learning mechanism once it has been paired with a real kernel of corn on only one or two occasions. Thus, the pecking of the key is rapidly established and is maintained over a long period of time. This behavior continues even when no food is forthcoming. Considering the diet required by a pigeon to survive, the existence of neuroconnections in the brain that facilitate learning of this type is of obvious evolutionary significance for the species. Without this prepared learning, the pigeon might not eat appropriately. The question is whether or not there are any examples of prepared learning in human beings.

As described in chapter 3, one type of prepared human learning may be phobias. Phobias are fears of objects that seem to be out of proportion to the actual danger the objects may pose.

From our point of view, the notion of "preparedness" seems to imply the existence of a specific organization of neurons and neural connections in the brain that, once activated, determine the alignment of the organism to its environment. This occurs on both a cognitive (insofar as this may be present in less developed organisms) and certainly behavioral level. Interestingly, Seligman considers the possible significance of "symbolism" in terms of preparedness:

> So, for a biologically oriented learning theorist, to what can the notion of symbolism amount? A is symbolic of B, if and only if human beings are prepared in the sense defined, to learn that A is associated with B. If humans can acquire with A the properties of B, after only minimal input, then is it meaningful to say that A is symbolic of B.
>
> Even more speculatively, does preparedness range beyond simply symbolic associations? Are there ways of thinking in which humans are particularly prepared to engage, as [E. H.] Lenneberg has argued for language and cognition? If association, causal inference, and forms of cognition, are prepared, are there stories that man is prepared to formulate and accept? If so, a meaningful version of the racial unconscious lurks close behind.[15]

This last conclusion is rather startling coming from a learning theorist, but it does indicate that biological science may be on the threshold of being able to give a solid empirical and physical foundation to some of the findings of such diverse scholars as Jung and Claude Lévi-Strauss. Although the evidence is not yet conclusive, all of this presents us with the real possibility that there is some sort of prepared recognition of important persons or elements in our environment. In other words, there is a prepared recognition for persons or objects in our environment that, from an evolutionary perspective, either are essential for our survival or represent serious threats to our survival. Furthermore, we must face the real possibility that not only is there a prepared recognition of elements in our environment that are related to fundamental survival, but there also may be a prepared way of relating these elements to each other and to the ego-self. Such a prepared way of relating these elements would presumably be the optimal or most adaptive configuration for survival. The organism would be driven as much as possible to organize the real world to conform to the configuration that would maximize the chances of survival. This tendency would suggest that the prepared patterns of behavior are genetically driven such that the behaviors most important to survival would enter into the overall gene pool of a given species.

It would appear that early in the evolution of human beings, the organism may have become "prepared" to recognize or learn certain imaginal-conceptual complexes that represented the motivational source for behaviors highly conducive to survival. It is these complexes, undoubtedly representing fairly "hardwired" neural connections, that we propose constitute what Jung called archetypes or archetypal themes. We propose that as the human brain evolved the capability of transforming cognitive activity into more complex functions, including those of the cognitive operators, the archetypes themselves undoubtedly became subject to possible transformation. At this point in evolution, the archetypal myth could be seen as only one surface structure of a deep cognitive structure. Thereafter, human beings may have developed the capability of transforming archetypal myths into alternate surface structures for various purposes, generating alternative stories. The original form of the myth (the archetype), however, presumably still retained primary survival value, and it is in the archetypal form that myths arise from the unconscious into dream material and comprise the preponderant content of fairy tales and mythology.

Jung sees fully constellated archetypes arising at critical points in our lives. These points are either critical developmentally or because of environmental contingencies. For example, the constellation of the mother archetype from the infant's interaction with her real mother provides the necessary information and motivation to interact both with the real mother and with maternal figures of various types throughout life. In a similar fashion, the archetype of the child provides the content and motivation for rebirth or renewal experiences throughout life. Related to this is the archetype of the solar hero, conquering dragons and overcoming all sorts of impediments in order to attain his transcendent goal. Likewise, the themes of death and rebirth or resurrection are both a way of comprehending failure and a means of, and motivation for, transcending it. The appearance in dreams of the wise old man archetype is usually correlated with a scanning of our environmental circumstances searching for a deeper meaning or significance to otherwise mundane daily experiences. These are but a few of the archetypal symbols or archetypal myth themes that Jung has proposed as being developmentally primitive. These archetypes are universally present in all cultures and are likely highly conducive to survival and optimal adaptation to the environment. This is the class of phenomena in which we propose to place the near-death experience.

IS THE NEAR-DEATH EXPERIENCE AN ARCHETYPAL COMPLEX?

As we have described, studies of NDEs within the past few decades have suggested that it is an overwhelmingly positive experience; however, the phenomenon may be more complicated. Quite a few cases reported in our own time and culture have indicated that NDEs can be a most unpleasant and often horrifying experience, but in keeping with our culture's optimism in these matters, these negative, and less common forms of NDEs, are often played down and occasionally not even reported.

In an excellent comparison of the NDE as reported in medieval and modern times, Zaleski noted that although there are many similarities between the two, there are also pronounced differences. The greatest and most obvious difference is that medieval reports suggest otherworld journeys that are primarily of the negative type, involving visions of hell and purgatory. It is only at the end of these medieval NDEs that there may be a glimpse of the light and of "heavenly" phenomena that are similar to what we understand currently to make up the usual NDE. Apparently, the medieval moralists did not wish to describe the heavenly termination of the otherworld journey in any great detail. They tended to minimize positive aspects of NDEs, perhaps because they were convinced that morality was maintained primarily through fear. Thus, it is uncertain whether people simply did not have as many positive NDEs similar to those reported in more modern times, or whether there truly was a preponderance of negative elements.

Lest we think that medieval Europe cornered the market on horrifying NDEs, initial horrifying experiences prior to the attainment of either bliss or reincarnation seem to be the rule in the classic Asian NDE. As we alluded to earlier, the description of the *Chönyid* state in the Tibetan Book of the Dead is quite as horrible as any medieval European description of hell or purgatory: "Then, the Lord of Death will place around thy neck a rope and drag thee along; he will cut off thy head, tear out thy heart, pull out thy intestines, lick up thy brain, drink thy blood, eat thy flesh, and gnaw thy bones; but thou will be incapable of dying. Even when thy body is hacked to pieces, it will revive again. The repeated hacking will cause intense pain and torture."[16]

Thus, both the classic Western and Eastern NDEs began with gruesome experiences before passing into a state similar to contemporary NDEs.

Considering that horrifying experiences occur even in contemporary reports, it seems clear that they must be at least considered as part of the overall NDE.

The universality of the NDE across cultures, races, and sexes would seem to suggest that it is a pattern of behavior or cognitive function that arises in near-death situations and somehow has become embedded in virtually all people. In fact, the NDE carries many of the components of archetypes in that they are universal and also arise at a critical point during a person's life. Furthermore, they appear to come from the unconscious mind and manifest themselves in images that profoundly affect the individual. Thus, the NDE may be a programmed behavior that has been in place since the early evolution of the hominid line.

We have hypothesized that two archetypes are sequentially activated during the NDE. The first we have called the archetype of dissolution. In its full form, it consists of images of torture, being hacked, burned, and other horrifying conditions symbolic of the immanent death, fragmentation, and dissolution of the self. This is followed by an activation of what we have called the archetype of transcendent integration. It is this archetype that terminates the classic otherworld journeys in both the East and West and that makes up much of the entire experience of contemporary NDEs. The archetype of transcendent integration consists of a sense of peace, tranquillity, wholeness, and light. It is interesting that most contemporary NDEs do commence with an experience of darkness and often buzzing or some other distinctly unpleasant sound. This fairly nondescript unpleasant-to-neutral phase is brief in contemporary NDEs, but it might possibly represent a *forme fruste* (rudimentary form) of the archetype of dissolution. We would agree with Zaleski's emphasis on the cultural influence upon the tenor of NDEs in that it is probably our society's generally optimistic beliefs in a possible afterlife, along with the general elimination of any vivid transcendent sense of personal sin and guilt, that aborts the full constellation of the archetype of dissolution in most contemporary NDEs. Thus, the contemporary experiencer of an otherworld journey may move quickly through a brief and vague unpleasantness, or at best, neutrality, into a fully transcendent archetypal integration. On the other hand, it may be that the negative aspects of the NDE are not remembered as easily. This has been suggested by some reports in which negative NDEs are more often related when the person is interviewed shortly after the experience rather than much later. We will consider later how memory might be altered during an NDE. One final reason that negative NDEs are not as frequently described may be reporting bias, since a person who has had a negative NDE might be less willing to admit it.

We must state that Zaleski does not present a model of dual archetypal activation for the generation of NDEs. She simply compares the total NDE as described in the Middle Ages with the typical contemporary NDE and explains their differences solely in terms of cultural input. We maintain that if cultural input were the sole determinant of NDEs, then they should be more radically diverse than they are. In fact, when one compares the classic accounts in both the East and West and considers the rare horrifying contemporary NDE, one must conclude that there are two separate constellations of elements, both of which remain remarkably similar across cultures. The problem is that one constellation of elements tends to be suppressed or remembered in the modern NDE.

CAN THE NEAR-DEATH EXPERIENCE BE DESCRIBED USING NEUROPHYSIOLOGY?

If we were to hazard an anatomical localization of the archetypes based on our current state of knowledge, we would be forced to state that they are most probably localized near the junction of the temporal and the occipital lobe. Further, the location probably resides more in the right than in the left hemisphere, and mostly involves the lower part of the temporal lobe (including, of course, the amygdala and hippocampus). The groundbreaking work of Roger Penfield involving electrical stimulation of various parts of the brain indicated that these regions, and particularly the lower temporal lobe, are involved in eliciting vivid memories, complex hallucinations, dreamlike states, and other sensations.[17] Furthermore, stimulation of these areas results in an unusual attribution of emotional significance to otherwise neutral thoughts and experiences. Subsequent investigators have confirmed and expanded Penfield's original work.[18] The eliciting of vivid memory and/or complex vivid hallucinatory phenomena can occur in states of either markedly decreased input into the brain regions mentioned above or following specific electrical stimulation of these areas. It is especially interesting that, with markedly decreased input, these regions begin to extract or assign meaningful significance to what may be random neural events or to whatever input they might receive. Thus, one finds that subjects will hallucinate when placed in sensory-deprived environments or even when movement is markedly restricted.

One also finds that hallucinations become increasingly complex as stimulation is applied to areas that have more complex functions. Thus, stimulation of the tertiary association areas will elicit more complex hallucinations than will stimulation of the primary sensory areas. It has frequently been reported that the most complex forms of hallucinations involve activation of both the hippocampus and the amygdala in conjunction with other parts of the temporal lobe. We must emphasize that stimulation of these parts has been shown to produce both archetypal symbols and archetypal themes. In this regard, it appears that limbic activation is necessary to bring elements that are being processed in the temporal lobes to the realm of conscious understanding. It is interesting that the hallucinatory effect of LSD, which often produces archetypal elements, appears to be generated in the right temporal lobe.

Wherever the neuroanatomical circuitry underlying archetypes may be localized, the question of the mechanism of archetypal activation remains a difficult one. Apparently, archetypes can be fully or partially constellated (i.e., filled with content and come to conscious reality). This activation may result from direct electrical stimulation of the temporal lobe; from stimulus deprivation (deafferentation) of parts of the temporal lobes; from intrinsic chemical alteration of neurotransmitter balance by pharmacological agents; or from a person's interactions with the environment in certain ways during critical periods of development. Jungian psychology is most interested in the fourth mode of activation since it is in this way that the archetypes are most involved in personality development.

As we shall expand upon shortly, we feel that the archetype of dissolution is always, or almost always, constellated by chemical alterations that occur in the very early stages of dying. Thus, the constellation of the archetype of dissolution is the imaginal representation of the actual dissolution of the body (i.e., the body actually dying). Therefore, we maintain that the archetype of dissolution is rarely, if ever, constellated unless a person is actually *physiologically* near death. The archetype of transcendent integration, on the other hand, seems to be constellated more typically by the *perception* of almost certain death. This perception may be generated by means of the experience of the archetype of dissolution, in which case the perception is accurate and the subject is seriously physiologically compromised. On the contrary, the perception may be generated by external circumstances that frequently result in death but that may not result in the individual actually being close to death. In this case, the archetype of transcendent integration may be activated without any physiological distress whatsoever.

Earlier, we considered a number of physiological mechanisms that have been proposed by various researchers to explain the activation of the NDE. Among these were the postulated effects of decreased oxygen to the brain, temporal lobe seizure-like activity, limbic hyperexcitation, extreme electrolyte imbalance, generation of endorphins, and production of endopsychosins. We would argue that the true cause of NDEs may be a complex combination of several of these mechanisms, as well as the psychological perception of almost certain death.

There are two problems with a simple model of direct physical activation of both of the NDE archetypes as the only mode of activation. The first, and perhaps most telling, is that there are numerous documented NDE experiences in which there was only a *perception* of almost certain death, without any physiological changes. The second objection is that archetypes, in general, seem to be activated by interaction with the environment during critical periods, whether these be developmentally critical or the result of external crisis. This does not preclude the possibility of direct physical activation. It is just that clinical observation suggests that some sort of interaction with the environment is the usual mode of activation. If NDEs truly represent the activation of archetypes, then they also should be capable of being activated by perceived environmental triggers just as other archetypes are. It seems clear to us that the *perception* of death is at least an extremely frequent trigger of the emotionally positive NDE archetype (the archetype of transcendent integration). A person may have this perception when caught in an avalanche, after jumping off a bridge, or possibly even after hearing the talk of surrounding people during resuscitation efforts. It is important to note, however, that not all of those who experience NDEs have reported knowledge of their own death, but certainly all people who have these experiences initially are in states of extreme stress either physiologically, psychologically, or both.

In modeling the activation of the NDE archetypes we must consider two situations: (1) when the subject is actually experiencing physiological distress or the very first stages of actual death, and (2) when the subject is not experiencing physiological distress but only the conscious perception of almost certain death or impending doom.

These two situations are clearly different. As far as we have been able to determine from the literature, the horrors of the archetype of dissolution and the out-of-body experience do not seem to be experienced when there is no physiological distress. Thus, they do not occur when the subject is simply conscious of impending death, but only when the person is actually in the physical process of dying. We therefore propose that the archetype of dissolution, with its assorted horrors, is precisely the imaginal representation of the earliest stages of actual physical disintegration (or dissolution) that is ordinarily a harbinger of death. We propose that there is no single physiological mechanism that activates the archetype, but rather the totality of the earliest signs of physical disintegration. Thus, decreased oxygen to the brain, electrolyte imbalance, production of endorphins, and probably a dozen or more chemical changes may initiate an automatic physiological stress response (perhaps measured in terms of increased norepinephrine or alterations in other neurotransmitter levels). The physiological stress response results in an arousal drive that, when it becomes intense enough, activates the fear centers in the amygdala.

In our model, this amygdalar stimulation sets off an interaction with some parts of the temporal lobe, including the visual association area, generating hyperlucid visions with a terrifying content corresponding to the terror experienced from the arousal stimulation of the amygdala. We maintain that there is a quality about the arousal drive generated by the stress of the early stages of actual physical disintegration that is specific for activating fear centers in the amygdala with the consequent activation of the archetype of dissolution. Then, as the arousal system achieves maximal stimulation, one begins to get break-through of the quiescent system. We propose that this state of maximal arousal acitivity with quiescent breakthrough tends to activate the OBE as well as deeply quiescent and peaceful feelings. The fact that most modern experiencers of NDEs first have feelings of peace suggests that this quiescent stimulation is crucial to the generation of the NDE, particularly those aspects that follow any horrific aspects of the archetype of dissolution. Further, the fact that most people maintain these quiescent feelings throughout the course of the NDE indicates that quiescent drive is likely responsible for the remainder of the NDE following the hyperarousal stage. As the quiescent stimulation continues, the experiencer eventually activates the archetype of transcendent integration, but we will consider this activation later.

The OBE might result from hyperstimulation by the arousal system of the right orientation association area (remember that this area gives us a "sense of body") followed by a partial deafferentation of that area caused by the "spillover" activation of the quiescent system. Rhawn Joseph cites evidence that there is a sensory representation of the entire body within the right hemi-sphere, separate and distinct from the primary representation of the whole body in the primary receptive areas of the left and right parietal lobes.[19] We maintain that it is this whole-body representation in the right orientation association area that is "projected" outward in the classic OBE. It is this right hemispheric body gestalt that may be the sensed ethereal body experienced in some out-of-body states. We propose that the mechanism of projection of this right hemisphere "body gestalt" involves the rotation and manipulation of space and spatial coordinates that is known to be a function of the orientation association area on the right side. The partial deafferentation of the orientation association area resulting from the "spillover" quiescent-hippocampal stimula-tion, and coupled with some, albeit decreased, sensory input from the envi-ronment may allow for an out-of-body feeling, with an absence of pain and an objective observer vantage point during the time near death. This sense of bodily separation, in addition to an ongoing auditory and perhaps somates-thetic perception of what is going on, may explain why some people who have OBEs actually experience sensory aspects of the entire situation. This is spec-ulation, of course, but at least it can give us an explanation about how OBEs are neurophysiologically possible.

We postulate that continued spillover, with progressively increasing quies-cent drive, eventually results in sufficient hippocampal stimulation that vivid, hyperlucid, positive, and even blissful visions occur. This is the point in the activation of the arousal and quiescent systems that results in the activation of the archetype of transcendent integration. Thus, the entire sequences of an NDE that is initiated by severe physical distress should theoretically result in activation of the archetype of dissolution, followed by the OBE, followed by the activation of the archetype of transcendent integration.

The fact is that, although some modern experiencers of the NDE do report experiencing the entire sequence, the great majority either do not experience, or do not remember, the archetype of dissolution. One possible explanation is that modern experiencers of the NDE are usually in no way prepared by the culture for such grisly horrors. Both medieval and Asian cultures possessed beliefs in hells or purgatories replete with the most ghastly tortures as punishment for sin. In addition to holding such beliefs, people in these societies often witnessed extended public punishments involving protracted torture and death for certain criminals. Most modern near-death experiencers, on the other hand, have no preparation for such terrifying visual and auditory experiences. We propose that, in the absence of any cultural preparation, the brain may repress memory of the archetype of dissolution in a fashion similar to its repression of some nightmares or to its repression of the memories of severe physical abuse associated with the genesis of multiple personality disorder. We postulate that ND experiencers, therefore, may dissociate themselves from their terrifying experiences followed by repression of all memory of their horrors as a fundamental coping mechanism. As we have noted, the experience of the tunnel or the occasional unpleasant buzzing noise either may represent a *forme fruste* of the archetype of dissolution or else may represent the final elements of that archetype, which may be retained in memory even when its more horrifying aspects are repressed. In effect, the tunnel may represent the last element of the archetype of dissolution taking the person far away from his or her body. Thus, the archetype of dissolution may be either fully constellated and fully remembered (rare in contemporary NDEs), fully constellated but repressed and forgotten (completely or partially), or expressed as a *forme fruste*.

Let us now briefly consider the second mechanism by which an NDE can occur. This is the situation in which a person does not physically come close to dying, but rather has the conscious perception that death is imminent, such as when an individual falls off a cliff but lands unharmed. We propose that there is an initial brief phase of terror, representing an intense arousal drive, that rapidly, almost instantaneously, reaches maximal capacity with consequent quiescent spillover. We believe that in this situation, the movement toward maximal arousal capacity is much more rapid than in the case initiated by actual physiological distress. Thus, there is insufficient time for activation of the archetype of dissolution, and one moves rapidly to the phase of quiescent spillover and the activation of the archetype of transcendent integration. Likewise, the level of mild activation of the quiescent system responsible for the OBE seems to be quickly passed through in the *perceived* near-death situation until a relatively stable quiescent state is attained in the hippocampus at a level of stimulation that activates the archetype of transcendent integration. This would explain why in the *perceived* near-death situations, the experiencer almost never reports the horrible elements of the archetype of dissolution and only very rarely an OBE. It is possible, however, that either of these sequences might happen in those who are actually physically near death or those who perceive themselves to be in a life-threatening situation. But based on current reports, it seems reasonable to divide the two mechanisms of generating the NDE as we have done in this chapter.

In NDEs, the light is perceived as beautiful, but it is also perceived as a presence, which some have argued is the transcendent self. It might be maintained that a similar activation of the archetype of transcendent integration can occur during certain hyperlucid visions obtained through meditation. But, because the meditator is approaching this archetypal activation in a different mode (namely, a conscious attempt to reach the transcendent self) there is a somewhat different perception of this archetype. There seems to be little doubt, however, that both meditative and near-death experiences cause major, and similar, changes in a person's attitudes toward life and death.

Another feature of NDEs is the life review that people experience. This might be explained by the continued activation of the hippocampus during NDEs, since this area is intimately involved in memory. The hippocampus may also be involved in the perception of various beautiful images and music during immersion in the realm of light. Such perceptions can be activated by hippocampal (and amygdalar) stimulation of memory centers, thereby producing images and sounds. These experiences, in the context of the archetype of transcendent integration, are apprehended in a vivid, startlingly clear (hyperlucid) fashion and are expressed in superlative terms. It is clear that this archetype is an overwhelmingly positive experience.

We propose that similar activation of memory centers (especially in the temporal lobes) during an NDE may be responsible for the perceptions of people who have died. Thus, a person might "meet" a deceased relative or perhaps a religious figure. The rare reports of people meeting others whom they did not know had died might represent either coincidence or unconscious knowledge obtained by overhearing conversations in the room while the person was ill. Reports of meeting living people during NDEs would suggest that the ND experiencer really does not meet the person, but only has the perception of that person as it is triggered by the activation of the memory centers. Hippocampal inhibition may also result in repression of the memory of the early, negative aspects of the NDE.

All of this brings us to the question regarding the selective advantage of archetypal activation in general, and the activation of the NDE archetypes in particular. We would suggest that the sense of calm and tranquillity accompanying activation of the archetype of transcendent integration increases the chances of survival by decreasing the likelihood of neurogenic shock from sheer terror. The tranquillity probably results from the spillover phenomenon within the autonomic nervous system that occurs when arousal discharge becomes so intense that it begins to generate an activation of the quiescent system, thus preventing neurogenic shock. An added advantage is that the NDE, or at least the neurophysiological response to being in a life-threatening situation, seems to allow for a clearer appraisal of the environmental circumstance when the NDE is not accompanied by loss of consciousness. This might enable someone to use rational thinking to escape from a life-threatening danger. Clearly such functioning of the brain would be a marked survival advantage.

It is still unclear, however, why NDEs have evolved. Several scholars have argued that there is no evolutionary reason for a blissful death experience because this would in no way increase the probability of producing offspring. People at the threshold of death are not likely to reproduce, and "nature does nothing for nothing."[20] Our model, on the other hand, offers the possibility that the NDE is the result of evolutionary forces and natural selection. The potential selective advantage of a pleasant NDE might also be to allow the sick and elderly of a population (human or otherwise) to be more amenable to dying and, consequently, not becoming a burden to healthier group members by struggling to survive and using up valuable resources. This would help the group in general, and their kin in particular, to survive better by not expending scarce resources on members who cannot contribute to the maintenance and propagation of the group.

Another, and perhaps stronger, argument for the selective advantage of the NDE can be found in our neurophysiological model, in which the NDE arises initially from the simultaneous activation of the quiescent and arousal nervous systems via the limbic system. Since the quiescent system, the arousal system, and the limbic system are among the evolutionarily oldest brain structures, we would suggest that responses to life-threatening situations, similar to those that occur in human beings, occur in other animal species as well. The ability to remain calm in the face of life-threatening danger would have been very selective among animals, particularly for those in their reproductive prime. Further, animals face such situations much more frequently than do humans, both as prey or as predators. Thus, it would be surprising if the rudiments of the NDE were not present in many animals, specifically those with developed autonomic-limbic systems.

As the neocortex developed in human beings, the ability to tie the near-death response into a highly developed cognition and affect would have greatly enhanced human survival capability. This increased survival capability would be due to an individual's ability not only to remain calm in life-threatening situations but to think clearly, rationally, and often in "slow motion." Thus, human beings would be able to rely upon their most valuable asset in times of extreme crisis—they would be able to use their brains efficiently, indeed, hyperefficiently. Further, connections of the limbic system and the neocortex, which probably evolved for other purposes, would likely have resulted in the more expanded version of the NDE, including hippocampal activation with consequent life review and the perception of the light.

ARE NEAR-DEATH EXPERIENCES REAL?

Our purpose here has been to propose a theoretical neuropsychological model of the NDE in keeping with our overall model of the functioning of the mind/brain. This model was developed upon the presumption that the NDE is generated by the activation (or partial activation) of two archetypes—the archetype of dissolution and the archetype of transcendent integration. If we accept that these archetypes form the fundamental aspects of the NDE, then the involvement of various brain structures in the activation of these archetypes rounds out the account of the generation of the NDE.

We believe that this model can explain why NDEs can be either horrible or wonderful or both. Beyond simply explaining the two aspects, positive and negative, of the NDE, our model explains virtually all aspects of the "core experience" of the positive version; from feelings of peace and tranquillity via quiescent system activation, to the experience of the tunnel and the light via activation of the temporal lobe, to the reason for meeting others during the NDE via activation of the hippocampal memory centers, and finally, the sense of oneness that the person experiences via a hyperstimulation of the arousal and quiescent systems and subsequent deafferentation of the orientation association area. This model also suggests that the hippocampus might be involved in the generation of the panoramic life review, and may be responsible for the frequent repression of memory of the horrible or hellish aspects of the NDE. This model can also explain many of the anomalous events that have been reported such as OBEs and the ability to perceive things such as the immediate environment through sensory stimuli despite the NDE being in progress. This model suggests that the NDE might have a survival benefit for a person or his or her kin by allowing the person to remain calm in life-threatening situations where remedy of the situation is possible as well as by facilitating imminent death when remedy is impossible.

This model includes the psychological aspects of NDEs. NDE archetypes, like all archetypes, possess a certain quality of exaggerated reality compared to baseline reality. It is for this reason that archetypes are often the basis of mythology, "divine reality," or the mysterious "hyperreal" underlying baseline experience. In their fully constellated or developed form, archetypes appear in only two phases of consciousness, that is, dream consciousness or the hyperlucid consciousness of mystical visions. And it is only in their full presentation in dream consciousness or in the hyperlucid consciousness of mystical visions that their divine or semidivine qualities are fully manifest. It is in this sense that the archetype of dissolution and the archetype of transcendent integration may be classified as mystical visions.

Thus, the fully constellated NDE archetypes possess a hyperlucidity that gives to the experiencing individual the sense of being in contact with a reality that is "realer" and more profound than ordinary baseline reality. This is confirmed by the reports of hundreds of people who have had NDEs. Not only do they almost universally report a persistent sense of the ultimate reality of the NDE, even after they return to this world, they also experience a transformation in their everyday lives as a direct result of experiencing that reality. A number of investigators have reported that individuals who have NDEs tend to be less materialistic, more altruistic, have greater compassion for others, and lack a fear of death. This clearly demonstrates the profound psychological implications of NDEs. Thus, they are powerful neuropsychological events with implications across cultures and times as well as in the life of the individual experiencer. They are, for all intents and purposes, equivalent to the hyperlucid visions of the mystic in their vivid reality compared to baseline, in the profound numinous sense they inspire, and in the fruits of compassion and caring they produce in the after-experience lives of those who have had them. In a way, the NDE is "every person's" mystical experience.

Part Three

Neurotheology and the Paradox of Phenomenology

Chapter Eight

The Origin of Religion

A DEFINITION OF RELIGION

We are now ready to begin to explore the theological implications of approaching religion from a neuropsychological perspective. The first step in such an analysis is to examine the neuropsychological origins of religion. By examining the origins of religion, we can eventually begin to explain the theology that arises from religion. The definition of religion is a notoriously difficult task. Indeed, there are many who maintain that the concept has no single referent. This is easy to understand since the term *religion* often encompasses such disparate elements as Eastern monism, Western dualism, divine immanence, divine transcendence, attempts at controlling nature and the environment, achieving and maintaining a plethora of interior states, emphasis on moral behavior, and so on. It is difficult to see much in common between the religion of various primitive societies and, say, the exalted spiritual awareness of Theravada Buddhism. Likewise, it is often very difficult to see much similarity between certain practitioners of the same religion. Thus, a behavioral analysis, and to a certain extent a cognitive one, would see very little in common between the Catholicism of a rural South American Indian and that of a Meister Eckhart or of an Anselm of Canterbury. In view of such differences can we even hope to arrive at anything like a unitary definition of religion?

Until the late eighteenth century, there had been practically no attempt at defining religion per se. Consequently, religions, particularly in the West, were defined by their cognitive content or dogmatic formulations. It is only with Friedrich Schleiermacher in the late eighteenth century that an attempt was made to define religion as such by switching the emphasis from a cognitive or doctrinal one to a more visceral or intuitive one. Schleiermacher defined religion as a "feeling of *absolute* dependence." Since his day, all attempts at a general definition of religion have relied heavily on emphasizing the intuitive, emotional, or visceral. A major step forward in the attempt to formulate a general definition of religion was the rise of anthropological and sociological theory. This approach asserted that religion is always embedded in a cultural matrix and that religious beliefs, customs, and rituals must be understood in a radical relationship to the cultures in which they arise. Émile Durkheim, in his *Elementary Forms of the Religious Life,* maintained that "a society has all that is necessary to arouse the sensation of the divine in minds, merely by the power it has over them."[1] Thus, in the Durkheimian analysis, religion is nothing more than a transform of society. On the other hand, psychologists from Sigmund Freud to B. F. Skinner have seen in religion a projection either of various intrapsychic dynamics or of hopes and expectations based on previous experience.

Since the beginning of the twentieth century, however, there have been scholars who began to devote themselves to the phenomenology of religion on its own terms. They believed that there were phenomena that needed to be explained that eluded both sociological and psychological determinism. An example of such an approach has been to analyze religion in terms of an awareness of the "sacred" and the "holy." Rudolf Otto, in *The Idea of the Holy,* defined the essence of religious awareness as "awe."[2] This he understood as a mixture of fear and fascination before the divine. Otto saw the essential religious experience as a *mysterium tremendum et fascinans.* Otto betrayed his Western origins, however, by understanding this as a sensed "wholly other" of the divine being. Such an approach began to get at a dominant form of Western mysticism but was not so applicable to Eastern religions or to primitive ones.

The most recent and subtle reworking of Otto's concept of the "sacred" as the central core of all religious experience has been done by Mircea Eliade.[3] For Eliade, no longer is the sacred to be found almost exclusively in Otto's god-encounter type of experience. Rather, every culture exemplifies the existential sense of the sacred in its rituals and symbols, especially primitive and Asian cultures. Commenting on Eliade, Winston King notes:

> It [the sacred] is embodied as sacred space, for example, in shrines and temples, in taboo areas, even limitedly in the erection of dwellings in accordance with a sense of the axis mundi, an orientation to the center of the true "sacred" universe. Indeed, structures often symbolically represent that physically invisible but most real of all universes—the eternally perfect universe to which they seek to relate fruitfully. This sense of sacredness often attaches to trees, stones, mountains, and other like objects in which mysterious power seems to reside. Many primitive rituals seek to sacramentally repeat the first moment of creation, often described in myth, when primordial chaos became

recognizable order. Sacred time—that is, eternal and unfragmented time—is made vitally present by the reenactment by such myths.[4]

In *The Sacred and the Profane,* Eliade writes, "Every religious festival, every liturgical time, represents the reactualization of a sacred event that took place in a mythical past, in the beginning" (pp. 68–69). In fairness it must be stated that Eliade's position, though intriguing and subtle, is hard to verify in actual cases across cultures. Many anthropologists, linguists, and psychologists question whether the concept of the "sacred" is identifiable as such in an analysis of the language, experience, and thought of most primitive societies. Such scholars assert that religious experience is not sui generis, but is rather an amalgam of diverse cultural phenomena and experiences.

This cursory review of the history of our Western attempt to understand religion leaves us in a somewhat confused state. Perhaps the best current working definition of religion is given by Winston King in an attempt to define religious salvation. After first making the point that salvation is but another name for religion in general, he writes:

> Are there distinguishing characteristics of religious salvation? The first is that religious salvation tends to concentrate on the needs that a culture defines as most fundamental, neglecting needs that a culture defines as less important. Religious means of salvation, often indirect and extrahuman, seek to use supersensible forces and powers either in addition to or in place of ordinary tangible means. The second distinguishing characteristic is that religious salvations tend to aim at total, absolute, and sometimes transcendent fulfillment of human needs. As defined by the cultural context, this fulfillment ranges all the way from the fullness of physical satisfactions to the eternal ecstasy of union with the Absolute.[5] (P. 288)

It seems, then, that religious behavior arises from the operation and interrelationship of two distinct neuroanatomical and neurophysiological mechanisms in the brain. The first of these is the perception of causal sequences in the organization of reality. This results in an attempt to impose control over the world through the manipulation of posited causal constructs such as gods, demons, spirits, and other personalized causal agencies. The second mechanism is the result of neurophysiological evolution culminating in the potential to develop altered states of consciousness. Such experiences are often interpreted as glimpses into the world of the supernatural and tend to confirm the existence of the personalized power sources generated by the first mechanism just mentioned. Furthermore, in and of themselves, such experiences can often facilitate both a reorganization of the personality structure and a realignment of the individual toward the cosmos.

In this chapter, we are proposing that there are two neuropsychological mechanisms that underlie the development of religious experiences and behaviors. These two mechanisms represent two lines of neurological development, involving the evolution of structures that comprise the causal operator, on the one hand, and the holistic operator, on the other. It is interesting that these two neural operators seem to generate the two essential characteristics in King's definition of religion, namely, the use of supersensible forces and powers to control the environment in such a way as to attain those needs that the culture defines as fundamental, and the tendency toward the fulfillment of human needs in a total, absolute, or transcendent fashion often involving unusual subjective states or experiences. We maintain that the first of these mechanisms (i.e., the manipulation of the environment by manipulating the power of gods, spirits, and other personalized powers) is primarily aimed at self-maintenance. The second of these mechanisms is aimed primarily at self-transcendence, but also allows the temporary neurological destabilization requisite for the possibility of self-transformation. It is necessary, however, to understand the neuropsychological basis for the concept of deity prior to expanding on the basis of religion in general.

THE NEUROPSYCHOLOGICAL BASIS
FOR THE CONCEPT OF DEITY

By now it should be clear that the concept of some form of supernatural (inferred rather than naturally observed) power or higher state of being, be it God, demons, spirits, or whatever, is required by the internal dynamics of myth. We have described how myths are structured in terms of pairs of polar opposites, usually consisting of human beings and some supernatural force. This supernatural force is crucial for giving human beings the power to resolve the problem of the specific myth. Usually, the myth problem cannot be resolved by human logic or by any method of human thought. Thus, the internal dynamics of myth require the relation of human beings to the supernatural power being in order to resolve the problem.

The concept of a god or supernatural power being arises, however, not only because of the internal dynamics built into the binary structure of myth by the binary operator, but also from the necessary operation of the causal operator. The binary and causal operators force the necessity for a superhuman being to resolve the myth problem and allow for causality to exist in the universe. This is simply the way the operators work, and human beings have little choice over this internal functioning of the mind/brain. This dynamic represents necessary neurophysiological functioning. The resulting subjective correlates of this mind/brain activity necessarily produce the notion of supernatural power beings or gods. Thus, the traditional proofs given for the existence of God, the *quinque viae* of Saint Thomas Aquinas, are subtle elaborations of argumentation by means of abstract causality. They represent various approaches to the application of the causal operator to the entirety of physical reality.

To expand upon the need for the causal operator to generate superhuman beings, we have mentioned that when the causal operator is applied to a limited strip of reality, the initial cause of which is not given in the environment, the operator automatically and necessarily tries to find a primary cause. If no cause can be found that is humanly comprehensible, then the causal operator produces a "causal being" to explain that strip of reality. Furthermore, these causal beings derive their essential causal characteristic from the functioning of the operator itself. The result is the generation of the concept of a limited god or of a spirit or demon that has particular association with that strip of reality.

If the mind/brain applies the causal operator to the totality of reality at any given moment, the result is the generation of the subjective sense of *pure causality* or the affirmation of the absolute cause of the universe. Many people assume that the traditional arguments for the existence of God from efficient causality suggest a regression through time to the cause of the first "big bang." This certainly is one approach, but, it represents a rather naive, eighteenth-century approach that was not that of medieval theologians. Aquinas, for example, maintained that in theory there is no reason why the universe could not be eternal. If this were the case, then the universe would necessarily have to be eternally caused. Aquinas believed that the universe was created at the first moment of time in order to correspond to the biblical account of creation. But he was very specific that, in principle, the universe could be eternal, and that this would not negate the argument from causality. His application of causality, therefore, was without time and therefore eternal. It represented his experiencing the functioning of the causal operator on the entirety of material reality. Of course the mere fact that he could conceptualize such a reality represents the application of the abstractive operator not to any specific series of empirical individuals, but to all empirical individuals. This conceptualization was achieved by the total functioning of the abstractive operator.

By total functioning of an operator, we mean that a particular operator is operating essentially on nothing. This is to say, the operator is deafferented and is cut off from any input. Thus, the operator in "total functioning" is not organizing reality, but is, as it were, operating on itself. This produces the subjective sensation of the "essence" of the operator applies to the totality of reality ("everything" and "nothing" being the same at this level of perception). Alternatively, the "essence" of the operator can be experienced as the totality of reality itself. Thus, for example, the total functioning of the causal operator generates the sensation that reality is causality, or, at least, that causality is the single underlying principle of the totality of reality. The total functioning of a cognitive operator is an unusual state that is not experienced by many philosophers or theologians. Furthermore, it may be that metaphysics arises from the application of various cognitive operators to the totality of physical reality as opposed to individual pieces of physical reality on which they ordinarily operate. Thus, we would suggest that the various schools of metaphysics and all the major metaphysical questions derive their absolute generality from the subjective experience of the total functioning of various cognitive operators. We will consider this in the next chapter.

There appears to be an even more important source for the concept of deity besides the application of the causal operator either to various strips of reality or to the totality of reality. This involves the total functioning of the holistic operator. In normal awareness it is difficult for the holistic operator to function in isolation. This isolation may occur in certain cases, usually produced by altered physiological states such as intense meditation or prayer. The holistic operator can be made to function briefly in an absolute sense so that the entire universe is perceived as a unity. When this perception occurs, even the self-other dichotomy is dissolved and the experience so often described by mystics in both the East and the West is obtained. We have called this state absolute unitary being. Once again, this experience represents the subjective awareness of the total functioning of the holistic operator. This state is so ineffable that a person who experiences such a state almost invariably affirms that it represents the only true reality. The everyday awareness of the non-holistic, individuated reality is affirmed to be only illusory. The absolute functioning of the holistic operator is associated not so much with the concept of God (causal operator) as with the *experience* of God.

To paraphrase Ken Wilber, the core experience of this holistic state is that the innermost consciousness of human beings is identical to the absolute and ultimate reality of the universe, known variously as Brahma, Tao, tathagata, Christ, dharmakaya, Allah, the Godhead, or absolute mind.[6] The mystical traditions that arise from such an experience assert in one way or another that the mystical mind is what there is and all there is, spaceless and therefore infinite, timeless and therefore eternal, outside of which nothing exists. Erwin Schrödinger, the founder of quantum mechanics, stated, "The only possible alternative [to the hypothesis of the plurality of souls] is simply to keep to the immediate experience that consciousness [i.e., mind] is a singular of which the plural is unknown; that there is only one thing and that what seems to be a plurality is merely a series of different aspects of this one thing, produced by a deception; the same illusion is produced in a gallery of mirrors, and in the same way Gaurisankar and Mt. Everest turned out to be the same peak seen from different valleys."[7]

The Ch'an Master Huang Po stated: "All the Buddhas and all sentient beings are nothing but the One Mind, beside which nothing exists. This Mind, which is without beginning, is unborn and indestructible. It is not green or yellow, and has neither form nor appearance. It does not belong to the categories of things which exist or do not exist, nor can it be thought of in terms of new or old. It is neither long nor short, big nor small, for it transcends all limits, measures, names, traces, and comparisons. Only awake to the One Mind."[8]

On this level, human beings are identified with the universe as a whole. The practitioners of profound meditation and mature contemplation experience actually becoming the universe. According to the *psychologia perennis,* this experience is not an abnormal or altered state of consciousness. This state is the only real state of consciousness, and all others are considered essentially illusions.

In short, the innermost human consciousness—known variously as the Atman, pneuma, Adam Kadmon, ruarch Adonai, purush, al-insan al-Kamil, the Christ, Tathagatagarbha—is identical to the ultimate reality of the universe. Thus, to quote Schrödinger again: "Inconceivable as it seems to ordinary reason, you—and all other conscious beings as such—are all in all. Hence this life of yours you are living is not merely a piece of the entire existence, but is in a certain sense the whole. Thus you can throw yourself flat on the ground, stretched out upon Mother Earth, with the certain conviction that you are one with her and she with you. You are as firmly established, as invulnerable as she, indeed a thousand times firmer and more invulnerable."[9]

We maintain that these mystical traditions arise from the experience of the total functioning of the holistic operator via the neurophysiological mechanisms described in chapter 6. For any operator, particularly the holistic operator, to function in a total fashion is a difficult state to attain. Nevertheless, when alterations in the activation of the arousal and quiescent systems occur as during meditation or ritual performance, such an effect can be achieved and is regularly attained by adepts of all mystical traditions.

We would conclude that the high Western religions—Judaism, Islam, and Christianity—appear to derive a concept of deity primarily from the total functioning of the causal operator on all of external reality. This, of course, corresponds more with the Western emphasis on causality and on reasoning based on causality. Eastern traditions, particularly Hinduism and Buddhism, derive a concept of deity or absolute being from the total functioning of the holistic operator. It should be noted, though, that the high Western religions contain elements derived from the functioning of both the causal and holistic operators. Mystics of all religions achieve an immediate sense of God via the total application of the holistic operator to the totality of reality. Combinations of both approaches are noted in many great Western theologians. Of all the great Western approaches to a demonstration of God, probably only Saint Anselm of Canterbury derived his formal presentation almost purely by the application of the holistic operator. Even his position, however, was couched in terms of the "proof" required by medieval disputation. To really get the "point" of Anselm's "proof," one had to have had such a mystical experience as to make dialectics both ludicrous and impossible. But if one had not experienced such a state, the mere verbal presentation of Anselm's "proof" tended to collapse in on itself.

SELF-MAINTENANCE: CONTROL OF THE ENVIRONMENT THROUGH THE MEDIATION OF PERSONALIZED POWER SOURCES

Religion itself is highly dependent upon the development of the concept of deity. We propose, however, that religion also becomes a method of self-maintenance. This occurs through the presumed contractual agreements with power sources or gods. These power sources, as described above, likely are derived from the function of the causal operator. We have suggested that gods, powers, spirits, or in general what we have come to call personalized power sources, or any other causative construct, are automatically generated by the causal operator. Note that in speaking of Western science we have not been speaking of Western scientists. The restrictions imposed on human thought in the Western sciences are of a social and contractual nature, but the brain of the scientist functions no differently from that of anyone else. Although he or she may reject the idea of gods, spirits, demons, and any other type of personalized power source, he or she nevertheless experiences them in dreams and fantasy life. Any practicing psychiatrist or clinical psychologist can point to these phenomena in the fantasy life of the most rational person. The causal operator simply operates spontaneously on reality, positing an initial causal terminus when none is given.

If this analysis is essentially correct, then human beings have no choice but to construct myths peopled by personalized power sources to explain their world. As we have described, myths may be social in nature or they may be individual in terms of dreams, daydreams, and other fantasy aspects of the individual person; as long as human beings are aware of the contingency of their existence in the face of what often appears to be a capricious universe they must construct myths to orient themselves within that universe. Thus they construct gods, spirits, demons, and other personalized power sources with whom they can deal contractually in order to gain control over a capricious environment. Once unknown or mysterious causes of strips of reality are perceived as persons or personalized forces, they can be dealt with as one would deal with powerful persons. They can be offered gifts in return for their beneficence. Thus the concept of sacrifice, such as the *do ut des* of the ancient Roman religion, is the most primitive contractual obligation entered into by human beings with power sources or gods. All this is inherent in the obligatory functioning of the neurostructures we have just considered. Since it is unlikely that humankind will ever know the first cause of every strip of reality observed, it is highly probable that it will always generate gods, powers, demons, and other entities as first causes to explain what it observes. Indeed, people cannot do otherwise.

The development of higher cortical functions may be regarded as a blessing insofar as they allow humans abstract problem solving, an adaptive mechanism in any environment. These higher functions can also be regarded as a curse. Because humans can think abstractly and causally, they can transcend their immediate perceptual field. From experience, they can postulate probable events under given circumstances. Most of all, these functions make them acutely aware of their own mortality and of the contingency of their existence in an unpredictable world. This realization is the basis of the existential anxiety that all humans bear within them. It is to relieve this "curse of cognition," this existential anxiety, that humankind first seeks mastery over its environment by attempting to organize it mythically and by attempting to control it through the intervention of personalized power constructs. We can cite numerous examples from the Judeo-Christian tradition. In the early books of the Old Testament there are many references to Yahweh's being pleased by the "sweet odor" or "sweet fragrance" of the sacrifices offered to him. Indeed, in some of the more primitive references the attention of Yahweh is sought by the fragrant odor of the sacrifice. Once his attention is obtained by the odor and by the gift, prayers may then be offered for whatever the original intention of the sacrifice may have been.

We maintain that this control aspect of religion is a self-maintenance system. It may not be immediately obvious why this observation is valid, since clearly such attempts at controlling the world are probably not actually efficacious. At least they are not efficacious in producing the specific desired ends of those who are attempting to utilize the power of the god or gods. What is efficacious is the *sense* of control over the environment itself that such religious practices give. It is clear that the human psyche requires some sense of control over the environment in order not to become dispirited, discouraged, or even depressed. It has been noted by several researchers as well as by clinicians that the essence of a clinical depression is a sense of loss of control over one's life, over one's fate, or over the environment. We have presented the hypothesis in a previous work, drawn from Sade's observations of his macaque colony, that depression may have evolved in an attempt to give stability to primate groups. Thus, when an alpha male is challenged in an antagonistic display, and when he loses the confrontation, he develops all the outward or behavioral signs of depression, complete with psychomotor retardation and movement to the periphery of the group. We have postulated that this state allows for the new alpha male to maintain his control over the group in a way that is unchallenged by the former holder of that position. This acquiesance would seem to prevent prolonged and fierce power struggles that would disrupt the structure and function of the group. Whether this submission, in fact, is the origin of clinical depression among humans or not, it is certain that the sense of a loss of control of the environment is profoundly debilitating, paralyzing, and destructive.

This control aspect of religion is a self-maintenance system par excellence in that it allows for a sense of control over the environment that preserves the necessary positive psychological outlook to allow individuals and social groups to perform the actual manipulations in the external world that, in fact, do lead to some measure of control and ultimately to survival. This control aspect of religion, involving the brain generating gods, spirits, and powers and their manipulation through sacrifice, prayer, and other contractual situations, is probably the most primitive form of religion. It is the predominant form in primitive societies and during the early historic period, especially in the West. The example of early Roman religion is particularly pointed in that it was a state religion that concerned itself almost exclusively with the manipulation of deities for the purposes of the state. Although this control, manipulative, and contractual aspect of religion is very primitive and predominates in primitive societies and in the early historic phases of the higher cultures, it is nevertheless present, to some extent at least, even in the most developed and advanced religions. This is true both theoretically and certainly in terms of popular individual religious practice.

We maintain that the attempt to control the environment via the positing of and control of personal power sources is sufficient in and of itself to constitute religion. In fact, almost all religions comprise other elements, which we will address shortly, but this aspect is never wholly absent, and in and of itself, generates behaviors that can properly be called religious without any admixture of other elements. We are somewhat arbitrarily restricting the noun *religion* and the adjective *religious* to attempts to control the environment via personalized power sources. We should note that the causal operator may also impose a spurious causality relating inanimate objects directly to each other, not through the mediation of personalized power sources. This process we have chosen to call magic and not religion. Thus, when a direct causal connection is seen between sticking a pin in a doll and a victim's having a heart attack, we would call this magic in our system. Religion understood in the sense that we are presenting it requires the mediation of the personalized power constructs. Thus the *ex opere operantis* theory of sacramental efficacy of classic Protestantism would be seen as a religious model whereas the *ex opere operato* theory of classic Roman Catholic sacramental theology would be seen as magical by this analysis.

SELF-TRANSCENDENCE: THE RELIGIOUS
INTERPRETATION OF ALTERED STATES
OF CONSCIOUSNESS

There is a second neural mechanism that produces phenomena that are quite distinct from the control aspect of religion, but which are nevertheless seen as intrinsically religious when they occur. In most of the world's high religions, the class of phenomena arising from this second neural mechanism is usually seen as expressing the summit or the ultimate in each respective religious tradition. In point of fact, however, it is extremely rare for this class of phenomena to exist independently from some aspect of religion generated by the control mechanisms discussed in the previous section. What we are talking about here is the mystical phenomena or altered states of consciousness generating a sense of some interaction with another and mysterious world perceived in some way as ultimate or transcendent. These altered states include the mystical experiences described earlier in this book such as absolute unitary being (AUB) or near-death experiences. Therefore, it is necessary to reconsider mystical experiences in the more general description of religions. Specifically, we must explore how mystical experiences are incorporated into religion to gain a better understanding of the neuropsychological basis of religion.

Since the early 1960s there have been many attempts on the part of philosophers of religion and others to define mystical experiences and to categorize them. Gimello gives a good general definition:

A mystical experience is a state of mind, achieved commonly through some sort of self-cultivation, of which the following are usually or often the salient, but not necessarily the only, features:

A feeling of oneness or unity, variously defined.

A strong confidence in the "reality" or "objectivity" of the experience, i.e. a conviction that it is somehow revelatory of "the truth."

A sense of the final inapplicability to the experience of conventional language, i.e. a sense that the experience is ineffable.

A cessation of normal intellectual operations (e.g. deduction, discrimination, ratiocination, speculation, etc.) or the substitution for them of some "higher" or qualitatively different mode of intellect (e.g. intuition).

A sense of the coincidence of opposites, of various kinds (paradoxically).

An extraordinarily strong affective tone, again of various kinds (e.g. sublime joy, utter serenity, great fear, incomparable pleasure, etc.—often an unusual combination of such as these).[10]

Initially, many scholars felt that mystical experiences are basically one and the same across cultures. It became clear, however, that there were various sorts of mystical experiences that seemed to be fundamentally different, even allowing for the differences in cultural expression and the differences in interpretation of what happens during a mystical experience in terms of the religious tradition in which it is embedded. Thus, Frederick Streng notes that "the term mysticism has been used to refer to a variety of phenomena including occult experience, trance, a vague sense of unaccountable uneasiness, sudden extraordinary visions and words of divine beings, or aesthetic sensitivity. For our purposes we will narrow the definition to: an interior illumination of reality that results in ultimate freedom. Ninian Smart has correctly distinguished mysticism in this sense from 'the experience of a dynamic external presence.'"[11]

We would like to pick up on this commentary regarding Smart's distinction between the experience of Otto's "wholly other" and the internal sense of ineffable unity defined as a mystical experience, predominantly, though not exclusively, in Asian traditions. Smart has argued that certain strains of Hinduism, Buddhism, and Taoism differ markedly from prophetic religions such as Judaism and Islam and from religions related to the prophetic-like Christianity, in that the religious experience most characteristic of the former is "mystical" whereas that most characteristic of the latter is "numinous."[12] Of these two terms, it is the numinous that Smart seems to have an easier time explaining, since it obviously arises more spontaneously out of Western religious traditions.

Somewhat similar to Smart's distinction between the mystical experience, properly so called, and the numinous experience is that of W. T. Stace, who distinguishes between what he calls extrovertive mystical experiences and introvertive mystical experiences:

Extrovertive mystical experiences:
    1. The unifying vision—all things are one
    2. The more concrete apprehension of the One as an inner subjectivity, or life, in all things
    3. Sense of objectivity or reality
    4. Blessedness, peace, etc.
    5. Feeling of the holy, sacred, divine
    6. Paradoxicality
    7. Alleged by mystics to be ineffable

Introvertive mystical experiences:
    1. The unitary consciousness; the One, the Void; pure consciousness
    2. Nonspatial, nontemporal
    3. Sense of objectivity or reality
    4. Blessedness, peace, etc.

5. Feeling of the holy, sacred, or divine
6. Paradoxicality
7. Alleged by mystics to be ineffable[13]

Stace then concludes that characteristics 3 through 7 are identical in the two lists and are therefore universal aspects of mysticism in all cultures, ages, religions, and civilizations of the world. It is in characteristics 1 and 2, however, that Stace distinguishes between extrovertive mystical experiences and introvertive mystical experiences. One can easily see a similarity between Stace's extrovertive mystical experience and Smart's numinous experience and between Stace's introvertive mystical experiences and Smart's mystical experience proper.

In his critique of both Smart's and Stace's typology, Steven Katz asserts that not only are those critics naive who maintain that all mystical experiences are essentially one but even that neither typology does justice to the variety and essential differences of mystical experiences as presented in the literature.[14] Katz maintains that mystical experiences differ in terms of the language of the culture in which they are embedded in explaining them and also that their very content is altered by the cultural experience the mystic brings to them.

The bottom line in understanding the phenomenology of subjective religious experience is to understand that every religious experience involves a sense of the unity of reality at least somewhat greater than the baseline perception of unity in day-to-day life.[15] This is another way of saying that a more intense application of the holistic operator to incoming stimuli, over and above its baseline function, and coupled with the limbic or emotional stimulation that accompanies such increased functioning, always results in experiences that are described as religious or spiritual in varying degrees. Thus, whether one is in the state of AUB, cosmic consciousness, trance states such as those achieved by members of flagellant sects during the Middle Ages, states known to be achieved by Taiwanese mediums, or states attained by practitioners of voodoo in Haiti and the Umbanda of Brazil, all involve increasing one's sense of unity with some higher order of reality.

It is clear that all these experiences involve self-transcendence in one way or another. We believe that this is the second manifestation of religion. Theoretically, it can stand on its own, but it rarely, if ever, does. It is usually integrated in one form or another, at least minimally, with the first aspect of religion mentioned above—that is, the attempt to control the external environment. One might ask why one would wish to transcend oneself. It is intuitively obvious why human beings would wish to control their environment. It is not immediately so obvious why one would wish to transcend the self. The answer is obvious to those who have had mystical experiences. It is clear that such experiences are characterized, at the lower end of the unitary continuum, by a sense of insight into the world of the mysterious bordering on the supernatural, and at the extreme end of the continuum by a sense of attaining absolute reality, union with God or the Absolute, a sense of either bliss or utter tranquillity, and, perhaps most important of all, a lack of fear of death. It is almost universally reported from those who have experienced the final two stages of the unitary continuum (i.e., either cosmic consciousness or AUB) that they simply have no fear of death. This is not necessarily because they believe in an afterlife. They may or may not depending on the general structure of the religious beliefs they hold separate from their mystical experiences. Even if they do not believe in a specific afterlife, mystical experiences tend to generate a sense of the ultimate goodness and appropriateness of reality, and death is simply perceived as an ordinary part of that reality, something that is not to be feared. Thus, it is easy to see why self-transcendence is highly prized. To a greater or lesser extent it makes an individual invulnerable to the exigencies of life and to the effects of evil in the world.

It is something of a paradox that this second manifestation of religion, at least toward the end of the unitary continuum, seems to involve a surrender to God, the Absolute, or to the universal ultimate reality. It is in some ways the opposite of the first manifestation of religion that we considered in this chapter (i.e., the attempt to control the environment). Paradoxically, it represents a surrender to absolute reality. In its more perfect or complete forms, this second aspect of religion positively rejects any attempt at control of the physical universe or even of one's own life as being inimical to spiritual development. The benefit is, in some sense, a greater control by achieving union with the rest of the universe. Thus, control is lost to the individual self, but it is gained as part of the entire universe.

This being the case, it is curious that rarely does either the first or the second manifestation of religion stand on its own. In most cultures, they are integrated to a greater or lesser extent. The first manifestation of religion, control of the environment, is more likely to stand on its own, but even in primitive religions shamans or witch doctors enter the "other world" of the gods and spirits and return to testify to its reality. Indeed, it is not too difficult to see how the second mystical manifestation of religion can help the first. Insofar as altered states of consciousness can be perceived as experiencing the world of the gods, they can be seen as immediate empirical verification of the existence of the personal power sources that are automatically constructed by the causal operator. It is not so immediately obvious why those religions that are primarily mystical in nature tolerate a significant admixture of the first manifestation of religion. The answer is probably that human beings are human beings. Religions are not primarily composed of mystics or people who have attained advanced spiritual states. They are composed by and large of ordinary people who must face ordinary problems in life. For them the control of the environment represents a necessity of day-to-day living. They may occasionally experience altered states at the lower end of the unitary continuum. These experiences may lend credibility to the powerful witness of mystics. But for the ordinary person such experiences, and the testimony of mystics, function to support the power of the gods or personalized power sources. It is thus that mystical religion tends to reinforce the first manifestation of religion, namely, the control of the environment.

SELF-TRANSFORMATION: A FUNDAMENTAL CHANGE OF UNDERSTANDING

Self-transformation is not so much a third manifestation of religion as it is a consequence and corollary of self-transcendence. As individuals move up the unitary continuum and impose ever more holistic views on reality, there is noted an increased emotional discharge via the rich connections which Gary Schwartz, Richard Davidson, and Foster Maer have described between the non-dominant hemisphere and the limbic system.[16] This increased emotional discharge (especially when associated with a high arousal state) is known to cause a certain degree of neural instability, allowing for the forming of new connections between neurons. If the new connections form in a certain way, the result may be a realignment of one's understanding of one's self and the world in relation to the mystical experience.

In other words, a state of relatively sustained emotional excitement can facilitate the reorganization of our cognized environment. This is akin to what Anthony Wallace called mazeway resynthesis and to what the great psychoanalyst Franz Alexander called a corrective emotional experience. Any intense emotional arousal such as "hitting bottom" in Alcoholics Anonymous can facilitate a personal transformation. Such an experience is accompanied, however, by a surrender of the ego in one way or another to a higher power. This may be to the general process in psychoanalysis, to the higher power in Alcoholics Anonymous, or to a more traditional concept of God. But there is no doubt that heightened emotionality in a context of surrender increases the possibility of self-transformation. One does not have to move far upward along the unitary continuum for the possibility of transformation to become more and more probable. Indeed, at the extremes of the unitary continuum, transformation of one's life becomes almost inevitable. We know of no mystic, properly so called, who attained the levels of either cosmic consciousness or absolute unitary being, whose view of himself and the world was not radically transformed. But more ordinary religious experiences, and even extremely intense aesthetic experiences, can often catalyze self-transformation to more desirable alignments of one's self to the cosmos.

OTHER ACTIVITIES PERCEIVED AS RELIGIOUS

One final point regarding the neuropsychological basis of religion and ritual is that there are many activities that may be perceived as more or less religious or having a religious flavor. This is particularly the case since such activities likely utilize the neurophysiological mechanisms that are manifested most strongly in either the first or second aspects of religion just described. That is, insofar as a human activity exerts control over the physical environment or involves the union of the self with other persons or things, such an activity can be perceived as having a religious flavor or even as being strongly although not essentially religious. Sports, politics, science, or almost any human activity that utilizes the mechanisms either of control of the environment or of imposing relative unity over multiplicity can be considered religious under certain circumstances.

Furthermore, any activity, whether or not it involves control of the physical environment or the theme of unity, can be perceived as religious if it is perceived as contributing to humanity's fundamental sense of well-being. This is because religion, in either its first or its second manifestation, is paradigmatic in this regard. Indeed, as King pointed out in his definition of religion, all religion tends to fulfill the fundamental needs of an individual as often defined by the culture in an absolute or transcendent way. Since this fundamental need-fulfillment role is essential to religion, any activity that participates in satisfying fundamental needs can be seen as participating in the religious paradigm.

Chapter Nine

Neurotheology

REFRAMING THEOLOGY FROM A NEUROPHYSIOLOGICAL PERSPECTIVE

We have now described how many mystical and religious experiences might be related to the function of various brain structures, both individually and together. This has led to a model that explains how meditation occurs and why it and other mystical experiences have such profound impacts on those who experience them. We have also seen how neuropsychology can help explain the development of religion. Therefore, neurophysiology not only is useful for describing mystical and religious phenomena but also has a significant relationship to the development of theology. In this chapter, we will consider in detail how various aspects of neurophysiology and neuropsychology manifest themselves in theology. In particular, we will examine how the cognitive imperative, the cognitive operators, and our model of mystical experiences relate to theology. It is important to mention that we will not consider any specific theological constructs in detail, but rather will explore how general concepts in theology may be derived from an analysis of neurophysiology. This approach will lead to the development of a metatheology that does not have specific theological content, but explains the essential components of any specific theology.

A REASON FOR THEOLOGY

To begin with, neurophysiology helps explain why theology exists at all. In its most general definition, theology is a deductively reasoned analysis applied to some foundational myth of a given religion or culture. In particular, theology can be approached in a number of ways. It must always begin, however, with a foundational myth, and then, from that, theology derives various concepts and conclusions based on rational thought processes. One might wonder why human beings create theology in the first place. For this answer, we turn to the notion of the cognitive imperative. We proposed this concept early in this book and described it as the ingrained need in human beings to organize their world cognitively. This need is applied to both internal and external stimuli from the world. From the evolutionary perspective, the cognitive imperative seems adaptive for *Homo sapiens* since it is human cognition that has proved an invaluable tool for finding food, avoiding dangers, constructing shelters, and surviving in general. But if the cognitive imperative is applied to whatever things are experienced in the world, it is also applied to religion and God. In other words, the cognitive imperative is an absolutely general function of the human mind/brain.

Thus, human beings seem destined to use their rational mind/brain to wonder about God and the mysteries of religion. Whatever myths arise regarding God or some other power source, and however irrational such myths may be, nevertheless, these myths can be considered rationally and conclusions can be derived from them. In fact, once there exists a foundational myth that includes a power source, then the cognitive imperative, which created the myth in the first place, necessarily begins to analyze the myth rationally. Cognitive operators such as the causal and holistic operator are then brought to bear on that myth.

THE COGNITIVE OPERATORS AND THEOLOGY

We can now turn to an analysis of theology and theological constructs from a neurophysiological perspective. In particular, theological concepts can now be interpreted based on the specific operators that might be manifesting themselves either singly or in combination with others. Thus, in the remainder of this chapter, we will use the notion of cognitive operators to help explain the development of various theological concepts.

We mentioned in the beginning that theology concerns itself with that which is ultimate. Thus, it certainly seems appropriate that theology should involve some supernatural power being that is considered to be the ultimate cause of the universe (if derived from the causal operator) or the ultimate unity of the universe (if derived from the holistic operator). We would argue, however, that the driving force behind this desire to seek out ultimate things is based partly on the cognitive imperative and partly on the experience of the absolute functioning of various operators on all of reality. In fact, whenever there is a total functioning of the operators, we derive some sense of the ultimate, since when an operator is functioning exclusively, no other analysis of the external world can occur. The entire world is a manifestation of that operator. Since the conditions that exist within which an operator can maintain absolute function require unusual activity of the arousal and quiescent systems, there is usually a strong affective content to these experiences. After these experiences, the cognitive imperative again takes over such that we have the burning desire to understand what the experience actually represented. Thus, there is a strong emotional drive to explore the ultimate since these are perhaps the most emotional states that can be achieved. Furthermore, the drive is derived from the strong evolutionary selection for the cognitive imperative.

Indeed, we have proposed that the sense of what underlying reality "really is" in various philosophies, and derivatively in various theologies, originates in a sudden flash of insight in a thinker. We maintain that the flash of insight arises from total deafferentation of any given cognitive operator. We suspect the sequence of events is something like the following: The philosopher or theologian thinks very intensely in a particular way. Let us say that the person is thinking, almost meditating, about how things are caused. The intensity of this use of the causal operator eventually may produce total deafferentation of the causal operator. Suddenly, our thinker experiences a profound sense of all of reality as cause and effect. This sensation is not yet a philosophical concept. It is infinitely more powerful than a concept. It is the profound sense that one has had a glimpse into the ultimate and that, in this case, it is cause and effect. After our philosopher's or theologian's flash of insight (when he or she recovers from the total deafferentation of the causal operator, in this case), he or she develops philosophical or theological concepts, derived from the experience. The philosopher or theologian then goes about constructing a logical system in the firm certainty that he or she has fundamentally comprehended what is "real." Of course, as we shall see, this can happen with any cognitive operator, generating diverse ultimate realities and diverse philosophies and theologies.

Now that we have gained insight into why humans are driven to seek out the ultimate, various problems in theology can be reframed in terms of the function of the mind/brain. Since we have already described theology as a rational deduction from a foundational myth, we must consider how this rational deduction arises. Rather than selecting specific theological concepts and describing them from a neurophysiological perspective, we will examine each of the cognitive operators individually to determine how theological concepts, in general, might be derived. Further, the derivation of various theological concepts seems to arise from the absolute function of a number of cognitive operators. Specifically, the implication is that, at any given time, only one of the operators functions, and it appears to function on all of reality. In order for this event to happen from the neurophysiological perspective, the structures of the brain that underlie any given operator have to be deafferented from the rest of the brain. This deafferentation has already been described in the chapter regarding the neurophysiological model of meditation in which the orientation association area is totally deafferented. We have proposed, however, that other operators and association areas may also be deafferented, leading to the ultimate development of various fundamental perceptions of reality and concepts about reality based on those perceptions. In terms of overall theological constructs, there likely needs to be some degree of absolute functioning of an operator to generate a profound sense of the underlying nature or reality and consequent ideas about the ultimate. Many "lesser" theological derivations may require lesser degrees of deafferention (i.e., partial) of a given operator, thus focusing its function on a smaller strip of reality. Lesser theological concepts may also result from the combination of the function of two or more operators. Either way, these operators must eventually be brought to bear on the foundational myth for theology to arise. For the purposes of this book, we will focus primarily on the absolute functioning of the operators and, thus, on more general or universal theological issues.

THE HOLISTIC OPERATOR

The holistic operator has already been related to the notion of the experience of deity with the subsequent development of a concept of God. This operator is fundamentally important, since it continually forces theology to account for God's omnipresence, omniscience, and ability to bind together and maintain the entire universe. Thus, any serious consideration of the implications of the absolute functioning of the holistic operator necessitates, at least, considering the expansion of any foundational myth to apply to all of reality, including other people, other cultures, other animals, and even other planets and galaxies. In fact, as human knowledge of the extent of the universe has evolved, the notion of God has evolved to incorporate the expanding sense of the totality of the universe. The holistic operator requires that whatever new reaches of the universe astronomers can find, God must be there. No matter how small and unpredictable a subatomic particle might be, God must be there, too.

The developments of science in the twentieth century, therefore, have been particularly difficult for continuing to invoke the holistic operator with regard to the concept of God. This difficulty arises not so much because of the problem in explaining how God might actually maintain a holistic nature, but because human beings are necessarily limited in their cognitive understanding of infinity. We can state that something is absolutely holistic or that it is infinite, but we cannot cognitively comprehend these constructs. The mystical literature of all traditions acknowledges that absolute unitary being cannot be described cognitively. In fact, the true mystic will maintain that it is impossible to experience this state humanly (especially since in these states, there theoretically is no discrete existence that allows for human experience). Thus, even though such a state may be attained through meditation or related practices, the experience is so ineffable as to defy any real human understanding. Unfortunately, for the theologian, this mystical notion of absolute unitary being (AUB) must be incorporated and maintained within the foundational myth if the foundational myth is to be experienced as valid. Any rational deductions derived from this myth must keep in mind the function of the holistic operator.

That the holistic operator must be taken into account when evaluating foundational myths is never more apparent than in the Christian concept of the Trinity consisting of the Father, Son, and Holy Spirit. Christian thought has generated great effort to maintain the notion of the Trinity in the face of the holistic need of God's being an absolute unity. Thus, the three components of the Trinity are traditionally understood to be discrete as regards *persons* (rational subjectivities), but all are said to possess the same, single, and absolutely undifferentiated divine nature. Attempts to explain this seeming contradiction have included each person eternally and perfectly proceeding from the others as well as each person being eternally and perfectly immanent in the others. But there is always that perfectly undifferentiated divine nature that prevents the Trinity from deflating into tritheism. Rationally, this lack of differentiation presents immense problems in terms of how the trinity and the wholeness of God can be juxtaposed. It is particularly the holistic operator, however, that has, in some sense, forced the issue and made the situation far more complex (in terms of human understanding) than perhaps it would have been without the holistic operator.

There is one other important point to be made regarding the holistic operator and our neurophysiological approach to mystical and theological concepts. It is interesting to note that many religions seem to exclude the possibility of other religions. One may wonder why this should be the case. We have often considered that if God is truly infinite, then God should have infinite manifestations. Why, then, should any particular version of God be set completely apart and exclusive of any other version? We have described earlier that ritual in religion tends to lead to the development of a group cohesiveness that excludes others not in the group. Even as one proceeds upward along the unitary continuum, it seems that some of the highest unitary states manifested in practitioners of a given tradition still maintain a certain degree of exclusivity.

Absolute unitary being itself cannot have exclusivity because of its infinite and undifferentiated unity. The question then is, Can slightly lesser unitary states be exclusive? A neuropsychological analysis of this question would suggest that the highest unitary states short of AUB can, in fact, be exclusive. When one considers the underlying neurophysiology, the only way to achieve AUB is to totally deafferent the orientation association area. This is really the last step of the model, although there are other areas that are deafferented and activated simultaneously. If an individual falls just short of AUB, then one would expect that there is incomplete deaffereniation of the orientation association area even though the person may feel totally absorbed into the given focus of the meditation (i.e., God, Christ, and so on). Because there is still some input to the orientation association area, specifically from the area of the brain concentrating on the given object of focus, there is the generation of a sense of everything being one with that object. This state is one of total absorption into that object, but it is not a state of universal absorption. Thus, the entire universe is perceived to be that object to the exclusion of all other things, since anything other than that object must be a part of that object or must not exist in reality. If something were to exist in reality outside of the object of focus, it would present an irreconcilable paradox. The resolution of that paradox is that the abnormal object is really part of the object of focus even though it does not seem so. Therefore, any notion of Christ, Brahma, God, or Allah that results in a total absorption into that object necessarily excludes all other interpretations. If, however, the person were able to go one step further to AUB, then there can be no exclusivity and all things can be considered to be inclusive. Certainly, the problem of exclusivity is prevalent throughout theologies. All religions must somehow come to terms with the existence of other religions. This neuropsychological approach may help show a method by which the problem can be solved or at least explained. Further, knowledge of the neurophysiological necessity for exclusivity may help our overall understanding of the conflictual nature of religions.

THE REDUCTIONIST OPERATOR

The antithesis of the holistic operator is the reductionist operator. The absolute functioning of the reductionist operator on all of reality leads to a primary intuition and existential sense that the whole is made up of the sum total of the parts. Of course, this sense of underlying reality quickly develops into the theological/philosophical concept that the whole is composed of, and only of, the sum of the parts. When applied to the foundational myths of the monotheistic religions, the result is the notion that God is actually the totality of all of the parts of the universe. This is akin to the concept of pantheism in which God is considered to be the universe. Clearly, it seems that the absolute function of the reductionist operator would not lead to the notion of a transcendent God.

Certainly, the notion of divine transcendency has garnered its share of theological literature. The absolute functioning of the reductionist operator necessarily contradicts the notions derived from the holistic operator, however. In fact, it seems that the absolute functioning of the holistic operator usually takes precedence over the absolute functioning of any other operator such that all of the parts previously perceived as being discrete are now considered to be one. Thus, in its absolute functioning, the holistic operator actually combines both the reductionist and the holistic functions of the mind/brain.

There may be another application of the reductionist operator that is in the scientific realm. It seems that the reductionist operator underlies the general process of science in which a given object is broken down into its component parts in order to learn what it is and how it works. In terms of a scientific methodology, this reductionist approach clearly has its benefits for providing an accurate analysis of material reality. For science to occur, it is important that a small, clearly defined object is studied to eliminate the possibility of confounding factors. Thus, science often strives to isolate a given part of reality, and it is here that the reductionist operator functions at its best—on a small piece of reality that is irreducible. Recent scientific thought has realized the limitations of such an approach, however, and has sought new avenues for understanding wholes rather than parts. The fields of cosmology and ecology have been particularly interested in the holistic understanding of the universe. Emerging disciplines such as chaos theory allow for the development of models that take into consideration the whole rather than the parts. More practically, holistic medicine has become popular as a total approach to health of the mind and body. Where this exploration of the parts and the wholes will end is difficult to determine. Certainly, science has recently made great strides in combining the holistic and reductionist operators, but science is just begining to realize the importance of looking at the whole in addition to the parts.

THE QUANTITATIVE OPERATOR

The quantitative operator functions to quantify various objects in the external world. If this operator is applied to the totality of objects, the result is the notion that mathematics underlies all things. Similar to the reductionist operator, the quantitative operator clearly both underlies and supports science and the scientific method. Science essentially is based on a mathematical description of the universe. This notion is particularly true when one considers the fields of quantum mechanics and particle physics. Both of these fields attempt to discover the fundamental nature of the universe using highly complex mathematical models. In terms of philosophical and theological implications, the quantitative operator appears to have heavily influenced the ideas of Baruch Spinoza, who often used mathematical concepts such as geometry to help explain the nature of God and the universe.[1] Further, religions throughout history have placed strong emphasis on a certain magic inherent in numbers and mathematics, partially out of the need for control over the environment that we described earlier as being a major facet of religion. Primitive religions certainly relied heavily on mathematical concepts in their interaction with their gods. Numbers abound in the Bible and lend their significance in terms of time, people, and places. Various numerologies in the folk practices of Christianity and Islam as well as the Gematryiah in Judaism all bear witness to the powerful force of the quantitative operator to impress the mind with the "mysticism" of numbers. For example, the number 18 in Hebrew represents the symbol for life.

It seems that the quantitative operator has played a major role in religion. When applied to God and broader theological concepts, however, the quantitative operator appears to have its shortcomings. The quantitative operator appears to be too narrowly focused to allow for the more holistic and, certainly, the more emotional aspects of God. This consideration is evident in the thinking of many scientists such as Albert Einstein, who have been concerned that too much dependence on mathematics tends to lead one away from how God is immediately manifested in the universe.

THE BINARY OPERATOR

We have already considered the significance of the binary operator in the formation of myth structure. This operator is clearly important for theology as well. The opposites that are set by the binary operator allow for the concepts of good and evil, justice and injustice, and man and God, among many more. Many of these polarities are encountered throughout religious texts of all religions. Much of the purpose of religions and their myths is to solve the psychological and existential problems created by these opposites. Theology, then, must evaluate the myth structures and determine where the opposites are and how well the problems presented by these opposites are solved by the myth structure. In particular, this concept, similar to the Hegelian triadic concept of thesis, antithesis, and synthesis, is crucial to the development of theology, because it is ultimately the foundational myth, and specifically the power of God, that brings together the problematic opposites.

THE CAUSAL OPERATOR

The causal operator is also crucial to theology. We have described how the causal operator functions to try to find the cause for any given strip of reality.

When applied to all of reality, it forces the question of what is the ultimate cause of all things. This question eventually leads to the classic notion of an uncaused first cause. For montheistic religions, the foundational myths posit that God is the cause of all things (i.e., is the uncaused first cause). This very question of how something can be uncaused is a most perplexing problem for human thought, and in fact, theologians and philosophers alike have tangled with causality as integral to understanding the universe and God. Aristotelian philosophy postulated four aspects of causality: efficient causality, material causality, formal causality, and final causality. These notions of causality led to the understanding of a metaphysic that would later be integrated into traditional Christian theology. The question of causality thus became applied to God to determine how, in fact, God could cause the universe.

The problem of causality in the world leads to many other related theological issues, foremost among them the notion of free will, which relies heavily on causality. The issue revolves around who or what is causing things. If someone can be considered the cause of a given sequence of reality, then they can be accountable for that sequence. If the cause of a sequence of reality lies beyond that sequence, then a person within that sequence cannot be responsible. Whether or not causality exists within a given sequence of a people's reality is what determines if they have free will. Therefore, causality within a sequence of reality allows for free will, while causality that exists external to a given sequence leads to determinism.

Free will is of particular interest to Christian theology, but clearly it is important in other religions. Free will is a necessary part of Christianity's foundational myth particularly with regards to the notion of sin, in particular, original sin. Free will must be maintained in order for someone to be responsible for committing a sin. If everything is predetermined, then a sinful act cannot be ascribed to the person committing that act, since he had no choice. If the person freely chooses to commit a sin, then he can be held accountable for that sin. Free will is also the sine qua non of ethics. In order for ethics to be viable, free will has to exist. Thus, the notion of causality in relationship to free will becomes an important issue within theology.

Eastern traditions have a slightly different perspective in terms of causality. The Buddhist and Hindu ideologies concede true causality only for the realm of the absolute unitary being (i.e., only through the absolute function of the holistic operator). The individual ego and material reality are seen more or less as an illusion, with AUB being the true reality. Causality, as well as free will, exist only on the level of AUB and do not apply to material reality or the human ego. This restriction still presents a problem, however, with the issue of practical ethics and the accountability of individuals. These traditions suggest that once AUB is attained, there is a natural flow of right behavior that derives from it and that this type of behavior is what constitutes ethics. In such a system, the only way to gain a true understanding of right and wrong, free will and determinism, is by attaining AUB.

THE ABSTRACTIVE OPERATOR

The abstractive operator is tied into the brain structures that underlie the verbal-conceptual association area. As we have described earlier, the abstractive operator creates general concepts from a larger group of objects. Thus, oak, pine, willow, and maple are grouped into the abstract category of "tree." In some senses, this operator functions to derive the essential characteristics of whatever types of objects it is working on. In other words, this operator presents us with a sense of "thingness" or "being" because it generates the basic components of any object and reifies that object as a particular thing. Going back to the example of the different trees, each of them is grouped into the category "tree" by virtue of their characteristics that define them as a tree—namely, they all have a trunk, roots, and leaves.

As with the other operators, we can consider what would happen if the abstractive operator functioned in an absolute way, not just on a particular set of objects, but on the set of all objects in the universe. The basic element derived would be conceptual or abstract "thingness" as opposed to the concrete "thingness" implied by the reductionist operator. The "conceptual thingness" of the totality of reality is akin to the Greek concept of being, either in the Platonic or in the Aristotelian sense. It is the formal and organizing element indwelling matter and giving matter meaning. Thus, the total functioning of the abstractive operator gives a profound sense that reality is fundamentally pure being, having the same relationship to gross matter as the pure concept "tree" has to the billions of concrete trees in the world. From this profound sense soon arises philosophical/theological concepts such as Plato's the good, Aristotle's hylomorphism, Thomas Aquinas's essences, or Paul Tillich's "ground of being" as a description of God. This "ground substance of being" could be attributed to God. Certainly, the foundational myths of the Western religions imply that God is not only the creator of all things in the universe, but continues to give substance and existence to all things all the time. Theology must then be forced to explain how God can be the ground substance of all being while performing other roles stipulated in the foundational myths. Certainly, the issue of whether God constantly supports existence or simply wound up the clock and lets things work out on their own lies at the heart of important theological controversies. It seems, however, that the notion of God as the ultimate being and supporting all of existence would be a natural consequence of the absolute functioning of the abstractive operator.

THE EMOTIONAL VALUE OPERATOR

The remaining operator—the emotional value operator—is the only one that refers not to cognition but rather to emotion. This operator imparts emotional values to whatever is presented within our experience. If this operator functions in an absolute way, it applies its value function upon the totality of the universe. The result might be that the entire universe is related only to an emotional response. Thus, all of existence is simply felt rather than cognized.

Although the absolute function of the emotional value operator theoretically generates all emotions simultaneously, this may not be experienced as such a chaotic display of affect. More likely, a person will interpret the absolute functioning of the emotional value operator in one of three ways—positive, neutral, or negative.

If there is a positive interpretation, then the result is that the entire universe appears to be an overwhelmingly beautiful, blissful, and loving place. When applied to mystical states such as AUB, as we have mentioned earlier, the experience is perceived (after the fact) in a personal manner such that the person has become one with God or some form of a divine being. When applied to the concepts of theology, God is the primary driver for this overwhelmingly positive affect that pervades the universe, and therefore God is essentially pure love and benevolence. This notion immediately presents large theological problems, however, since the pain and suffering that exist in the world must somehow be explained in light of the overwhelming love of God. In other words, we are left with the chronic question, If God is ultimate love, then how can God allow all the suffering that occurs? This question clearly has been a very difficult one for all religions to address.

If the absolute function of the emotional value operator is perceived as neutral, then all is considered to be impersonal. In terms of mystical experiences (as described earlier), this neutral affect likely is associated with void consciousness or Nirvana in which there is an empty, impersonal consciousness that lies at the foundation of the universe. When the neutral affect is applied to theological or philosophical concepts, it may underlie the notions elaborated upon in existentialism. Existentialism is based on the notion that all we can do is exist and "feel" our way through. Other than our emotional sense, we can get at no other understanding of that reality. From a theological perspective, the conclusions drawn from the neutral interpretation suggest that God is impersonal or perhaps that there is no God at all and everything simply is without purpose or even meaning. Although this existential approach is antithetical to most theistic religions, theology must contend with the possibility of an existential universe.

The final interpretation of the absolute functioning of the emotional value operator is a negative one. The result is that the entire universe is viewed as intrinsically evil and horrible. There are very few examples of absolute negative emotions in the mystical literature. AUB itself has rarely, if ever, been associated with a negative affect. Indeed, anecdotal reports have suggested that such a state is impossible to attain while maintaining normal life functions, which suggests in turn that a negative state of AUB may actually be incompatible with life. While there is no solid documentation of this bizarre notion, there are occasional rumors and anecdotal reports of mystical sects that try to achieve such a state. Whether they truly exist remains unknown. The negative interpretation applied to theology may be responsible for the notion of hell in which all of existence becomes horrible and terrifying. In Judeo-Christian theology, though, it becomes difficult to explain how such a negative existence can be maintained alongside the generally positive image of God.

One can begin to see the interplay between the various interpretations of the absolute functioning of the emotional value operator. With the help of the binary operator, it may be that the positive and negative aspects of God are combined in theology as presented in the battle between good and evil. Further, it is dyadic concepts such as original sin and redemption through the love of Christ that bring these two opposing forces to some resolution. Good and evil are similarly considered in other religions with the resolution ultimately being derived from the interaction of human beings with God or some other power source.

THE ATTENTION ASSOCIATION AREA

There remain two other parts of the brain whose absolute functioning may bear on mystical and theological concepts. These are the attention association area and the orientation association area. If the attention association area functions in an absolute manner on all of reality, it would likely generate a sense that everything is derived from intention or will. This is similar to the concepts elaborated upon by Arthur Schopenhauer in *The World as Will and Idea*.[2] In this work, he presents the notion of will as the striving from which all things are derived. Schopenhauer goes further, however, in describing that with increased will, there is increased suffering. This ultimately explains why there is so much human suffering, because human beings are endowed with an enormous amount of will.

The notion that the entire universe is derived from will also leads to several theological implications. Certainly, the will of God has a prominent place in Western religion. God used will to create the universe and to carry out all divine actions. Thus, it could be argued that will is the driving force of the universe, only in religion, it is God's will. That human beings have a part of the universal will also leads to an analysis of free will. Schopenhauer actually addresses this issue and argues that will does act with freedom. However, it is only our conscious analysis of our actions that leads to the conclusion a posteriori that there is no free will. The point of this description of the absolute functioning of the attention association area is to indicate that it leads to certain concepts that are an integral part of theology, particularly when considering the will of God and free will.

THE ORIENTATION ASSOCIATION AREA

The final structure whose absolute function we will consider is the orientation association area. We have already taken into account in our model of meditation that the orientation association area is involved in generating the sense of no time or infinite time and no space or infinite space. When the absolute functioning of this area is related to the external universe and God, it leads to several more theological concepts. In terms of time, the orientation association area can generate the sense of eternity or timelessness that is often considered to be a characteristic of God. This has particular relevance in terms of free will, since God's ability to exist in an eternal realm allows for God to have knowledge of all things even "prior" to their occurrence in the physical universe. Despite the fact that the universe is known by God to unfold in a certain manner, physical reality still preserves free will because God's knowledge of the universe is, in some sense, outside of time. Similarly, God can be thought of as being spaceless even though God can be manifested also in the space that exists within material reality. Thus, the orientation association area can be useful in generating certain theological concepts related to time and space.

BEYOND NEUROTHEOLOGY

We undertook this somewhat lengthy analysis of the absolute functioning of cognitive operators and association areas to show how an understanding of neuropsychology and neurophysiology can lead to theological concepts, and undoubtedly has led to theological concepts arising from the experiences of mystics and mystically oriented theologians. Although one could take any theological issue and break it down to its various neuropsychological components, we felt it would be more useful to build some of the basic concepts of all theologies from the operators up. We feel certain, however, that any specific theological idea may eventually be reducible to neuropsychological functions. Lest this idea be considered overreductionistic, we would point out that the overall models presented in this book suggest just such a reductionism. This reductionism applies not only to theology but to ritual, religion, and mysticism, as well as to baseline reality. We are still left with the problem that, based on such an analysis, all of reality, including the analysis itself, can be similarly broken down. As we shall see in the next chapters, we do not feel in any way that a neuropsychological analysis of theology or mysticism alters their true spiritual and possibly transcendent nature. It merely indicates how human beings *perceive* these phenomena. Furthermore, as we shall soon describe, the entire approach of using neurophysiology to explain religious and mystical phenomena can be turned around. This can also lead to neurotheology as a metatheology and even a megatheology. We will leave that for the next chapters, however.

Chapter Ten

Consciousness and Reality

We are now almost ready to see how neurotheology can generate a metatheology and a megatheology. By metatheology, we mean the most overarching approach to fundamental reality comprising the general principles that regulate and constrain the construction of any and all concrete specific theologies. In this sense, a metatheology is devoid of all theological content (although not of neuropsychological content) in that it describes how any theology, regardless of its content, must be structured.

By megatheology, we mean the most overarching theological content available in terms of current knowledge. Such general and basic theological content, derived from neurotheology, is what we have called megatheology. Megatheology can serve as a basis for a new and more universal specific theology by which human beings may guide their lives. Or, because of its generality, it may serve as a fundamental elaboration of most, if not all, of the existing specific theologies of the world's great religions.

The generation of a metatheology and a megatheology seems to be a heavy task to place upon neurotheology. Nevertheless, we are firmly convinced that neurotheology is clearly the best and most effective approach to attacking the problems of a metatheology and a megatheology. We hope to demonstrate the basis for this conviction in the next chapter. But before we can do so, it is essential that we consider, in some detail, first, the relationship of consciousness to external reality and, second, what the concept of "reality" can possibly mean. Once we have considered these ancient philosophical problems within the context of neurotheology, we will be equipped to consider seriously the problems of a metatheology and a megatheology.

CONSCIOUSNESS, THE MIND/BRAIN,
AND EXTERNAL REALITY

The relationship of consciousness to the mind/brain is anything but clear. Therefore, to understand the problems of consciousness, it is first necessary to understand the problems that consciousness poses in general, and particularly how it may relate to any physical reality. To an adult human being with a normally functioning mind/brain, reality, at first pass, seems to be composed of two vividly real categories. The first is the conscious self and the second is external reality composed of things that appear to have an inherent reality separate from the conscious self. The things in external reality also appear to be represented in, or known by, the conscious self. Thus, the classical philosophical problem of subjectivity versus objectivity is only a problem because the mind/brain, under ordinary conditions, insists on processing reality in this manner. To the naive observer, there is an absolutely certain sense that there is a reality external to the self that appears to be characterized by a heavy, substantive reality often termed *matter* or *material* reality. The naive observer also has the absolutely certain sense of a conscious self that seems to have a light, changeable, and ethereal quality often termed *mind, spirit,* or sometimes *soul.* The naive terminology is anything but exact.

These two senses of reality are so vivid and appear so real that early philosophy did not seriously question the fundamental nature of this duality. For the first thousand years of its existence in the West, philosophy began its work by concentrating primarily on the substantiality of reality. This was the heyday of ontology. Beginning with René Descartes, followed by the radical empiricism of Bishop George Berkeley, among the British empiricists, and with Immanuel Kant, on the Continent, the shift to the emphasis on the mind as the philosophical starting point and on how we can "know" external reality, or anything at all for that manner, began. Since the seventeenth century, therefore, we have seen the dominance of epistemology with its emphasis on how we know, and in its extreme manifestation, with the assertion that all reality is mind. At first, modern science entered in on the side of the old ontology, naively assuming the existence of external reality as represented in consciousness. Since the beginning of the twentieth century, and particularly since the development of quantum theory, science finds itself caught between ontology and epistemology, with old certainties vanishing like smoke. Bertrand Russell expressed the state of this confusion manifested in the conversation around his childhood dinner table. His parents apparently were given to discussing the nature of reality. The joke was, "Is reality mind? No matter! Is reality matter? Never mind!"

As just noted, the problem of the relationship of subjective awareness to external material reality began to achieve a modern focus with Descartes's clear and unabashed dualism. Descartes saw the mind as a subjective awareness that contained ideas either corresponding or sometimes not corresponding to what was actually in the external world. For Descartes, the mind ordinarily represented the world in a one-to-one correspondence except for the occasional glitches that generated error.[1] This view of the mind as representational of the external world reached its apogee in the work of Franz Brentano. According to Brentano, all states of awareness are *of* or *about* something. For Brentano, mental states must necessarily have "reference to a content" or "direction toward an object," a characteristic of mental states he called "intentionality."[2] This vivid directedness or intentionality was, for Brentano, the defining characteristic of the mind.

Edmund Husserl, often called the father of phenomenology, was one of Brentano's students. Husserl began his work trying to develop a specific procedure for examining the structure of intentionality, which, of course, was the structure of experience itself, without making any reference whatsoever to a factual empirical world and especially without any assumption of its actual existence. This rigid formal procedure he called *epoché* or "bracketing," for it required that one bracket, or suspend belief in, one's ordinary judgments about the relation between experience and the world "out there." Husserl maintained that these ordinary judgments, which must be temporarily suspended or bracketed, represent a "natural attitude." When this natural attitude is raised to the level of a philosophical school, it is called "naive realism." By bracketing what he came to see as the "hypothesis of the natural attitude," Husserl attempted to study the intentional contents of the mind purely internally, that is, without tracing them back to what they *seemed* to refer to in the external world. By this approach, he claimed to present a new domain of knowledge that was absolutely prior to any empirical science. Starting with pure experience, and eschewing all assumptions implicit or explicit about the nature of reality, Husserl embarked upon a sort of philosophical introspection which he called *Wesenschau* or "intuition of essences." By this process, Husserl attempted to reduce experience to essential structures and then demonstrate how our human world was generated from them.[3] We can now see how far Husserl's rigorous approach to subjective awareness eventually led him from Descartes's and Brentano's mental representationalism.[4] Husserl's rigorous phenomenological approach had put an independent isomorphic external world on very shaky ground, indeed.

Expanding upon the work of Husserl, Maurice Merleau-Ponty recognized the enormity of the problem for both science and philosophy of trying to meaningfully relate subjective awareness to the vivid sense of external reality or to the sense of world. In his *Phenomenology of Perception,* Merleau-Ponty wrote, "The world is inseparable from the subject, but from a subject which is nothing but a project of the world, and the subject is inseparable from the world, but from a world which the subject itself projects."[5] Merleau-Ponty recognized the need for a bridge between self and world, between the apparent inner and the apparent outer. Unfortunately, his astuteness in defining the problem was not matched by his ability to solve it.

If we add to all of this rigorously derived confusion the current ferment among cognitive scientists of various persuasions, mutually attacking each other and rushing off to write books claiming to explain consciousness based on the most recent blips on an oscilloscope or on the most recent positron emission tomography or functional magnetic resonance imaging studies of the brain, we can begin to understand the chaos surrounding the relationship of subjective awareness to external material reality. It is probably the most important general scientific and philosophical problem of our time.

It has been suggested that if philosophy begins with the reality of external existence, it can never adequately explain the development of consciousness. And if philosophy begins with consciousness, it can never adequately explain the development of external reality. Let us consider these two approaches separately to see if we can develop a reasonably integrated approach, to the consciousness/brain problem.

EXTERNAL REALITY AS PRIMARY

If external reality is accepted as primary, the question we must answer is, How is consciousness generated by the mind/brain and nervous system and how can this phenomenon be understood in an evolutionary context?

We must realize that neuropsychology up to the present, and parallel to Brentano's philosophy, has always understood consciousness to refer to consciousness of something. That pure consciousness, devoid of content, might exist has generally not even been entertained as a problem in science. Therefore, there has been little attempt at understanding the physical basis of pure consciousness. We will return to the issue of pure consciousness below. First, let us consider the basic and classical neuropsychological problem of how consciousness of anything is possible. Here we are using consciousness in its very simplest sense of awareness. We do not mean consciousness of self, or how the self comes to be conscious. In other words, we are not referring to the reflexive self-consciousness of which human beings are capable. In this context, we are simply referring to consciousness as subjective awareness, whether in lower animals or in human beings.

To this point, we have been using the words *consciousness* and *awareness* interchangeably in a naive sense. We must now define these concepts more carefully and use them more precisely:

We define *subjective awareness* as any and all mental content that inheres in a subject, excepting only a reified sense of self.

We define *consciousness* as any and all mental elements that inhere in a subject, one of which elements is a reified sense of self.

Strictly speaking, consciousness involves the generation of a self as an element in subjective awareness. We have proposed that the mind/brain becomes aware of a certain set of sensory input that ultimately arises from the body or from the body's interaction with the external world. In other words, the mind/brain perceives its multiple activities and organizes them into a reified category that we call the self. Considered evolutionarily, such a process becomes possible only with the evolution of the inferior parietal lobule and its interconnections with various sensory association areas. These structures are known to underlie the reification of classes of objects generating abstract categories. If they indeed do so, then the neuroanatomical requirements of "selfhood" must restrict the clear sense of self to higher primates, and especially to the *Homo* lineage. There is, in fact, good evidence that this is so. For example, only higher primates respond to their image in a mirror as if it were a representation of themselves. All other animals apparently perceive another beast.

Finally, the inferior parietal lobule and interconnected sensory association areas can operate on, and reify, the self perceiving the self, generating what has been called "reflexive consciousness." It is generally thought that reflexive consciousness is only a property of *Homo sapiens*. This is still an open question, however, and some anthropoid apes may possess it.

Having more carefully defined our terms, we must note that we are more concerned in this chapter with the implications of simple subjective awareness common, to one degree or another, to all sentient creatures, than we are with the evolution of consciousness of "self" and of reflexive consciousness.

Perhaps the biggest problem currently faced by neurophysiologists and neuropsychologists is how recognition or awareness of sensory input comes about. This has come to be known as the "binding" problem. It is known that the mind/brain breaks down sensory input into many constituent parts. These constituent parts are analyzed and physically stored in different brain structures. Within each sensory modality, the specific identifying elements or "recognition features" are stored in physically different locations within the brain's association areas for that modality. For recognition of a sensory input, it is necessary to somehow bring together at least the essential recognition features both within a given sensory modality and then across modalities. One can see the magnitude of the problem when one realizes that any given sensory input is broken down according to the various sensory components—

visual, auditory, tactile, and possibly olfactory and gustatory as well. Each of these elements of the sensory input is then divided into many recognition features that are physically stored separately. Most neuroscientists agree that the binding of these disparate elements to match new sensory input, generating recognition, is a temporal and not a spatial phenomenon. In other words, the various recognition features stored physically apart are probably not reassembled in one place in the brain, like a mosaic, to form a picture, which is then compared with input, thus generating recognition. Rather, it seems that all of the relevant features are somehow activated where they are stored at precisely the same time. It is this temporal binding of recognition features that apparently underlies conscious awareness and recognition.

At New York University, Llinas has obtained intriguing evidence regarding how binding is possible.[6] Recent extension of his earlier work indicates that the initial breakdown of recognition features either has already occurred prior to the stimuli reaching the thalamus or else occurs at the thalamic level. The cells in the thalamus that encode each recognition feature send pulses of a certain frequency that generate corresponding pulses in the neurons storing these recognition features throughout the brain. The simultaneous pulses of the same frequency in all the relevant storage areas, even across sensory modalities, somehow result in the binding of these features, resulting in recognition of the incoming material. According to Llinas, just imagining a scene may involve the reverse phenomenon of multiple bits of stored information all beginning to pulse at the same frequency and at the same time, creating an activation of corresponding cells in the thalamus. Thus, awareness and recognition of incoming sensory input, or imagining objects in a scene, all result from a sort of thalamic/cortical dialogue. This model, which would solve much of the binding problem, allowing awareness of our external environment or even of imagined entities, still has many problems and raises many questions. Almost everyone agrees that the amygdalas and hippocampi are somehow involved in the generation of awareness, through their connections with the thalamus, with sensory association areas, and with other cortical regions. The precise role of the amygdala and hippocampus is not yet clear in Llinas's model.

Whatever the ultimate mechanism of binding may be that underlies conscious recognition and imagination, it is becoming clearer that the association areas involved with each sensory modality seem to be somehow responsible for subjective awareness in that modality. The evidence is particularly strong with vision. The phenomenon of "blindsight" is a rare but well-documented pathological condition. It was first described before the beginning of the twentieth century. In this disorder, the primary visual area (the calcarine cortex) is left intact, but there is destruction of most of the visual association areas. Patients claim that they are totally blind. They can, in fact, see nothing, at least consciously. However, such patients can walk through rooms of furniture, through doors, up and down staircases, and even on busy streets without ever bumping into anything or taking unusual chances. In other words, they behave as if they were sighted, but they have no conscious visual awareness of the world around them. There is some evidence that a similar condition may obtain with other sensory modalities when their association areas are destroyed, but when their primary cortical areas are intact. If further evidence bears this out, especially in sensory modalities other than vision, it is reasonable to assume that subjective awareness arose with the evolution of secondary sensory association areas.

The binding problem and the specific function of the sensory association areas are two major research issues that neuropsychologists are currently investigating to obtain an understanding of subjective awareness either of the external world or of imagined gestalts. All of this discussion refers to the mechanisms underlying *awareness of something*.

Over the years, we have become interested in understanding pure consciousness, that is, consciousness devoid of content, sometimes described as a clear and vivid consciousness of nothing, or perhaps of everything at the same time.[7] In preceding chapters, we have described in detail the state of absolute unitary being. AUB is described in the mystical literature of all of the world's great religions, and it has been attested to by modern secular mystics. In AUB, there are no boundaries of discrete beings, no sense of the passage of time, and no sense of the extension of space; moreover, the self-other dichotomy is totally obliterated. In other words, the state consists of an absolute sense of unity without thought, without words, without sensation, and without being sensed to inhere in a subject. We have proposed that total deafferentation of the posterior superior parietal lobule, especially on the right, results in this state. This area of the mind/brain is responsible for the orientation of objects in three-dimensional space. If it is denied of all input as a result of mechanisms generated during profound meditation, it creates a sense of pure space. Since space has subjective reality only if it relates things to each other, the subjective experience is one of total spacelessness or of total perfect unity. It is interesting, as we have noted earlier, that there is evidence that the posterior superior parietal lobule in the left hemisphere may be responsible for the self-other dichotomy. During profound meditation, we have proposed that the posterior superior parietal lobule on both sides is totally deafferented, resulting not only in the sense of absolute space, but in the obliteration of the distinction between self and other.[8]

We described our study of practitioners of Tibetan Buddhism who have meditated on a average of one to three hours per day for the past fifteen years, using the nuclear imaging technique known as single photon emission computed tomography (SPECT).[9] Our pilot study strongly supports the model we have proposed. Thus, it seems that a state of pure consciousness can be achieved in intense meditation by deafferentation of a certain part of the parietal lobe bilaterally.

COMMENTARY ON BEGINNING WITH EXTERNAL REALITY

The problem with everything that we have discussed in this chapter up to this point is that while neurophysiological mechanisms are correlated with awareness and may even be the causes of awareness, they do not explain the stuff of awareness itself. In this regard, Penrose notes:

> If it were not for the puzzling aspects of consciousness that relate to the presence of "awareness," . . . which as yet seem[s] to elude physical description, we should not need to feel tempted to look beyond the standard methods of science for explanation of minds as a feature of the physical behavior of brains. . . . It may well be that in order to accommodate the mystery of the mind, we shall need a broadening of what we presently mean by "science," but I see no reason to make any *clean break* with those methods that have served us so extraordinarily well.[10]

We can certainly agree with Penrose that a clean break with traditional science is neither required nor desirable. But we also strongly agree that a broadening of what is meant by science, perhaps a total realignment toward cognitive science, is required for any systematic study of consciousness or awareness.

If we look at the traditional Aristotelian four types of causality that were considered necessary to explain a phenomenon fully—efficient causality, material causality, formal causality, and final causality—we find that our scientific explanation of awareness satisfies only one of the four requirements, efficient causality. Efficient causality is knowledge of a phenomenon in terms of anterior sequential causes. It is what we ordinarily mean by causality in modern parlance. Material causality is knowledge of the constitutive substance of the phenomenon. Clearly, we do understand what the stuff of awareness actually is. Formal causality is knowledge of a phenomenon in the organization of its constituent parts. Awareness itself has no constituent parts. The contents of awareness are its objects and not part of what it is itself. It would seem that awareness itself is simple and hence has no formal cause. Final causality is a knowledge of things in their purpose or, in modern terminology, in terms of their adaptive function. Although final causality as originally formulated is subject to the critique of teleology, its reformulation as teleonomy has an important function in the philosophy of science.

We come to the biggest problem of all when we begin our analysis with the primacy of external reality. Why should subjective awareness exist at all? If every change in awareness, every change in the contents of awareness, and even the generation of pure awareness itself, are all caused by physical (i.e., neural) events, as we suggest they are, then why should awareness exist? There is no reason why the entire social universe that we know, with every product of our individual endeavors, every product of our social interactions, and, in short, every psychological or cultural product, from science through art and religion, should not be produced by biologically evolved robots that do not possess subjective awareness. In other words, an objective observer from another galaxy could view everything as it is on Earth today, including the appearance of subjective awareness, without there ever having to be any actual subjectivity. The central nervous system is an electrical input/output system of immense complexity. But it is no more than that, or so it would appear. No matter what degree of complexity the nervous system has attained or will attain in the future, this complexity never implies in itself the existence of subjective awareness. It might produce the appearance of subjective awareness to an external observer, but there is no reason why subjective awareness should, in fact, exist. Actually, there is no reasonable hypothesis to explain subjective awareness arising out of an electrical input/output system, no matter what its complexity. The material nature of the causes of awareness and awareness itself, we maintain, are incommensurable, although obviously, awareness depends on its neurophysiological substrate. Again, all this is true only if we begin the philosophical analysis of reality with the primacy of external material reality.

One often hears it said that subjective awareness had to evolve because input becomes so complex in higher animals that awareness is required to process it. But if the material, physical, and neural processing of the mind/brain is not adequate for the job, then are we to believe that subjective awareness comes into being and somehow lifts off its neuroanatomical base, as it were, to perform the required complex analyses, and then presumably settles down again on its physical base? If such a circumstance were to occur, if awareness for even a moment were free of its neurophysiological base, then we would most certainly have the ghost in the machine—we would have demonstrated a substantial soul separate from neurophysiological functioning.

If awareness never lifts off of its neurophysiological base, as indeed we cannot believe it does, then what is the purpose of awareness? All the physical mechanisms underlying awareness are operating to analyze reality and to respond to it. It would seem that subjective awareness is epiphenomenal. Again, why should such an epiphenomenal reality exist at all? We do not claim to have the answer to this question, but we are left with a mystery and a fundamental paradox.

It seems to us that if we start our philosophical analysis with the reality of matter and the external world, then there are fundamentally two great discontinuities in the universe. The first discontinuity is the big bang, or more specifically, why there is something rather than nothing. This is, of course, the question that plagued Martin Heidegger and many philosophers since. The second great discontinuity in the physical universe is the existence of subjective awareness. It simply represents an unexplainable jump from material organization to a level of reality of another order, analogous to the jump from nothing to something. Again, we must keep in mind that all these statements are true only if we assume the primacy of material reality as our philosophical starting point.

Another major problem with assuming the priority of external physical reality is the problem of isomorphism between subjective awareness and the external world. This problem can be summarized by the simple question: How do we know that the world as known to us corresponds in some significant way to the external world? Since we have begun our analysis by acknowledging the priority of external material reality over subjective awareness, and by assuming that subjective awareness evolves from the evolution of physical and biological systems, we can fairly safely assume that some degree of isomorphism between external reality and subjective awareness exists or else the organism simply could not adapt to the world in which it finds itself. But what degree of isomorphism is required for an individual organism to adapt to its environment? The answer simply is not known. Perhaps only a mild to moderate degree of isomorphism is biologically required to select for an organism's perceptual apparatus. There is actually evidence that different species perceive the world in remarkably different ways, but always in a manner conducive to their survival. If such is the case, the assumption of the priority of matter from which subjective awareness evolves can only lead to adaptability as an epistemological inference and never to truth. If the traditional definition of truth as the *adaequatio intellectus ad rem* be taken at all seriously, then truth can be at best an approximation, perhaps a fairly weak one at that.

To this point, we have been considering the pros and cons of an analysis of the world in which external material reality is primary, and subjective awareness is presumed to derive from it. A careful phenomenological analysis can strongly challenge this basic premise, however. Indeed, as Husserl implied, from the point of view of any careful conscious examiner of the world, the only thing that is certain is that all aspects of material reality, including the laws of science and the mind/brain itself, exist within subjective awareness. Whether they have any other substantive reality is an open question, but what is certain is that they exist within awareness. Furthermore, what also exists within subjective awareness is the vivid sense that the external world is substantively real and that matter is something other than consciousness. But this vivid sense likewise exists within awareness or is an aspect of awareness. Thus, it would appear that all the vividness of the reality of the material world is at least a subset of awareness, whatever else that vividness may or may not imply. So let us see what happens to our analysis of the relationship between subjective awareness and external material reality when we give subjective awareness ontological priority.

SUBJECTIVE AWARENESS AS PRIMARY

What are the advantages and disadvantages of starting our analysis of the relationship of subjective awareness to external material reality by granting the primacy to subjective awareness? The greatest advantage is that the problem of explaining the development of subjective awareness evaporates because subjective awareness is the fundamental given matrix that permeates everything. In this case, the problem becomes one of explaining how external material reality comes into being. Thus, it is not a question of subjective awareness arising out of material reality but of material reality in some sense arising out of subjective awareness. From this perspective, all of physical reality exists in present subjective awareness, including the knowing brain, all the laws of science, the compelling sense of the otherness of external material reality, of a past of completed events, and of a future of possible ones. Since all of material reality exists at least in the mind of the analyzing knower, and since one would have to step outside of subjective awareness to ascertain whether any reality other than subjective awareness exists (a patently impossible situation), then one is constrained to see material reality (its past and future), the laws of nature, and science itself as aspects of present subjective awareness. As disagreeable as such an epistemological position might be to those of us trained in Western science, it is the only possible rigorous stance unless one wishes to make a complete act of faith that the vivid sense of the otherness of external reality, which certainly exists in subjective awareness, reflects an isomorphic referent outside of subjective awareness. From a pragmatic point of view, such an act of faith is not so terrible. We all make it almost all the time, and we use it as a basis for our actions. But if one wishes to take a rigorous phenomenological approach, it is clearly impossible to get outside of subjective awareness to determine the existence of a corresponding alternate reality. One clear advantage of approaching the problem through the priority of subjective awareness is that, in such a system, there are no discontinuities. The big bang itself becomes an aspect of subjective awareness, a conclusion tending to support the strong anthropic principle, although for reasons somewhat different from those usually put forward in support of it. And with the priority of subjective awareness, there is no question of subjective awareness per se evolving from a material system, since material externality is itself an aspect of subjective awareness.

The major disadvantage of such an approach is solipsism, or rather, not so much solipsism itself, but solipsistic behavior. If indeed there is a world of other subjectively aware beings as external realities with whom the subjectively aware philosopher must interact as if they have individual external integrity, then any behavior based on a solipsistic belief might appear psychotic.

So finally we must ask: Is there any solution to the nasty dilemmas that occur both when we assume the priority of external material reality and when we assume the priority of subjective awareness?

AN INTEGRATED APPROACH TO THE PROBLEM
OF SUBJECTIVE AWARENESS AND MATERIAL REALITY

One way to try to get a handle on the problem of subjective awareness and material reality is to consider the phenomenon of absolute unitary being. As we have described, AUB is a state of pure awareness without the perception of discrete reality, without the sense of the passage of time, without the sense of the extension of space, and without the self-other dichotomy. In short, it is pure awareness or awareness without content. Its existence is amply attested to cross-culturally in the mystical literature of all the world's great religions as well as by living mystics, whether of the religious or of the secular variety. Furthermore, our neurophysiological model of how this state is generated (i.e., by deafferentation of areas of the parietal lobe) seems to be confirmed in our brain-imaging studies of mature contemplation in Tibetan Buddhist meditators. Thus, there can be little doubt that AUB exists, even if it is a relatively rare state. From the point of view of our concerns here, AUB has an interesting property. Neither during the experiencing of AUB nor upon subsequent recollection is this state ever perceived as subjective. Although it is attained by going deeply within the subject, once it is attained, it is perceived as neither subjective nor objective. Indeed, from a phenomenological perspective, AUB or pure awareness seems to be anterior to either subject or object. Of course, awareness *of something* is clearly perceived to be a subjective state. But as difficult as this notion may be to understand, pure awareness seems to be neither subject nor object when analyzed by the meditator after the fact. It seems to be the only state to which humans have access that eludes the categories of subjectivity and objectivity. If we approach AUB from the stance of giving material reality ontological priority, then AUB or pure awareness, although intrinsically neither subject nor object, can nevertheless be said to be generated by the simple or absolute functioning of the deafferented posterior superior parietal lobules. But even in this case, when one can clearly define the physical antecedent causes of AUB, it nevertheless carries the characteristic of "absolute reality," as we shall see later in this chapter. If, on the other hand, we approach AUB or pure awareness from the position of giving subjective awareness ontological priority, then we must conclude that AUB or pure awareness represents absolute reality, in itself neither subjective nor objective, but from which both subjects and objects are derived. As counterintuitive as it may seem, such an approach requires that both individual subjective awareness and external material reality must derive from pure awareness.

We must now clearly differentiate subjective awareness from pure awareness. In fact, even from the perspective of the priority of external material reality, it seems that the self or conscious ego (as the locus of subjective awareness) has no a priori status but is a practical construct arising from physical evolution. While it is beyond the scope of this book to describe in detail how the self or the conscious ego may evolve, suffice it to say that certain brain structures must have evolved before a conscious self could be constructed. Most important among these structures is the inferior parietal lobule, which Luria and others have demonstrated is intimately associated with abstract classification and, more generally, with reification. Thus, as we have noted, the mind/brain observes its functioning and this functioning serves as input back into the mind/brain. The diverse elements of this mind/brain input are reified by the inferior parietal lobule, interacting with the sensory association areas in the same manner that these structures can classify a dogwood tree, a birch tree, and a giant redwood all in the same category, which eventually receives the name of "tree" when processed through the language centers. This reification of the perceived diverse functions of the mind/brain is the conscious self. Once this system of reification is set up, it can operate with infinite redundancy, resulting in the self being aware of the self being aware of the self and so forth.

The point of all this is that even from the perspective of the priority of the external material world, the conscious self is a construct of evolutionary processes, is always aware of "the other," and is unquestionably distinct from pure awareness or AUB. Thus, whether one approaches the problem of the relationship of subjective awareness and material reality from the point of view of the priority of material reality or from the priority of subjective awareness, it is clear that individual consciousness or the ego is a secondary reality deriving, on the one hand, from organic evolution and, on the other, from pure awareness.

To return to the phenomenological analysis of AUB or pure awareness, one must conclude that, unlike ego or individual subjective consciousness, pure awareness is nonlocal and unlimited. Again, this is counterintuitive from the point of view of Western science, but arises as a necessary conclusion from a phenomenological analysis of the state of AUB and from an epistemological analysis of what the concept of reality can possibly mean in any context. This is as far as we can go with a phenomenological analysis of AUB or pure awareness, an ineffable state that has tempted many mystics and some philosophers to speculate that AUB is not only nonlocal but creative. In such an understanding, not only is pure awareness anterior to subjectivity and objectivity, but it actually creates those categories and possibly the contents of those categories. At this point, one can see the possibility of an eternally creating God or ground of being beginning to emerge. We shall return to this topic at the end of this chapter.

Up to this point, this chapter has been a counterpoint between the concepts of subjective awareness and material reality. We have seen that subjective awareness can be understood first as deriving from the mind/brain and organic evolution (priority of material reality) and second as deriving from a phenomenological analysis of the knowing subject (priority of subjective awareness). We can now see the great difficulty of relating awareness even to its own primordial machine, the brain.

By now it should be obvious that for the individual subject seriously contemplating his or her "knowing," there is no absolute priority either for external reality or for the subject's own subjective awareness. Both are insistent and demand priority; neither can be ascribed priority necessarily. Clearly, the subject's culture is highly determinative in ascribing priority. The cultures of the Far East tend to favor consciousness or subjective awareness as prior. The cultures of the West tend to ascribe priority to external reality. But, in principle, there is no way to choose except by cultural prejudice or personal aesthetics. As scientists, we have chosen to place our "act of faith" consciously and explicitly in the priority of external reality. We feel that this approach allows for better science, although it may not be best in other aspects of life. Nevertheless, we are never unaware that it is, and must necessarily be, an act of faith. We would maintain that it is an act of faith for all scientists, at least implicit in their doing science. Personally, certain scientists may prefer to give priority to consciousness. We maintain that faith in the priority of external reality, at least unconsciously and implicitly, underlies the performing of science. Thus, our entire approach here has been "scientific," if only because of our insistence of working within the Western tradition of prioritizing external reality over consciousness. But even operating within the Western tradition, there comes a point where one can go no further with external reality, and a phenomenological analysis of consciousness is required. Such a point occurs when scientists or philosophers are forced to ask the question, What is the nature of reality?

THE NATURE AND DEGREES OF REALITY

One of the most ancient problems of philosophy is, How do we know that the external world corresponds, at least partially, to our mental representation of it? The question of what is "really real" has been considered, with various answers, since the time of the pre-Socratic Greek philosophers. The three most common criteria for judging what is real are as follows:

1. The subjective vivid sense of reality
2. Duration through time
3. Agreement intersubjectively as to what is real

In point of fact, we believe that it can be demonstrated that all three of these criteria determining what is real can be reduced to the first one: the subjective vivid sense of reality. For example, the sense of duration through time depends on the structuring of time in baseline reality. We have shown that the sense of time or, more properly, duration is structured by the brain. Alteration of function of this part of the brain, for any reason, results in significant distortion of the perception of time in a number of ways. As we have seen during AUB, there is no sense of time or duration while the person is in that state. Essentially, time vanishes for the subject in AUB. It becomes obvious that time and duration are not absolutes and that they derive their perceived qualities from brain function. Hence it begs the question to derive the reality of baseline reality from one of the qualia (time) which is itself structured by baseline reality (the brain). This same critique applies to any appeal for the reality of objects that depend on characteristics of baseline reality whose perception is known to be structured by the brain. The third criterion of the reality of entities (intersubjective validation) again arises from begging the question. The "subjects" who agree or disagree about entities' being real are themselves only images or representations within the sensoricognitive field of the analyzing philosopher. Thus, it is unfortunately true that any person analyzing his or her own experience must start out, at least, as a naive solipsist.

These analyses could continue ad infinitum. Suffice it to say that we are satisfied that each and every criterion of the reality of entities collapses into the first, namely, the subjective vivid sense of reality. Much follows from this point. The vivid sense of reality has been called many things by philosophers over the years. The Stoics called it the *phantasia catalyptica,* it is understood as "intentionality" by some phenomenologists, and certain contemporary German philosophers call it *Anwesenheit.* Whatever one wishes to call it, it is the compelling presence that generates a vivid and lucid sense of reality.

If we are forced to conclude that reality is ultimately reducible to the vivid sense of reality, then what are we to make of states that appear to the experiencing subject as more real than baseline reality, even when they are recalled from within baseline reality? If we take baseline reality as our point of reference, it appears that there are some states whose reality appears to be inferior to baseline reality and some states whose reality appears to be superior to that of baseline reality when these states are recalled in baseline reality. And this is the crucial point. We are not talking about various alternate phases of consciousness appearing real while one is experiencing them. We are talking about certain alternate phases of consciousness appearing more real than baseline reality *when recalled from within baseline reality*. Thus, individuals almost always refer to dreams as inferior to baseline reality when they recall and discuss them within baseline reality. The same is true of psychotic hallucinations after they are cured by phenothiazines or other psychotropic medications. A person having emerged from such a state will recall it as psychotic, often commenting "I was crazy then," or "Of course the voices or visions were not real . . . I was in a psychotic state."

The same cannot be said, however, of other alternate phases of consciousness that appear to be "more real" than baseline reality and are vividly described as such by experiencers after they return to baseline reality. This observation is true of a number of the states that we have described in this book. It is certainly true of the experience of AUB; it is true of cosmic consciousness, certain trance states, hyperlucid visions (usually of religious figures, religious symbols, and dead persons), and the core near-death experience (NDE). So real do these experiences appear when recalled in baseline reality that they have the ability to alter the way the experiencers live their lives. For example, those who have had a core NDE clearly behave more altruistically, more kindly, and with greater compassion toward other human beings than they showed before the experience. Furthermore, there is a marked tendency for near-death experiencers not to fear death. And these salutary changes do not last for just a short time after the NDE, they persist for years. Perhaps they will show themselves to endure throughout the experiencers' lives. Enough time has not passed for us to make that statement, but it appears to be the direction in which the evidence is pointing.

Again, if it is true that all of the proposed criteria by which reality is judged to be real can be reduced to the vivid sense of reality, then we have no choice but to conclude that in some sense, these states are, in fact, more real than the baseline reality of our everyday lives. And the word *real* is not here used poetically or metaphorically. It is used in the same sense as in the utterance "This rock and this table are real." In the next chapter, when we consider how a "megatheology" can be generated from neurotheology, we will compare the essential properties of baseline reality and hyperlucid unitary states. Suffice it to say that, whether one begins with the primacy of external reality or with the primacy of subjective awareness, "reality" is a slippery concept, often manifesting itself in profoundly counterintuitive ways to the scientist or philosopher.

But there is a strange theological conclusion to be drawn from the fact that individuals and cultures have an irreducible choice whether "external" reality or "subjective" consciousness is primary. In the first case, one can conclude with certainty that the concept and experience of God, and all religious phenomenology, are generated by the brain and nervous system. In the second case, one can conclude with equal certainty, from a rigorous phenomenological reflection on experience, that God (absolute unitary being or pure consciousness) generates the world (including the brain) and subjective experience itself. Since it is in principle impossible to determine which starting point is more "fundamental," external reality or the awareness of the knower, one is forced to conclude that both conclusions about God (AUB) are in a profound and fundamental sense true—namely, that God is created by the world (the brain and the rest of the central nervous system) and that the world is created by God.

Chapter Eleven

Metatheology and Megatheology

METATHEOLOGY

As we described at the beginning of the preceding chapter, a metatheology can be understood as the overall principles underlying any and all religions or ultimate belief systems and their theologies. A metatheology comprises both the general principles describing and, implicitly, the rules for constructing any concrete theological system. In and of itself, a metatheology is devoid of theological content, since it consists of rules and descriptions about how any and all specific theologies are structured. We propose that neurotheology, as presented in this book, is the best current contender for the title of "ultimate metatheology." Indeed, barring a major Kuhnian shift in fundamental scientific paradigms, it is hard to see how neurotheology, in principle at least, can fail to constitute an ultimate metatheology. While building the case for neurotheology, most of this book has been, in fact, elaborating a metatheology. In other words, the principles by which any and all theologies are formulated are contained within the structure and function of the mind/brain as described in the previous chapters.

An ultimate metatheology must account for three things. First, it must describe how and why foundational, creation, and soteriological myths are formed. Second, it must describe how and why such myths are elaborated into complex logical systems that we call specific theologies. Third, it must describe how and why the basic myths and certain aspects of their theological elaborations are objectified in the motor behavior that we call ceremonial ritual.

Neurotheology addresses these three constitutive demands of a metatheology by referring to three basic neuropsychological explanatory elements of the mind/brain:

1. The cognitive imperative
2. The cognitive operators
3. Arousal/quiescent states and rhythmicity

The Cognitive Imperative

As we have explained, the cognitive imperative provides the motive force for explaining any phenomenon or series of phenomena either simply or systematically. We have called the cognitive imperative the "drive of the neocortex." It represents the impetus to apply the cognitive operators to incoming input in some understandable fashion. The predominant operator activated by the cognitive imperative is the causal operator. As we have seen, the mind/brain automatically sets up causal sequences to explain any phenomenon or cluster of phenomena. When the initial terminus of any strip of reality is not given in the sensorium, we have seen how the mind/brain generates an initial terminus or cause of that strip of reality in the form of a god, demon, numen, or some other power source. Only the artificial scientific social contract that developed in seventeenth-century Europe, and by which natural philosophers refrained from positing any initial terminus unless it was observed or immediately inferrable from sense-data, prevents modern science from generating gods, demons, and other power sources. It appears, however, that the mind/brain naturally posits such entities. Even the most rational of scientists and philosophers must occasionally construct and deal with such entities, if only in their dreams.

Thus, we see that the cognitive imperative is immensely powerful. Cognitive psychologists have generated a mountain of evidence that this is indeed the case, but a simple example here will serve to make the point. A number of years ago, a mild earthquake shook the Philadelphia area in the middle of the night. The noted physical anthropologist Solomon Katz, his graduate students, and one of the authors (Eugene d'Aquili) did an informal study involving random telephone calls to residents of the area to ask them questions about the earthquake. Some were asked, "What did you think happened last night?" and others were asked, "What was the first thing you did when you felt the earthquake?" The first question elicited, as one might expect, a broad spectrum of answers. Many correctly thought that it was a mild earthquake. Many others opted for a heavy truck passing outside or for a furnace exploding. There was even one bizarre answer: "The universe reached critical mass." All of these responses, whether common or bizarre, were predictable in that they were cognitive responses to the question, "What did you think happened last night?" The really interesting result of this study was with the responses to the question, "What was the first thing you did when you felt the earthquake?" In spite of the form of this question, virtually every respondent answered first by giving what he or she thought had occurred before going on to say what he or she did. The mind/brain forcefully and immediately seeks an explanation for an indeterminate stimulus, and gives that cognitive response later even when none is asked for.

Therefore, the cognitive imperative, the driver of the neocortex, compels human beings to try to understand their environment, to structure myths as explanatory stories, to generate gods or power sources "to fill in the causal gaps," and to squeeze every ounce of truth from the myth by the application of logic and deductive reasoning using the cognitive operators. Such is the force of the cognitive imperative that human beings have no choice but to structure myths whether in their scientific form (a special case) or in their more primitive form embodied in dreams, daydreams, fairy tales, folktales, and other manifestations of myths.

The Cognitive Operators

As we have considered in earlier chapters, the cognitive operators represent neural networks that operate upon sensory input to organize it and modulate it in specific ways. In the aggregate, this function forms our cognized environment. The causal and binary operators are particularly active in the generation of myth. The organization of the world, and myth content, into polar opposites or, at least, into contrasted dyads, is the obligatory function of the binary operator. The contrasting of myth elements into opposites often presents the "myth problem" that must somehow be resolved. The contrasting of pairs such as good and evil, divine and human, life and death constitutes the polar tension essential to the myth story. As we have elaborated, attempts at resolving such myth problems can be either cognitive, as part of the myth structure, or profoundly existential or emotional, as a result of incarnating the myth into a ritual matrix.

The mind/brain can then operate on a myth as it is elaborated by a particular culture, extracting explicit meanings from the myth and deducing various conclusions from elements of the myth. Such conclusions are not specifically contained in the myth. Rather, conclusions are derived in the form: if element A of the myth is true (as indeed the whole myth is believed to be true, at least in primitive societies), then X must necessarily be the case for A to happen, and Y must necessarily be concluded as a consequence of A. With this kind of reasoning, theology is born from religious myth. Since theology is based on logic and deductive reasoning, the causal operator (this time operating on abstract concepts), the abstractive operator, and the quantitative operator are all integral to the formation of the organized body of knowledge that we have traditionally called a theology.

Arousal/Quiescent States and Rhythmicity

Since all religions present their myths, and to some extent their theologies, within some sort of ritual context, from minimal to maximal, any inclusive metatheology must account for human ceremonial ritual. We have seen the effect of slow and fast rhythmicity on arousal/quiescent states and ultimately on the generation of pleasurable experiences, from mild satisfaction to ecstatic bliss. We have also seen how this rhythmic, arousal/quiescent system can briefly activate the holistic operator, generating powerfully unitary as well as pleasurable experiences. Finally, we have described how such unitary experiences can create the existential sense of the union of elements that are logically opposed in the myth prior to the myth's having been exposed to ritual expression. Such mystic unions of opposing mythic elements, as well as the sense of the mystic union of all participants in a ritual through activation of the holistic operator, provide experiences that are among the most intense that a religion can provide for one of its practitioners. Such experiences as manifestations of the divine often provide a retrospective "confirmation" of the truth both of the religion's foundational myth and of its theological elaboration.

Last, any metatheology must account for intense mystical experiences derived from meditation and to some extent from prayer. In chapter 6, we proposed neurophysiological mechanisms that account for all of the major religious and spiritual experiences generated by the mystical mind.

To summarize, then, we can see that neurotheology constitutes a great formal apparatus that is required for the structure and understanding of any specific myth, its theological elaboration, and its incarnation and resolution in ceremonial ritual, as well as the otherworldly, transcendent, or mystical experiences that certain practitioners of all religions enjoy. Although neurotheology as a metatheology is devoid of specific theological content, neurotheology is full of content at the level of the neuropsychology that both underlies and constitutes it.

MEGATHEOLOGY

Just as a metatheology is devoid of content, a megatheology should contain content of such a universal nature that it could be adopted by most, if not all, of the world's great religions as a basic element without any serious violation of their essential doctrines. Alternatively, a megatheology should have such universal content that it could be used as the basis for the development of a new specific theology, one, it is to be hoped, more universal in nature than those arising from the cultural exigencies of humanity's remote past. In addition to its strictly formal elements, which we have described in the first part of this chapter, can neurotheology generate content about which there can be meaningful speculation? At this point, we must turn our attention to hyperlucid unitary states, the reality of which, compared to baseline consciousness, we considered in the preceding chapter.

As we have seen, hyperlucid unitary states derive from various causes—meditation, effective ceremonial ritual, severe fasting or ascetic practices, and spontaneous mystical experiences. Major examples of such hyperlucid unitary states are vivid mystical visions, sensorially constellated archetypes, a vivid sense of the unity of being (cosmic consciousness), and absolute unitary being. Although it is true that all such hyperlucid unitary states have their basis in neuroanatomy, neurophysiology, and the flux of neurohumoral transmitters, it is equally true that baseline reality, or what we have called ordinary lucid consciousness, which both the average person and the average scientist construe to be really real, nevertheless is based on exactly the same parameters. Simply put, one can never get at what is "really out there" without its being processed, one way or another, through the brain.

Many find it deeply disturbing that the experience of God, the sense of the Absolute, the sense of mystery and beauty in the universe, the most profoundly moving religious and spiritual experiences of which humans are capable, might be reducible to issues of neural activity or even to specific patterns of blood flow or metabolism in the brain. Such an attitude misses a few important points. First of all, our experience of baseline reality—of chairs, tables, love, hate, indeed, of our whole physical and psychological environment—can also be reduced to neural blips and fluxes of brain chemistry. So what criteria can we use to evaluate whether God, other hyperlucid unitary experiences, or our everyday world is more "real"? Can we use our subjective sense of the absolute certainty of the objective reality of our everyday world to establish that that world is "really real"?

To simplify the issue, let us for the moment contrast the sense of reality of the most extreme hyperlucid unitary state, that of absolute unitary being (AUB), with baseline reality. In such an exercise there is absolutely no question that AUB wins out as being "more real." People who have experienced AUB, and this includes some very learned and previously materialistic scientists, regard it as being more fundamentally real than baseline reality. Even their memory of it is more fundamentally real. A number of years ago we interviewed several people who had had this experience. There is no doubt that it, and even the memory of it, carried the sense of greater fundamental reality than that generated in their day-to-day living. If we use the criterion, therefore, of the sense of certainty of the objective reality of that state, AUB wins hands down. The same is true, *mutatis mutandis,* of all hyperlucid unitary states, including the near-death experience.

From the point of view of neuropsychology, AUB is likely "caused" by the total deafferentation of the orientation association areas on both the left and right side. Other mechanisms are responsible for other hyperlucid states to which we have alluded in previous chapters. But we must keep in mind that baseline reality is a cognized environment and, as such, is molded by brain mechanisms just as hyperlucid unitary states are. As we noted in chapter 10, this is the point at which a strict neuropsychological analysis grinds to a halt. We are forced to move to a phenomenological analysis of these various states (including baseline reality) in order to determine what reality might mean and whether it has degrees. All of this we addressed in detail in chapter 10.

We would maintain that there is no way to determine whether the various hyperlucid unitary states or baseline reality are more "real," beyond the sense of reality described in chapter 10. In other words, outside of consideration of the sense of reality, we cannot tell which state represents more fundamental ontological reality without first making gratuitous and unsubstantiated assumptions. This being the case, it is a foolish reductionism indeed that states that because hyperlucid unitary consciousness can be understood in terms of neuropsychological processes, it is therefore derived from baseline reality. Indeed, the reverse argument could be made just as well. Neuropsychology can give no answer as to which state is more real, baseline reality (coherent, lucid consciousness) or hyperlucid unitary consciousness. As we have seen, a phenomenological analysis renders reality as the sense of reality. So, phenomenological analysis must yield hyperlucid states as more real. But in terms of neuropsychology, we are reduced to saying that each is real in its own way and for its own adaptive ends. This may not be epistemologically satisfying, but up to now any alternative has escaped us. We suspect that this is because of an inherent indeterminacy in brain functioning.

Let us now turn to an examination of the most extreme form of hyperlucid consciousness, namely, AUB. There can be no doubt that AUB exists. The mystical literature of all the world's high religions, certainly across cultures and centuries, provides startlingly similar, and even virtually identical descriptions. The same cannot be said of other hyperlucid states because they have discrete elements of perception and cognition; their superficial content is strongly influenced by the cultures from which they arise. We would maintain that their deep, unitary content is the same across cultures, but these other hyperlucid states are at least superficially different across cultures and religions. This argument does not apply to AUB, however. In addition, the reality of AUB is further supported by our brain-imaging research. The deafferentation of the orientation association areas, which we predicted in our model prior to these studies, has so far been supported and correlates with the peak experience of Tibetan meditators.

What can we say about this intensely powerful state, whose perfect simplicity seems to be identical in all places and times of which we have record?

It is almost universally described as being pure consciousness. It is clearly not local consciousness or subjective awareness. Individuals who have experienced AUB curiously describe it as neither subjective nor objective. Most would describe local consciousness as subjective and external reality as objective. But AUB appears to be logically, and perhaps ontologically, anterior to the categories of subjective and objective. What is shocking, and certainly counterintuitive, is that this pure consciousness, apparently undivided and unenduring in time, this nonsubjective and nonobjective entity, is real. At least, according to the only criterion by which we can judge reality, AUB is more "really real" than any other known phase of consciousness. At this point, one cannot refrain from asking, "Are we looking at God?" To go beyond this point is to speculate. But perhaps some speculation based on the reality of what we have presented thus far is not amiss. First of all, there is the temptation to speculate that, since AUB or pure consciousness is not experienced as either subjective or objective, the subjective and objective arise from it. This speculation would be tantamount to stating that from pure consciousness both the subjective local consciousnesses of individuals and the objective external reality are created. At least the sense of external reality might be thus created. Therefore, the two worlds, which at times seem to us incommensurable, may in fact relate to each other by both arising from a pure and creative consciousness.

One further speculation is permitted to us on the basis of the empirical observation that AUB comes in two forms. The absolute unity and simplicity of AUB can be perceived as suffused with positive affect. In such a case, the experiencer, whether Hindu, Sufi, or Christian, experiences AUB as personal and generally refers to it as God. The timeless and perfect simplicity of AUB can also be experienced suffused with neutral affect. This most often happens in the Buddhist tradition and is described after the fact as nonpersonal or void consciousness. One wonders whether it would be helpful in constructing a megatheology to see void consciousness as the anterior nature of God and to see AUB suffused with positive affect or bliss as the posterior nature of God. The anterior nature of God would represent a total and infinite conscious potentiality, as counterintuitive as the juxtaposition of the notions of consciousness and potentiality may be. The posterior nature of God might be seen as the total actuality. Thus, the phrase "anterior and posterior natures of God" is theological language reflecting the empirically different affects associated with the perfect unity and perfect simplicity of AUB arising out of different traditions. The concepts of an anterior and a posterior nature of God, the one representing the total potential consciousness and the other representing totally inclusive actuality, have the virtue of being able to unite God seekers and void consciousness seekers in one superordinate conceptual framework.

Thus, it appears that neurotheology can lead to a megatheology. Utilizing many sources of evidence, neuropsychology has been able to demonstrate that the hyperlucid unitary states described in the world's mystical literature not only can exist but probably *should* exist. But neuropsychology is going beyond what allowed us to construct our models a number of years ago. Our current research involving brain imaging of Tibetan Buddhist meditators while meditating has thus far been supportive of the model presented in this book. Thus, neuropsychology has brought us to understand the reality of AUB and other hyperlucid unitary states. A subsequent phenomenological analysis of what is meant by reality leads us to an area of speculation where angels have feared to tread. Nevertheless, our speculations are compatible with what is known empirically, and, we would say, our state of knowledge even urges them. Whether this megatheology deriving from neurotheology will be helpful to anyone, only time will tell.

Permit us one final epistemological observation derived from a comparison of baseline consciousness with the most extreme state of hyperlucid unitary consciousness, absolute unitary being. If we grant ontological priority to external reality, and if we grant that the laws of science and, hence, neurophysiology and neuropsychology as sciences reflect a reasonably significant isomorphism with external reality, and if, furthermore, we consider the transcendent certainty of the reality of absolute unitary being among those who have experienced it, and, finally, if we consider the intense functional certainty that we all have of the reality of our everyday world made up of multiple discrete interacting beings, then we must conceive the brain as a machine that operates upon whatever it is that fundamental reality may be and produces at the very least two basic versions, both accompanied by profound subjective certainty of their objective reality. Thus, it seems that both God and our everyday world can be perceived by the brain and generated by the brain. At this level of analysis both statements are probably equally true. Whatever is anterior to the experience of God and the multiple contingent reality of everyday life is in principle unknowable, since that which is in any way known must be a transformation wrought by the brain.

As counterintuitive and, in some ways, disturbing as these conclusions may be, they represent sober reflections upon our current knowledge of the functioning of the central nervous system. They derive from scholars who choose, like most of Western culture, to consider external reality to be primary and the findings of science to be a fairly accurate representation of reality. Yet, even this approach, when one considers its full implications, reveals a profound mystery in our understanding of external reality, God, and how they may interrelate through the brain.

But, as we described earlier, if one were to choose subjective awareness as primary, as a number of Eastern cultures do, and if, in this context, one were to experience AUB (or even believe that the state occurs in some other people), then a phenomenological analysis would tend to conclude that AUB or God or pure consciousness generates subjective experience and, with it, the world. All of these considerations make theology very much alive, and for those of us in Western tradition, a neuropsychological analysis can form the basis of a megatheology.

Chapter Twelve

Epilogue: Some Practical Reflections

The one whom I bow to only knows to whom I bow
When I attempt the ineffable Name, murmuring Thou,
And dream of Phaedian fancies and embrace in heart
Symbols (I know) which cannot be the thing thou art.
Thus always, taken at their word, all prayers blaspheme
Worshiping with frail images of folk-lore dream,
And all in their praying, self-deceived, address
The coinage of their own unquiet thoughts, unless
Thou in magnetic mercy to Thyself divert
Our arrows, aimed unskillfully, beyond desert;
And all are idolators, crying unheard
To a deaf idol, if thou take them at their word.
Take not, O Lord, our literal sense. Lord, in thy great,
Unspoken speech our limping metaphor translate.

—C. S. Lewis

We have seen that neurotheology is itself a metatheology that contains both the constraints upon and the rules for mythmaking, the generation of specific theologies, the formation and purpose of religious ritual, and the experiencing of the spectrum of religious experiences and altered phases of consciousness. Neurotheology has shown that the products of the mystical mind are real, at least as neuropsychological states. But the phenomenological analysis, which we have been forced to employ as a complement to our basic neuroevolutionary and neurophysiological approach, has powerfully demonstrated that hyperlucid states of consciousness and other products of the mystical mind must be understood as either more real or as real as base-line reality when recalled from baseline reality.

Thus, it seems that in spite of the fondest hopes of eighteenth-century *philosophes* and nineteenth-century materialist scientists, religion and theology will not go away. The reason is that, if we take external reality as primary for our ontology, then God appears to be "hard-wired" into the brain. On the other hand, if we take subjective awareness as having ontological primacy, then a phe-nomenological analysis of altered phases of consciousness reveals that certain individuals experience God, as the absolute unitary being (AUB), as a primary epistemic/ontological state. While the state of AUB occurs in very few indi-viduals, other hyperlucid states occur in many. These non-AUB hyperlucid states are not understood to be the direct experience of God *(unio mystica),* but they are, nevertheless, extremely powerful unitary/epistemic/ontological states. Since neuropsychology not only can document the possibility of these hyper-lucid states existing in terms of what is currently known about neurophysiology, but also is now beginning to demonstrate their reality (as neuropsychological states) in current brain-imaging studies, contemporary philosophy and science are forced to take them seriously. One can no longer dismiss the description of such states in the world's religious and mystical literature as the "silly imaginings of religious nuts." They must be accounted for and their claims and practical implications carefully examined.

We shall briefly consider four (among many others) practical implications of neurotheology that we have not explored in detail in this book, but which the reader may wish to reflect upon (they are given in no particular order):

1. Mystics are not crazy or, at least, not necessarily so.
2. Religions and their theologies necessarily arise from the machinery of the human brain operating within a social context.
3. Ritual can be an extremely powerful technology, which, in itself, is nei-ther good nor bad.
4. Neurotheology can generate a megatheology, described in the preced-ing chapter, that we believe could be adopted by all the world's great religions without prejudice to their individual doctrinal content.

The first concept, that mystics are not crazy, must be reconsidered from the neurotheological perspective. It is unfortunate that various psychological dis-orders are often associated with religious or spiritual phenomena. This fact has led to the long-standing bias in Western culture that mystics are crazy. That they are not is attested to by their prominence in many cultures and religious communities. Furthermore, as presented in this book, there is increasing evi-dence that these states are associated with particular brain states. In fact, the brain may have evolved in such a way that these experiences were possible.

When considering mystical experiences from a phenomenological perspective, their significance as real spiritual events becomes even more impressive. It is possible that with the advent of improved technologies for studying the brain, mystical experiences may finally be clearly differentiated from any type of psychopathology. Until then, neurotheology at least suggests that the reality of the mystical mind is crucial to the development of religion and spirituality.

The second practical implication deriving from neurotheology is that the general structures of theology and religion necessarily arise from the functioning of the human brain. We have seen that the functioning of the various operators lays the foundations for numerous theological concepts as well as the spiritual components of religion. The individual aspects of a particular religion and theology are then determined by the cultural and societal milieu. Thus, neurotheology offers a thoroughly integrated approach to understanding religion, spirituality, and theology, in terms of their general as well as their specific aspects.

Another interesting conclusion drawn from neurotheology is that ritual is an extremely powerful technology that in itself, is neither good nor bad. Neurotheology considers ritual only in terms of its overall effect on the person's psyche. Certainly, this effect can be tremendously positive by suffusing those participating in a ritual with a sense of unity and love and even a sense of absolute unitary being. Ritual can also, however, be used to powerful effect politically and even recreationally in addition to its use in religious ceremonial. As the Nazi Nuremberg torchlight parades forcefully demonstrate, ceremonial ritual can be demonic as well as angelic.

The fourth point, which considers the relationship between our megatheology and the major world religions, is an issue that needs to be expanded. We maintain that conceptually there is nothing to prevent this megatheology from being interpreted as foundational in all the world's high religions. Clearly much attention has to be given to the language used in expressing the megatheology, particularly with reference to Buddhism. The specific phrases "anterior nature of God" and "posterior nature of God" would have to be recast so as not to give offense to this nontheistic religion. There would be no problem with "anterior nature of God" being translated into Buddhist terminology since, as we have seen, it is identical with the Buddhist concept of void consciousness. The status of the "posterior nature of God," which we have proposed as totiactual and creative consciousness, is somewhat more problematic for Buddhism. We have seen the "posterior nature of God" as creative of at least the sense of external reality, so it would seem that Buddhism must find the "posterior nature of God" in whatever ontological state samsara arises from. Granted that samsara carries nothing like the positive emotional value of the Judeo-Christian concept of creation, nevertheless, a comparison of the structural similarities of samsara and creation and the state from which they arise would seem to provide fruitful material for ecumenical dialogue.

It is beyond the scope of this book to examine in detail how the mega-theology derived from neurotheology can effectively be seen as foundational to all the world's great religions. The most difficult problem is relating this megatheology to Buddhism, since one must be careful with the use of theistic language. We have just seen one example of how this problem can be effectively approached, but systematically expanding upon the relationship between our megatheology and the existing great theological systems will have to wait for a later time. It is nonetheless an extremely important subject because it may lay the groundwork for effective ecumenical dialogue.

This brings us to the question of what the stance should be of an individual who finds this neurotheological approach compelling, but who is not currently committed to any faith tradition. If such a person came from a specific faith tradition, should he or she return to it, and if so, under what intellectual and psychological conditions? Conversely, should a person who is persuaded of the validity of the neurotheological approach construct his or her private theology based on the megatheology presented here? These are difficult questions and have the potential of being very emotional ones.

One must respect the traditional religions and their theologies as being what Donald Campbell has called "well-winnowed" systems of behavioral and social control.[1] They are well winnowed in the sense that their various components have been selected for during the process of cultural evolution over extended periods of time. Although the traditional religious systems have been blamed for the killing of innumerable people in the name of God, their adaptive capabilities advance their societies and cultures, presumably allowing many more to live than were ever killed in religious wars, inquisitions, and the like. According to theoreticians such as Ralph Wendell Burhoe, the evolution of religion among hominids marks the true beginning of culture and to this day represents the link between cultural and biological evolution among *Homo sapiens*.[2] If Hobbes's famous description of primitive life as being "nasty, brutish and short" is correct, then it was the evolution of religions that made it less so, in spite of hominids' homicidal xenophobia. In the great calculus of adaptation, the modulation of hedonistic impulses and the promotion of transkin in-group altruism must have made religions, even the most primitive ones in service of the tribe or city-state, overall more life-giving than life-taking. As Donald Campbell and others have pointed out, traditional religions have been inordinately adaptive mechanisms for their societies and usually for the individuals in them.

It is fashionable in certain circles to maintain that traditional religions have outlived their usefulness and that they are no longer adaptive in modern technological society. Given the well-winnowed quality of traditional religions, their surprising endurance over even the most hostile of times, and the tight mesh between religiously motivated behavior and generally successful adaptation to the cultural environment, it is probably extremely dangerous to write off traditional religions as anachronistic. It is with this caution in mind that we suggest that those who are persuaded by neurotheology and its megatheology first consider realigning themselves with their faith community of origin before considering developing their own specific theology based on this megatheology. Of course, this may be difficult or impossible for a number of reasons. For example, there are those individuals who were emotionally traumatized in childhood by being exposed to an excessively rigid and literal theology. Such individuals usually had little contact with the life-giving elements of their tradition and more than a passing contact with the rigid and oppressive elements that usually guard the boundaries of a religious tradition as a system. For such individuals, the wounds are often too severe ever to consider a realignment with their tradition of origin, even under markedly changed psychological circumstances and even with a markedly changed understanding of what religion is all about. Such individuals may have no other option but to construct their own theology based on a megatheology such as that generated by neurotheology.

There may be other difficulties with an individual's ability to accept his or her tradition of origin, even if he or she is not a victim of severe emotional abuse. Depending on how conservative or literal (with respect to the foundational myth) a person's religion of origin may be, there may be a greater or lesser need for "mental reservation," especially with regard to any exclusive truth claims of one's tradition as well as with regard to a literal interpretation of every point of the foundational myth. Constantly reminding oneself of the metaphorical nature of much of what one's faith community claims to be literally (and factually) true can be an exhausting process. At some point, and this may differ for different individuals, the tension produced by many mental reservations may become inordinate and require the individual to disengage yet a second time from his or her faith community of origin.

Whether because of early emotional abuse or because of the development of issues that appear to become more one of intellectual honesty than of mental reservation, it may be impossible for certain individuals to be spiritually nourished by their faith community of origin, even when they reinterpret it through the perspective of neurotheology. Such individuals have little choice but to construct their own theology or their own life path, ideally one based on a meaningful megatheology such as that derived from the neurotheological considerations put forth in this book. We must keep in mind, however, that all the well-winnowed religious traditions, at their best, provide a path of access to the divine as neurotheology demonstrates they must. Unfortunately, other aspects of traditional religions may contradict the best principles of those traditions even to the point of becoming demonic.

The reader may have noticed a hesitancy on the part of the authors to jump to the conclusion that, since we have a megatheology derived from neurotheology, why not let everyone use it as the basis for constructing a personal theology. Our hesitancy derives from a bit of wisdom possessed by all the world's great religions, namely, that the greatest enemy of access to the divine or to wisdom or to enlightenment is ego. Ego is rapacious, self-seeking, hedonistic, acquisitive, materialistic, and above all else, proud. The best, the truest, and the wisest in all the great religious traditions know this fact well and attempt to protect their novices on the path to the divine. The lone individual, even with the best and most empirically derived megatheology as a base, is in grave danger of constructing a personal theology that ends in the worship and love of the ego rather than of God. This is not to state that the venture of constructing a meaningful and nourishing personal theology is impossible. But it is a path marked by significant dangers. Perhaps the best advice that can be given to anyone embarking on such an intensely lonely journey is to familiarize himself or herself with the mystical literature of all the great religious traditions, thereby avoiding at least most of the pitfalls that have been noted and charted by mystics who have gone before.

The road to God is paved with many stones: metaphor, poetry, music, ritual experiences, prayer, and meditative experiences. In our eagerness to avoid mythic literalism (biblical literalism in the Judeo-Christian tradition), we must be careful not to throw out the baby with the bathwater. Indeed, metaphor, poetry, music, ritual experiences, prayer, and even meditative experiences are culturally conditioned. But, relative as they are, they point to that which is "really real." Metaphor does not point to more metaphor, nor does religious poetic language point to more poetry. That which gives religious poetry and metaphor its meaning is real in an absolute, ultimate, and unconditioned way, as the experience of AUB clearly demonstrates.

We hope that the paving stones on the road to God will include some new ones such as neurotheology as a metatheology helping us to understand the nature of all the other paving stones. Perhaps the most important new paving stone on the road to God may be neurotheology as a basic megatheology, including both its neuroevolutionary aspect and its phenomenological analysis of reality. Neurotheology as a megatheology provides the basic theological content that we maintain is conceptually compatible with all the world's great religions. We hope that such an approach will eventually result in increased ecumenical dialogue between the world's great religious traditions, in an increase in understanding and tolerance among individuals of all religious traditions, and, ultimately, in an increase in compassion and love in a world that is desperate for them. Since the approach presented in this book is firmly based on the neurosciences, on neuroevolutionary theory, and on strict phenomenological analysis, we hope that it will carry a compelling plausibility, indeed probability, to twenty-first century readers steeped in a scientific culture and demanding proof.

Thus, the mystical mind has led us down a new and fascinating path toward the understanding of human beings and their relationship to religion, spirituality, and God. As we stated in our dedication, we certainly believe that neurotheology can help open us to a greater sense of the *mysterium tremendum et fascinans*—the tremendous and spellbinding mystery—and to the awareness that we, who are brought together in a love of truth, are the mystical minds seeking that mystery.

Notes

CHAPTER 1

1. E. G. d'Aquili and C. D. Laughlin, *Biogenetic Structuralism* (New York: Columbia University Press, 1974).

2. W. J. Smith, "Ritual and the Ethology of Communicating," in *The Spectrum of Ritual: A Biogenetic Structural Analysis*, ed. E. G. d'Aquili, C. D. Laughlin Jr., and J. McManus (New York: Columbia University Press, 1979).

3. P. Tillich, *Systematic Theology* (Chicago: University of Chicago Press, 1967), p. 18.

4. I. Barbour, *Religion in an Age of Science* (San Francisco: HarperCollins, 1990).

5. E. O. Wilson, *On Human Nature* (Cambridge, Mass.: Harvard University Press, 1978); J. Monod, *Chance and Necessity* (New York: Vintage Books, 1972).

6. D. Tracy, *Blessed Rage for Order* (New York: Seabury, 1975); D. Tracy, *Plurality and Ambiguity* (San Francisco: Harper & Row, 1987).

7. H. Rolston, *Science and Religion: A Critical Survey* (New York: Random House, 1987).

8. A. N. Whitehead, *Process and Reality* (New York: Macmillan, 1929).

9. P. Tillich, *Systematic Theology* (Chicago: University of Chicago Press, 1967).

10. P. Hefner, *The Human Factor: Evolution, Culture and Religion* (Minneapolis: Fortress Press, 1993).

11. A. E. Barnes, "Ces Sortes de Penitence Imaginaires: The Counter-Reformation Assault on Communitas," in *Social History and Issues in Human Consciousness*, ed. A. E. Barnes and P. N. S. Stearnes (New York: New York University Press, 1989).

12. A. Greeley, "Mysticism Goes Mainstream," *American Health* 6, no. 1 (1987): 47–49.

13. F. Streng, *Understanding Religious Life*, 3d ed. (Belmont, Calif.: Wadsworth, 1985).

CHAPTER 2

1. R. Joseph, *Neuropsychology, Neuropsychiatry, and Behavioral Neurology* (New York: Plenum Press, 1990); E. R. Kandel, J. H. Schwartz, and T. M. Jessell, eds., *Principles of Neural Science*, 3d ed. (Norwalk, Conn.: Appleton & Lange, 1993).

2. Kandel, Schwartz, and Jessell, *Principles of Neural Science*.

3. B. Lex, "The Neurobiology of Ritual Trance," in *The Spectrum of Ritual: A Biogenetic Structural Analysis*, ed. E. G. d'Aquili, C. D. Laughlin Jr., and J. McManus (New York: Columbia University Press, 1979), pp. 117–51.

4. Joseph, *Neuropsychology, Neuropsychiatry, and Behavioral Neurology*.

5. Lex, "The Neurobiology of Ritual Trance."

6. Kandel, Schwartz, and Jessell, *Principles of Neural Science*.

7. V. K. Somers, M. E. Dyken, A. L. Mark, and F. M. Abboud, "Parasympathetic Hyperresponsiveness and Bradyarrhythmias During Apnoea in Hypertension," *Clinical Autonomic Research* 2 (1992): 161–76; K. Koizumi and M. Kollai, "Control of Reciprocal and Non-Reciprocal Action of Vagal and Sympathetic Efferents: Study of Centrally Induced Reactions," *Journal of the Autonomic Nervous System* 3 (1981): 483–501.

8. E. G. d'Aquili and A. B. Newberg, "Religious and Mystical States: A Neuro-psychological Substrate," *Zygon* 28 (1993): 177–200.

9. Ibid.

10. E. G. d'Aquili and A. B. Newberg, "Liminality, Trance and Unitary States in Ritual and Meditation," *Studia Liturgica* 23 (1993): 2–34.

11. Ibid.

12. M. S. Gazzaniga and J. E. LeDoux, *The Integrated Mind* (New York: Plenum Press, 1978).

13. J. E. Bogen, "The Other Side of the Brain, II: An Appositional Mind," *Bulletin of the Los Angeles Neurological Society* 34 (1969): 135–62.

14. Gazzaniga and LeDoux, *The Integrated Mind.*

15. Kandel, Schwartz, and Jessell, *Principles of Neural Science.*

16. Ibid.

17. L. Weiskrantz, *Blindsight: A Case Study and Implications* (Oxford: Oxford University Press, 1986).

18. Joseph, *Neuropsychology, Neuropsychiatry, and Behavioral Neurology.*

19. R. Desimone and S. J. Schein, "Visual Properties of Neruons in Area V4 of the Macaque: Sensitivity to Stimulus Form," *Journal of Neurophysiology* 57 (1987): 835–67.

20. E. G. Jones and T. P. S. Powell, "An Anatomical Study of Converging Sensory Pathways within the Cerebral Cortex of the Monkey," *Brain* 93 (1970): 793–820; J. T. Wall, L. L. Symonds, and J. H. Kaas, "Cortical and Subcortical Projections of the Middle Temporal Area (MT) and Adjacent Cortex in Galagos," *Journal of Comparative Neurology* 211 (1982): 193–214.

21. L. Leinonen, J. Hyvarinen, J. Nyman, and D. Linnakoski, "Functional Properties of Neurons in the Lateral Part of Associative Area 7 of Awake Monkeys," *Experimental Brain Research* 34 (1979): 299–320.

22. J. C. Lynch, "The Functional Organization of Posterior Parietal Association Cortex," *Behavioral Brain Sciences* 3 (1980): 485–99.

23. V. B. Montcastle, "The World around Us: Neural Command Functions for Selective Attention," *Neurosciences Research Progress Bulletin* 14 (1976): 1–47; V. B. Montcastle, B. C. Motter, and R. A. Andersen, "Some Further Observations on the Functional Properties of Neurons in the Parietal Lobe of the Waking Monkey," *Brain Behavioral Sciences* 3 (1980): 520–29.

24. E. T. Rolls, D. Perret, S. J. Thorpe, et al., "Responses of Neurons in Area 7 of the Parietal Cortex to Objects of Different Significance," *Brain Research* 169 (1979): 194–98.

25. A. Benton, "Visuoperceptive, Visuospatial and Visuoconstructive Disorders," in *Clinical Neuropsychology*, ed. K. M. Heilman and E. Valenstein (Oxford: Oxford University Press, 1979), pp. 186–232; D. A. Ratcliff and G. A. B. Davies-Jones, "Defective Visual Localization in Focal Brain Wounds," *Brain* 95 (1972): 49–60.

26. Joseph, *Neuropsychology, Neuropsychiatry, and Behavioral Neurology.*

27. D. T. Stuss and D. F. Benson, *The Frontal Lobes* (New York: Raven, 1986), p. 25.

28. O. S. Adrianov, "Projection and Association Levels of Cortical Integration," in *Architectonics of the Cerebral Cortex*, ed. M. A. B. Brazier and H. Petsche (New York: Raven, 1978); N. Geschwind, "Disconnexion Syndromes in Animals and Man," *Brain* 88 (1965): 585–644.

29. Stuss and Benson, *The Frontal Lobes*, p. 24.

30. Jones and Powell, "An Anatomical Study of Converging Sensory Pathways within the Cerebral Cortex of the Monkey."

31. Stuss and Benson, *The Frontal Lobes*, p. 33.

32. W. Pohl, "Dissociation of Spatial Discrimination Deficits following Frontal and Parietal Lesions in Monkeys," *Journal of Comparative Physiological Psychology* 82 (1973): 227–39; M. Mishkin et al., "Kinesthetic Discrimination after Prefrontal Lesions in Monkeys," *Brain Research* 130 (1977): 163–68.

33. J. M. Fuster, *The Prefrontal Cortex: Anatomy, Physiology, and Neuropsychology of the Frontal Lobe* (New York: Raven, 1980), p. 61.

34. K. H. Pribram and A. R. Luria, *Psychophysiology of the Frontal Lobes* (New York: Academic Press, 1973), p. 297.

35. Ibid., p. 299.

36. K. H. Pribram and D. McGuinness, "Arousal, Activation, and Effort in the Control of Attention," *Psychological Review* 82 (1975): 116–49; K. H. Pribram, "Emotions," in *Handbook of Clinical Neuropsychology*, ed. S. K. Filskov and T. J. Boll (New York: John Wiley & Sons, 1981).

37. Fuster, *The Prefrontal Cortex*, pp. 114, 121.

38. M. Gerbner, "Study on the Functional Mechanism of the Dorsolateral Frontal Lobe Cortex," in *Psychophysiology of the Frontal Lobes*, p. 237.

39. W. J. H. Nauta, "The Problem of the Frotal Lobe: A Reinterpretation," *Journal of Psychiatric Research* 8 (1971): 167–87.

40. C. J. Bruce, R. Desimone, and C. G. Gross, "Both Striate and Superior Colliculus Contribute to Visual Properties of Neurons in Superior Temporal Polysensory Area of Macaque Monkey," *Journal of Neurophysiology* 58 (1986): 1057–76; H. Burton and E. G. Jones, "The Posterior Thalamic Region and Its Cortical Projections in New World and Old World Monkeys," *Journal of Comparative Neurology* 168 (1976): 249–302; B. Seltzer and D. N. Pandya, "Afferent Cortical Connections and Architectonics of the Superior Temporal Sulcus and Surround Cortex in the Rhesus Monkey," *Brain Research* 149 (1978): 1–24.

41. Kandel, Schwartz, and Jessell, *Principles of Neural Science*.

42. Joseph, *Neuropsychology, Neuropsychiatry, and Behavioral Neurology*.

43. Ibid.

44. Ibid.

45. Ibid.

46. Kandel, Schwartz, and Jessell, *Principles of Neural Science*.

47. Ibid.

48. Joseph, *Neuropsychology, Neuropsychiatry, and Behavioral Neurology*.

49. K. D. Hoppe, "Split Brains and Psychoanalysis," *Psychoanalytic Quarterly* 46 (1977): 220–44.

50. J. D. Green and W. R. Adey, "Electrophysiological Studies of Hippocampal Connections and Excitability," *Electroencephalography and Clinical Neurophysiology* 8 (1956): 245–62; W. J. H. Nauta, "Hippocampal Projections and Related Neural Pathways to the Midbrain in Cat," *Brain* 81 (1958): 319–40; R. Joseph, N. Forrest, D. Fiducis, P. Como, and J. Siegal, "Behavioral and Electrophysiological Correlates of Arousal," *Physiological Psychology* 9 (1981): 90–95.

51. Joseph, *Neuropsychology, Neuropsychiatry, and Behavioral Neurology*, pp. 116–20.

CHAPTER 3

1. E. G. d'Aquili, "The Neurobiological Basis of Myth and Concepts of Deity," *Zygon* 13 (1978): 257–75.

2. R. W. Sperry, M. S. Gazzaniga, and J. E. Bogen, "Interhemispheric Relationships: The Neocortical Commisures; Syndromes of Hemisphere Disconnection," in *Handbook of Clinical Neurology*, vol. 4, ed. P. J. Vinken and C. W. Bruyn (Amsterdam: North Holland, 1969); R. D. Nebes and R. W. Sperry, "Hemispheric Disconnection Syndrome with Cerebral Birth Injury in the Dominant Arm Area," *Neuropsychologia* 9 (1971): 249–59; M. S. Gazzaniga and S. A. Hillyard, "Language and Speech Capacity of the Right Hemisphere," *Neuropsychologia* 9 (1971): 273–80; J. E. Bogen, "The Other Side of the Brain, II: An Appositional Mind," *Bulletin of Los Angeles Neurological Society* 34 (1969): 135–62.

3. A. R. Luria, *Higher Cortical Functions in Man* (New York: Basic Books, 1966); A. Basso et al, "Neuropsychological Evidence for the Existence of Cerebral Areas Critical to the Performance of Intelligence Tasks," *Brain* 96 (1973): 715–28.

4. Luria, *Higher Cortical Functions in Man.*; K. H. Pribram and A. R. Luria, eds., *Psychophysiology of the Frontal Lobes* (New York: Academic Press, 1973); L. Mills and G. B. Rollman, "Hemispheric Asymmetry for Auditory Perception of Temporal Order," *Neuropsychologia* 18 (1980): 41–47; L. Swisher and I. Hirsch, "Brain Damage and the Ordering of Two Temporally Successive Stimuli," *Neuropsychologia* 10 (1971): 137–52.

5. D'Aquili, "The Neurobiological Basis of Myth and Concepts of Deity."

6. Luria, *Higher Cortical Functions in Man*; N. Geschwind, "Disconnexion Syndromes in Animals and Man," *Brain* 88 (1965): 585–644.

7. Luria, *Higher Cortical Functions in Man.*

8. Ibid.

9. E. G. d'Aquili, "The Myth-Ritual Complex: A Biogenetic Structural Analysis," in *Brain, Culture, and the Human Spirit*, ed. J. B. Ashbrook (New York: Lanham Press, 1993).

10. Geschwind, "Disconnexion Syndromes in Animals and Man."

11. P. Starkey, E. S. Spelke, R. Gelman, "Numerical Abstraction by Human Infants," in *Cognition* 2 (1991): 167–70.

12. d'Aquili, "The Myth-Ritual Complex."

13. C. Laughlin, J. McManus, and E. G. d'Aquili, *Brain, Symbol, and Experience* (New York: Columbia University Press, 1992).

14. M. E. P. Seligman, "Phobias and Preparedness," *Behavior Therapy* 2 (1971): 307–20.

15. Ibid.

16. M. S. Gazzaniga and J. E. LeDoux, *The Integrated Mind* (New York: Plenum Press, 1978); M. Kinsbourne, "Lateral Interactions in the Brain," in *Hemisphere Disconnection and Cerebral Function*, ed. M. Kinsbourne and W. L. Smith (Springfield, Ill.: Charles C. Thomas, 1974), pp. 239–59.

17. L. Weiskrantz, *Blindsight: A Case Study and Implications* (Oxford: Oxford University Press, 1986).

18. A. R. Luria, *The Working Brain* (New York: Basic Books, 1973); see also M. S. Gazzaniga, *The Social Brain* (New York: Basic Books, 1985); C. J. Golden, "The Luria-Nebraska Neuropsychological Battery: Theory and Research," in *Advances in*

Psychological Assessment, ed. P. McReynolds (San Francisco: Jossey-Bass, 1981), pp. 191–235.

19. E. H. Taylor and J. L. Cadet, "Social Intelligence, a Neurological System?" *Psychological Reports* 64 (1989): 423–44.

20. M. C. Diamond, M. R. Rosenzweig, E. L. Bennett, B. Lindner, and L. Lyon, "Effects of Environmental Enrichment and Impoverishment on Rat Cerebral Cortex," *Journal of Neurobiology* 3 (1972): 47–64; W. T. Greenough, "Structural Correlates of Information Storage in the Mammalian Brain: Review and Hypothesis," *Trends in Neuroscience* 7 (1984): 229–33; . F. Lindroos, M. L. A. Riittinen, J. V. Veilahti, L. Tarkkonen, H. Multanen, and R. M. Bergstrom, "Overstimulation, Occipital/Somesthetic Cerebral Cortical Depth and Cortical Asymmetry in Mice," *Developmental Psychobiology* 17 (1984): 547–54.

21. R. A. Cummins, P. J. Livesey, and P. A. Bell, "Cortical Depth Changes in Enriched and Isolated Mice," *Developmental Psychobiology* 15 (1982): 187–95; Greenough, "Structural Correlates of Information Storage in the Mammalian Brain."

22. J. L. Fuller, H. E. Rosvold, and K. H. Pribram, "Effect on Affective and Cognitive Behavior in the Dog of Lesions of the Pyriform-Amygdaloid-Hippocampal Complex," *Journal of Comparative and Physiological Psychology* 50 (1957): 89–96; P. Gloor, "Amygdala," in *Handbook of Physiology*, ed. J. Fried (Washington, D.C.: American Physiological Society, 1960), pp. 300–370. H. Kluver and P. C. Bucy, "Preliminary Analysis of Functions of the Temporal Lobes in Monkeys," *Archives of Neurology and Psychiatry* 42 (1939): 979–1000.

23. H. E. Rosvold, A. F. Mirsky, and K. H. Pribram, "Influences of Amygdalectomy on Social Behavior in Monkeys," *Journal of Comparative and Physiological Psychology* 47 (1954): 173–78.

24. Gloor, "Amygdala" Kluver and Bucy "Preliminary Analysis of Functions of the Temporal Lobes in Monkeys."

25. K. R. Jonason, L. J. Enloe, J. Contrucci, and P. M. Meyer, "Effects of Stimulation and Successive Septal and Amygdaloid Lesions on Social Behavior in the Rat," *Journal of Comparative and Physiological Psychology* 83 (1973): 54–61; D. R. Meyer, R. A. Ruth, and D. G. Lavond, "The Septal Social Cohesiveness Effect," *Physiology and Behavior* 21 (1978): 1027–29.

26. J. L. Bradshaw, M. J. Taylor, K. Patterson, and N. Nettleton, "Uptight and Inverted Faces, and Housefronts, in the Two Visual Fields: A Right and a Left Hemisphere Contribution," *Journal of Clinical Neuropsychology* 2 (1980): 245–57; E. DeRenzi, *Disorder of Space Exploration and Cognition* (New York: John Wiley & Sons, 1982); R. G. Ley, and M. P. Bryden, "Hemispheric Differences in Processing Emotions and Faces," *Brain and Language* 7 (1979): 127–38.

27. Ibid.; M. Suberi and W. F. McKeever, "Differential Right Hemispheric Memory Storage of Emotional and Non-Emotional Faces," *Neuropsychologia* 5 (1977): 757–68.

28. S. T. DeKosky, K. M. Heilman, D. Bowers, and E. Valenstein, "Recognition and Discrimination of Emotional Faces and Pictures," *Brain and Language* 9 (1980): 206–14; W. Heller and J. Levy, "Perception and Expression of Emotion in Right-Handers and Left-Handers," *Neuropsychologia* 19 (1981): 263–72.

29. R. Campbell, "Asymmetries in Interpreting and Expressing a Posed Facial Expression," *Cortex* 15 (1978): 327–42; H. A. Sackheim, R. C. Gur, and M. C. Saucy,

"Emotions Are Expressed More Intensely on the Left Side of the Face," *Science* 202 (1978): 424–35; J. C. Borod and H.S. Caron, "Facedness and Emotion Related to Lateral Dominance, Sex, and Expression Type," *Neuropsychologia* 18 (1980): 237–41.

30. E. DeRenzi, P. Faglioni, and H. Spinnler, "The Performance of Patients with Unilateral Brain Damage on Face Recognition Tasks," *Cortex* 4 (1968): 17–34; T. Landis, J. L. Cummings, L. Christen, J. E. Bogen, and H. G. Imhof, "Are Unilateral Right Posterior Cerebral Lesions Sufficient to Cause Prosopagnosia? Clinical and Radiological Findings in Six Additional Patients," *Cortex* 22 (1986): 243–52.

31. DeKosky, Heilman, Bowers, and Valenstein, "Recognition and Discrimination of Emotional Faces and Pictures."

CHAPTER 4

1. E. G. d'Aquili, "The Myth-Ritual Complex: A Biogenetic Structural Analysis," in *Brain, Culture, and the Human Spirit*, ed. J. B. Ashbrook (New York: Lanham Press, 1993).

2. C. Lévi-Strauss, *Structural Anthropology* (New York: Anchor Books, 1963).

3. M. Grossman, "A Central Processor for Hierarchically-Structured Material: Evidence from Broca's Aphasia," *Neuropsychologia* 18 (1980): 299–308.

4. Lévi-Strauss, *Structural Anthropology*; C. Lévi-Strauss, *The Savage Mind* (Chicago: University of Chicago Press, 1963); J. Piaget, *Structuralism* (New York: Basic Books, 1970); O. J. Harvey, D. E. Hunt, and H. M. Schreder, *Conceptual Systems and Personality Organization* (New York: John Wiley & Sons, 1961).

5. Lévi-Strauss, *Structural Anthropology*; Lévi-Strauss, *The Savage Mind*.

6. A. F. C. Wallace, *Culture and Personality* (New York: Random House, 1961).

7. C. G. Jung, *Psyche and Symbol* (New York: Doubleday Anchor Books, 1958). Lévi-Strauss, *Structural Anthropology*.

8. E. G. d'Aquili, "The Neurobiological Basis of Myth and Concepts of Deity," *Zygon* 13 (1978): 257–75; d'Aquili, "The Myth-Ritual Complex."

9. C. D. Laughlin and E. G. d'Aquili, *Biogenetic Structuralism* (New York: Columbia University Press, 1974).

10. M. G. Kenny, "Latah: The Symbolism of a Putative Mental Disorder," *Culture, Medicine, and Psychiatry* 2 (1978): 209–31.

11. M. W. Schein and E. B. Hale, "Stimuli Eliciting Sexual Behavior," in *Sex and Behavior*, ed. F. A. Beach (New York: John Wiley & Sons, 1965); N. Tinbergen, *The Study of Instinct* (London: Oxford University Press, 1951); J. S. Rosenblatt, "Effects of Experience on Sexual Behavior in Male Cats," in *Sex and Behavior*.

12. K. Lorenz, *On Aggression* (New York: Bantam Books, 1966).

13. V. J. Walter and W. G. Walter, "The Central Effects on Rhythmic Sensory Stimulation," *Electroencephalography and Clinical Neurophysiology* 1 (1949): 57–85; E. Gellhorn and W. F. Kiely, "Mystical States of Consciousness: Neurophysiological and Clinical Aspects," *Journal of Nervous and Mental Disease* 154 (1972): 399–405.

14. Ibid.; E. Gellhorn and W. F. Kiely, "Autonomic Nervous System in Psychiatric Disorder," in *Biological Psychiatry*, ed. J. Mendels (New York: John Wiley & Sons, 1973).

15. Lorenz, *On Aggression*, p. 72.

16. A. J. Deikman, "Experimental Meditation," in *Altered States of Consciousness*, ed. C. T. Tart (Garden City, N.Y.: Doubleday, 1969), pp. 208–9.

CHAPTER 5

1. E. G. d'Aquili and A. B. Newberg, "Religious and Mystical States: A Neuropsychological Substrate," *Zygon* 28 (1993): 177–200; E. G. d'Aquili and A. B. Newberg, "Liminality, Trance and Unitary States in Ritual and Meditation," *Studia Liturgica* 23 no. 1 (1993): 2–34.

2. R. Joseph, *Neuropsychology, Neuropsychiatry, and Behavioral Neurology* (New York: Plenum Press, 1990).

3. Ibid.

4. E. R. Kandel, J. H. Schwartz, and T. M. Jessell, eds., *Principles of Neural Science,* 3d ed. (Norwalk, Conn.: Appleton & Lange, 1993).

5. C. G. Jung, *Analytical Psychology* (New York: Pantheon Books, 1968); C. G. Jung, *The Archetypes and the Collective Unconscious* (Princeton, N.J.: Princeton University Press, 1968); C. G. Jung, *Mandala Symbolism* (Princeton, N.J.: Princeton University Press, 1969).

CHAPTER 6

1. J. H. Austin, *Zen and the Brain* (Cambridge, Mass.: MIT Press, 1998); J. L. Saver and J. Rabin, "The Neural Substrates of Religious Experience," *Journal of Neuropsychiatry and Clinical Neurosciences* 9 (1997): 498–510.

2. E. G. d'Aquili and A. B. Newberg, "Religious and Mystical States: A Neuropsychological Substrate," *Zygon* 28 (1993): 177–200.

3. Ibid.; see also R. Joseph, *Neuropsychology, Neuropsychiatry, and Behavioral Neurology* (New York: Plenum Press, 1990).

4. D'Aquili and Newberg, "Religious and Mystical States"; Joseph, *Neuropsychology, Neuropsychiatry, and Behavioral Neurology.*

5. D'Aquili and Newberg, "Religious and Mystical States."

6. Ibid.

7. Ibid.

8. Ibid.

9. Saver and Rabin, "The Neural Substrates of Religious Experience," 498–510; Austin, *Zen and the Brain*; L. O. McKinney, *Neurotheology: Virtual Religion in the 21st Century* (Cambridge, Mass.: American Institute for Mindfulness, 1994).

10. A. Newberg, A. Alavi, M. Baime, and E. d'Aquili, "Cerebral Blood Flow During Intense Meditation Measured by HMPAO-SPECT: A Preliminary Study," *Clinical Nuclear Medicine* 23 (1997); A. Newberg, A. Alavi, M. Baime, P. Mozley, and E. G. d'Aquili, "The Measurement of Cerebral Blood Flow During the Complex Cognitive Task of Meditation Using HMPAO-SPECT Imaging," *Journal of Nuclear Medicine* 38 (1997): 95P.

11. H. Herzog, V. R. Lele, T. Kuwert, K. J. Langen, E. R. Kops, and L. E. Feinendegen, "Changed Pattern of Regional Glucose Metabolism During Yoga Meditative Relaxation," *Neuropsychobiology* 23 (1990–91): 182–87.

12. A. B. Newberg and A. Alavi, "Neuroimaging in Neurological Disorders," in *Neuroimaging II: Clinical Applications*, ed. E. D. Bigler (New York: Plenum Press, 1996), pp. 25–71; A. B. Newberg and A. Alavi, "The Study of the Neurological Disorders Using Positron Emission Tomography and Single Photon Emission

Computed Tomography," *Journal of the Neurological Sciences* 135 (1996): 91–108.

13. See D. Schiller, *The Little Zen Companion* (New York: Workman Publishing, 1994) p. 332.

CHAPTER 7

1. G. Roberts and J. Owen, "The Near-Death Experience," *British Journal of Psychiatry* 153 (1988): 607–17.

2. K. Ring, *Life at Death: A Scientific Investigation of the Near-Death Experience* (New York: Quill Publishers, 1980); R. A. Moody, *Life after Life* (Atlanta: Mockingbird Books, 1975).

3. J. E. Owen, E. W. Cook, and I. Stevenson, "Near-Death Experience," *Lancet* 337 (1991): 1167–68.

4. M. Rawlings, *Beyond Death's Door* (London: Sheldon Press, 1980).

5. M. Rawlings, *To Hell and Back* (Nashville: Thomas Nelson Publishers, 1993).

6. C. Zaleski, *Otherworld Journeys: Accounts of Near-Death Experience in Medieval and Modern Times* (New York: Oxford University Press, 1987).

7. A. Heim, "Remarks on Fatal Falls," *Yearbook of the Swiss Alpine Club* 27 (1892): 327–37; R. Noyes Jr. and R. Kletti, trans. "The Experience of Dying from Falls," *Omega* 3 (1972): 45–52.

8. J. C. Lilly, *The Center of the Cyclone* (New York: Julian Press, 1972).

9. C. G. Jung, *Memories, Dreams, Reflections* (New York: Vintage Books, 1961), pp. 295–96.

10. Ibid., pp. 304–5.

11. V. S. de Laszlo, *Psyche and Symbol: A Selection of Writings from C. G. Jung* (Garden City, N.Y.: Doubleday, 1958), p. 292.

12. Ibid., p. 294.

13. Ibid., p. 293–94.

14. P. Brown and H. Jenkins, "Autoshaping of the Pigeon's Key Peck," *Journal of the Experimental Analysis of Behavior* 11 (1968): 1–8. A. R. Williams and H. Williams, "Automaintenance in the Pigeon: Sustained Pecking Despite Contingent Non-Reinforcement," in M. E. P. Seligman and J. L. Hager, *Biological Boundaries of Learning* (Englewood Cliffs, N.J.: Prentice-Hall, 1972) pp. 158–73.

15. M. E. P. Seligman and J. L. Hager, *Biological Boundaries of Learning* (New York: Appleton Century-Crofts, 1971), p. 460.

16. V. S. De Laszlo, *Psyche and Symbol*, p. 295.

17. W. Penfield and A. Perot, "The Brain's Record of Auditory and Visual Experience: A Final Summary and Discussion," *Brain* 86 (1963): 595–696.

18. R. Joseph, *Neuropsychology, Neuropsychiatry, and Behavioral Neurology* (New York: Plenum Press, 1990).

19. Ibid.

20. P. F. James, "Near-Death Experiences," *Lancet* 333 (1989): 1110–11.

CHAPTER 8

1. É. Durkheim, *The Elementary Forms of the Religious Life* (New York: Macmillan, 1926), p. 207.

2. R. Otto, *The Idea of the Holy* (New York: Oxford University Press, 1970).

3. M. Eliade, *The Sacred and the Profane* (New York: Harcourt Brace Jovanovich, 1959).

4. W. King, "Religion," in *The Encyclopedia of Religion*, vol. 12, ed. M. Eliade (New York: Macmillan, 1978), pp. 284–85.

5. Ibid., p. 288.

6. K. Wilber, "Psychologia Perennis: The Spectrum of Consciousness," *Journal of Transpersonal Psychology* 2 (1975): 105–32.

7. E. Schrödinger, *What Is Life? The Physical Aspect of the Living Cell and Mind and Matter*, (Cambridge: Cambridge University Press, 1967).

8. J. Blofield, *The Zen Teaching of Huang Po* (New York: Grove, 1970).

9. E. Schrödinger, *My View of the World* (London: Cambridge University Press, 1964).

10. R. Gimello, "Mysticism and Meditation," in *Mysticism and Philosophical Analysis*, ed. S. Katz (New York: Oxford University Press, 1978), p. 178.

11. F. Streng, "Language and Mystical Awareness," in *Mysticism and Philosophical Analysis*, p. 142.

12. N. Smart, *Reasons and Faiths: An Investigation of Religious Discourse, Christian and Non-Christian* (London: Routledge and Kegan Paul, 1958); *The Religious Experience of Mankind* (London: Macmillan, 1969); and "Understanding Religious Experience," in *Mysticism and Philosophical Analysis*.

13. W. T. Stace, *Mysticism and Philosophy* (London: Macmillan, 1961).

14. S. Katz, "Language, Epistemology, and Mysticism," *Mysticism and Philosophical Analysis*.

15. E. G. d'Aquili, "Myth, Ritual, and the Archetypal Hypothesis: Does the Dance Generate the Word?" *Zygon* 21 (1986): 141–60.

16. G. E. Schwartz, R. J. Davidson, and F. Maer, "Right Hemisphere Lateralization for Emotion in the Human Brain: Interactions with Cognitions," *Science* 190 (1975): 286–88.

CHAPTER 9

1. B. Spinoza, *Tractatus Theologico-Politicus*, trans. S. Shirley. (New York: Leiden, 1989).

2. A. Schopenhauer, *The World as Will and Idea* trans. by R. B. Haldane and J. Kemp (Garden City, N.Y.: Doubleday, 1961).

CHAPTER 10

1. R. Descartes, *The Philosophical Works of Descartes*, vol. 2, trans. E. S. Haldane and G. R. T. Ross (Cambridge: Cambridge University Press, 1911).

2. F. Brentano, *Psychology from an Empirical Standpoint* (London: Routledge and Kegan Paul, 1973), p. 88.

3. E. Husserl, *Ideas: General Introduction to a Pure Phenomenology*, trans. W. R. Boyce Gibson (London: Allen and Unwin, 1931).

4. E. Husserl, *The Crisis of European Sciences and Transcendental Phenomenology*, trans. D. Carr (Evanston, Ill.: Northwestern University Press, 1970).

5. M. Merleau-Ponty, *Phenomenology of Perception*, trans. C. Smith (London: Routledge and Kegan Paul, 1962).

6. R. Llinas, "The Intrinsic Electrophysiological Properties of Mammalian Neurons: Insights into Central Nervous System Function," *Science* 242 (1988): 1654–64.

7. E. G. d'Aquili and A. B. Newberg, "Consciousness and the Machine," *Zygon* 31 (1996): 235–52.

8. E. G. d'Aquili and A. B. Newberg, "Liminality, Trance, and Unitary States in Ritual and Meditation," *Studia Liturgica* 23, no. 1 (1993): 2–34; E. G. d'Aquili and A. B. Newberg, "Religious and Mystical States: A Neuropsychological Model," *Zygon* 28 (1993): 177–200.

9. A. Newberg, A. Alavi, M. Baime, P. D. Mozley, and E. d'Aquili, "The Measurement of Cerebral Blood Flow During the Complex Cognitive Task of Meditation Using HMPAO-SPECT Imaging," *Journal of Nuclear Medicine* 38 (1997): 95P; A. Newberg, A. Alavi, M. Baime, and E. d'Aquili, "Cerebral Blood Flow During Intense Meditation Measured by HMPAO-SPECT: A Preliminary Study," *Clinical Nuclear Medicine* 23 (1997): 58.

10. R. Penrose, *Shadows of the Mind* (New York: Oxford University Press, 1994), p. 50 (emphasis added).

CHAPTER 12

1. D. T. Campbell, "On the Conflicts between Biological and Social Evolution and between Psychology and Moral Tradition," *American Psychologist* 30 (1975): 1103–26.

2. R. W. Burhoe, *Toward a Scientific Theology* (Belfast: Christian Journals Limited, 1981).

Index

CPSIA information can be obtained
at www.ICGtesting.com
Printed in the USA
LVOW13s1128100118

562215LV00031B/182/P